MAKING

AND

MARKETING

MUSIC

Second Edition

MAKING AND MARKETING MUSIC

The Musician's Guide To Financing, Distributing, and Promoting Albums

JODI SUMMERS

ALLWORTH PRESS
NEW YORK

07 06 05 04 03   5 4 3 2 1

Published by Allworth Press
An imprint of Allworth Communications
10 East 23rd Street, New York, NY 10010
www.allworth.com

LIBRARY OF CONGRESS CATALOGING-IN-PUBLICATION DATA
Summers, Jodi.
Making and marketing music: the musician's guide to financing, distributing, and promoting albums/ Jodi Summers.—2nd ed.
p. cm.
Includes index.
ISBN 1-58115-387-2 (pbk.)
1. Sound recording industry—United States. 2. Sound recordings—United States—Marketing. 3. Popular music—Writing and publishing. I. Title.
ML3790.S84 2004
780'.68'8—dc22
2004017390

Cover design by Derek Bacchus

Page composition/typography by Sharp Des!gns, Lansing, MI

ISBN: 1-58115-387-2

Printed in Canada

*Dedicated to everybody who
has ever believed in me.*

Contents

Many Thanks to . . .

Jeff Abercrombie, *bassist for Fuel*

Steve Addabbo, *producer, Shelter Island Sound*

Elijah Blue Allman, *visionary and frontman for Deadsy*

Michael Badami, *DreamWorks Music Publishing*

John Bates, *silicon surfer at Radionet.com*

Fletcher Beasley, *soundtrack producer*

Frank Black, *solo artist*

Carl Bell, *guitarist and songwriter for Fuel*

Bryan Biniak, *director of business development for Harmonix
     Music Systems*

David Bowie, *singer/songwriter and visionary artist*

Scott Blum, *founder of Buymusic.com*

Richard Branson, *founder of Virgin Records*

Edgar Bronfman, Jr., *CEO of the Warner Music Group, among
     other things*

Biff Butler, *vocalist for Apartment 26*

Kathy Callahan, *senior director of western regional sales at
     BMG Music*

Jerry Cantrell, *guitarist for Alice in Chains*

Mariah Carey, *solo songwriter/singer*

Laura Cohen, *singer, songwriter, and former manager of
     publicity for Virgin Records*

Geoff Cottrill, *group director of music for Coca-Cola North America*

Jon Crosby, *the artist behind VAST*

Chuck D, *founding member of the multiplatinum rap band Public Enemy*

Joe Daniels, *drummer for Local H*

Rob DeLeo, *bassist for Stone Temple Pilots*

Brad Delson, *guitarist for Linkin Park*

Craig Devilliers, *editor and inspiration*

Matt Devine, *vocalist and guitarist for Kill Hannah*

Glenn Dicker, *cofounder of Yep Roc Records*

Cheryl Dickerson, *senior director of writer/publisher relations, BMI*

Ani DiFranco, *independent recording artist*

Thomas Dolby, *musician and president of Headspace*

Michael Dorf, *president of the Knitting Factory*

Gilbert Grant Dorland, *for becoming an example*

Chris Douridas, *A&R executive for DreamWorks*

George Drakoulias, *staff producer and A&R executive for American Recordings*

Sully Erna, *vocalist for Godsmack*

Nancy Ferguson, *cofounder of the progressive film company Atomika*

Lonn Friend, *former vice president of A&R West Coast for Arista Records*

Robert Fripp, *composer and recording artist*

Mary Gauthier, *composer and recording artist*

Marc Geiger, *chairman and CEO of ARTISTdirect and the Ultimate Band List*

Stone Gossard, *guitarist for Pearl Jam*

Sammy Hagar, *solo singer, songwriter, and guitarist, and periodic Van Halen frontman*

Tom Hamilton, *bass player for Aerosmith*

Kirk Hammett, *guitarist for Metallica*

Taylor Hanson, *keyboards and vocals for Hanson*

Emily Hay, *composer and flutist*

Pat Hayes, *guitarist, vocalist, and songwriter for the Lamont Cranston Band*

Jim Heath, *frontman and songwriter for the Reverend Horton Heat*

Liz Heller, *senior vice president for new media at Capitol Records*

Ken Hertz, *entertainment industry attorney*

Ted Hooban, *director of Digital Media for CDNOW*

Billy Howerdel, *guitarist for A Perfect Circle*

Chrissie Hynde, *vocalist for the Pretenders*

Mark Janowski, *drummer for Sister Hazel*

David Javelosa, *keyboardist and audio designer*

Jewel, *solo singer/songwriter*

John Keefe, *producer at First Generation Recording Studio*

Maynard James Keenan, *singer/songwriter for A Perfect Circle and Tool*

David Kessel, *president of IUMA/Offline Records*

Abbey Konowitch, *executive vice president at MCA Records*

Charles Koppelman, *chairman of CAK Universal Credit Corp. and former chairman of EMI Capitol Music Group*

Joey Kramer, *drummer for Aerosmith*

Mike Krupit, *vice president of technology at CDNOW*

Michael Laskow, *founder of Taxi A&R Service*

Michael Leventhal, *attorney at The Law Offices of Michael Leventhal*

Nick Lowe, *British pop star*

Scott Lucas, *singer/guitarist for Local H*

Melissa Macfadyen, *audience*

Frank McDonough, *president of Moir/Marie Entertainment*

Travis Meeks, *visionary behind Days of the New*

Ted Mico, *Internet consultant and developer for Virgin Records*

Kevin Miller, *drummer for Fuel*

Russ Miller, *studio drummer*

Mark Mothersbaugh, *mastermind behind the* Rugrats *music and cofounder of DEVO*

Oded Noy, *Java developer and technical director for Path, LLC*

Jim Olsen, *cofounder of Signature Sounds*

Ozzy Osbourne, *the godfather of heavy metal*

Hugh Panero, *president and CEO of XM Satellite Radio*

Donald Passman, *attorney with Gang, Tyre, Ramer & Brown*

Ellis Paul, *New England songwriter and performing artist*

Joe Pernice, *songwriter for the Pernice Brothers*

Steve Perry, *founder of the Cherry Poppin' Daddies*

Joey Peters, *drummer and percussionist for Grant Lee Buffalo*

Joe Pezzillo, *founder of Eclectic Radio's GoGaGa station*

Chuck Plotkin, *producer*

Keith Richards, *songwriter, guitarist, vocals for the Rolling Stones*

Jason Ringenberg, *founder of the country/hard rock band Jason and the Scorchers and solo artist*

Michael Robertson, *founder, MP3.com and Lindows.com*

Alicia Rose, *vice president, head buyer, general manager, slave driver, and queen of NAIL*

Larry Rosen, *chairman and CEO of N2K and Music Boulevard*

Brett Scallions, *vocals and guitars for Fuel*

Pierre Schroeder, *composer and French pop star*

James Schureck, *director of new media for Jeff McClusky & Associates*

Andy Secher, *editor of* Hit Parader *magazine*

Chad Sexton, *drummer for 311*

Jacoby Shaddix, *vocalist for Papa Roach*

Fred Siebert, *president of MTV Networks Online*

Steve Simon, *executive vice president, music division, for Clear Channel Entertainment*

Mike Sistad, *manager of A&R for Arista Records, Nashville*

Roger Stein, *president of Iguana Records*

Chris Stephenson, *senior vice president of marketing for House of Blues*

Alex Stone, *classical guitarist and composer*

Steve Summers, *vocalist for Sprung Monkey*

Jim Survis, *guitar tech for Aerosmith's Joe Perry*

Chuck Taylor, *radio editor for Billboard*

Steven Tyler, *vocalist for Aerosmith*

Lars Ulrich, *drummer for Metallica*

David R. Valenti, *president/sales for Kanakaris Communications and NetBooks*

Alex Van Halen, *drummer for Van Halen*

Edward Van Halen, *guitarist for Van Halen*

Butch Vig, *producer and drummer for Garbage*

Tom Viscount, *lead singer and the primary writer for Viscount*

Andy Voelkel, *bassist and composer*

John J. Volanski, *author of* Sound Recording Advice

Jake Walker, *cofounder of Disclive*

Perry Watts-Russell, *A&R West Coast for Capitol Records*

Steve Weisberg, *composer, conductor, and arranger*

Brad Whitford, *guitarist for Aerosmith*

Dar Williams, *folksinger*

Robert Williams, *director of sales and marketing for Demeter*
    Amplification

Todd Williams, *marketing director for IUMA*

Dan Wilson, *songwriter and vocalist for Semisonic*

Tony Winders, *president of InterActive Agency*

Ken Wirt, *Diamond Multimedia*

Rob Zombie, *hard rock artist*

CHAPTER ONE

Choosing to Make an Album

I don't think I create anything. I'm a receiver. Songs are zooming through this room right now, and if I had a guitar I'd sit around and play for a bit; I'd catch one. The idea of creation, I leave that to God.

—Keith Richards, The Rolling Stones

All musicians have an album in them. As kids, they all sat there practicing their instruments for hours on end, making music. The goal wasn't necessarily to play stadiums or release platinum albums; the goal was to make music.

"When I started playing guitar, I didn't really start playing to make a career out of it. I started to play because I thought it was so cool, what Jimi Hendrix was doing on guitar," observes Metallica's Kirk Hammett. "I never gave music as a career much serious thought, until three or four years of playing guitar. I decided I didn't really want to do anything else but play guitar. It was either make money working at Burger King, or play guitar. I played guitar while I worked at Burger

1

King. Then I started playing guitar all the time and I haven't stopped yet."

If you're a musician making music, recording an album is a perfectly natural progression. Get it down on disc, and save it for prosperity, so people can be listening to it two hundred years from now, like Mozart.

Music is about getting heard. And after you've been making music for a while, and realize that the talent goes far beyond your bedroom, you want to get out there and share your songs.

If you want to share your music, there are two ways you can do it. The first is by playing live gigs, hearing the cheers of the audience, figuring out by the response what works and what doesn't. The second way is by taking a stab at immortality and making an album. Certainly Johann Sebastian Bach never thought people would be listening to his music two hundred fifty years after he wrote it. Elvis Presley could have only hoped that his music would live long beyond his lifetime. You never know if people are going to embrace your art. *Making and Marketing Music: The Musician's Guide to Financing, Distributing, and Promoting Albums* will show you the easiest, most economical ways to make an album and get it heard. A common thread that you'll find is that among many successful musicians, having a successful band is a natural evolution that comes from making music together.

Brad Delson, guitarist for the multiplatinum, cross-genre, Grammy Award–winning band Linkin Park, highlights, "We started doing our music for fun, just as friends in Mike [Shinoda]'s bedroom. We really didn't plan on being a band. Eventually, we got a publishing deal and things just started to happen. When we realized this was more than just a hobby, we decided— just like everything else that you really are passionate about—let's do the best job that we can.

"We now have a lot of great people working on our team. From our manager, Rob McDermott at Andy Gould Management, to our record company, Warner Bros., our attorney, our business manager—we really have a great team of people around us, helping us to run our business. We all work together.

"We pay attention to people and read up on stuff and really take an active roll in not just our creative life, but also our business life. When you relinquish too much control to other people, they can really pervert and distort your goals and your artistic vision, so it is important to have your business life in order."

■ When Do You Make an Album?

At what point in your or your band's musical evolution do you choose to make an album? Dumb question? Maybe, maybe not. It depends upon when you have something to say that's worth listening to.

Fans of Boston-based alternative metal moshers Godsmack started asking for an album. As Godsmack vocalist Sully Erna shares:

"We kept hearing from people coming to our live shows that if we had a CD they would buy it; we only had this three-song sample cassette. We basically said, how much would it cost? I started asking around, and we ended up borrowing $2,500 off of a friend. There was this guy, Andrew Murdoch, who I had worked with before. He ended up hooking us up in his studio.

"He said, 'How many songs do you have?'

"I said, 'About eleven.'

"He goes, 'I'll do this for you.'

"I told him in return, 'If it goes well, we'll cut you in as a coproducer on the record and give you a couple of points. If it doesn't, we banged it out in a weekend, so it's not like you lost a lot of studio time.'

"When we got our deal, I never thought they'd use the record; I thought they'd rerecord. But they seemed to like the production enough that they remastered it and put some new artwork on it."

Were you surprised that you had made an album-quality release for $2,500?
SE: Yes, I was. I thought it sounded great. I was happy with it. The rest of the band was happy with it, but you really don't know. Remastering it thickened it up quite a bit, but all and all, it's the same record.

And how did you go about getting your record heard?
SE: For a while we were beating the clubs up in New England. When we made the CD, we passed it around to all the radio stations in our area and kept our fingers crossed because we didn't know anyone. About a month later, a guy named Rocco, who's a deejay at WAAF [a Boston rock music station, at 107.3 FM], called me up, along with the programming director. They said, "We got your record. We listened to it. IT'S GREAT! We want to get behind you guys, support you, make this thing happen."

So Rocco started plugging Godsmack every single night. From there, we called a bunch of stores and tried to stick it in here and there. There was this one local chain called Newbury Comics that had about eighteen stores in New England, and there was one consignment person who dealt with all eighteen stores, and that was easy. A lot of the other stores had one consignment person per store. The consignment person, Beth, took it in. She said, "I'll help you guys out, send me fifty copies of your album." And when the fifty went, she'd reorder another fifty.

Then, things started to build on top of each other. Because the airplay was doing well, the live shows would pick up and because the live shows would pick up, more CDs would sell, and it just kept snowballing until we were selling, like 1,000 records a week. Nearly 20,000 CDs were sold before we were signed.

It was the help of a couple key people like Andrew, Rocco, and Beth that took to us when nothing was happening. These people took a chance on it and it paid off. I can't thank them enough for what they've done for us. All that was before our manager, Paul Geary, stepped in and brought Godsmack to a whole other level.

■ Evolution of an Album

When you are ready to make an album is your own best guess. There is no the-time-is-right-to-make-a-record cliché; each situation tends to be unique. If you've got twelve songs that work together as a whole, then you're just about there. Do some preproduction on what kind of instrumentation you want to use—how you would make the song come alive.

"Then you figure out what instruments you want to bring in, and if you have the budget for it," explains soundtrack producer Fletcher Beasley. "As you figure your budget, you have to figure, Okay, I want to use cello, viola, violin, contrabass, taiko drums, and I'd like to have at least two taiko drum players, even though ideally I'd like to have five. Then there's bamboo flute on it, and that's essential."

So you know how you'd do it. The next question to ask yourself is why you want to make an album:

- Artistic satisfaction?
- Because people need to hear your music?
- To inflate your ego and get laid?

If your answer has anything to do with your music being heard by other people, then ask yourself one further question:

- If you make an album, will anybody care?

"You know the old adage: If a tree falls in the woods and nobody is there to hear it, does it make a noise?" asks Alex Van Halen, drummer for the seminal American rock band Van Halen. "A song is only half-written unless somebody else hears it. That's important. Yes, you have to satisfy your own creative urges, but without somebody else hearing it, what's the point?"

■ It's the Songs

What it takes to make an album is good songs. A good song is an obvious commodity. You can tell a great song on the worst four-track demo or the finest sixteen-track studio recording. Think about whether every song is of the caliber of "Can't Stop, Won't Stop," "Drift Away," or "The Boys of Summer." Explore whether you are creating something that's unique and desirable; or is it just a raucous tape of you and your buddies getting their rocks off?

What makes a song great? Again, it varies. It could be a riff, a chorus, a strong vocal, an attitude, a strong lyric, a personality, or just something that sticks with you. You can't explain what a great song is, but you know it when you hear it.

"When I heard 'Novocain for the Soul,' on the Eels' demo, it was obvious that it was a great song," recalls Lonn Friend, former vice president of A&R West Coast for Arista Records. "The 'Novocain' on the record was very much the 'Novocain' we heard on the demo. Very little was done to that. I listened to that demo over and over and over again, and I believe, to this day, we should have signed that act."

When you write songs, have a reason for writing the song—a riff, a melody line, a rhythm—something magic that appeals to people. Don't reach. Write songs you can sing. If you don't have enough of the right material, there's no reason to make a record. When you're finished, you should at least have something that's worth selling. You're not going to do a second CD if nobody liked the first one, unless you want to keep putting out bad CDs.

■ Biff Butler: Understanding Your Audience

Eclectic British metal band Apartment 26 blends hard rock, drum 'n' bass, and rave elements into their aggressive sound. Vocalist Biff Butler is the son of Black Sabbath bassist Geezer Butler.

Did musical chemistry come quickly to the members of Apartment 26?
BIFF BUTLER: In our first two years, we probably wrote three or four albums, worth of material. There's a whole collection we refer to as "Album 1.5." Wrote all that, scrapped the whole thing. There are film school–like things and other instrumental projects. We do have a load of songs.

Musically, you took a big step between your first record, Hallucinating, *to your second album,* Music for the Massive.

BB: We didn't really want to alienate our fans from the first record, but back then we were blissfully ignorant in that we just did whatever made sense to us. During our time off after the Ozzfest, we decided to put our heads down and learn our craft. We did well on our first album, but we don't want to make that album part two. We thought, if we're going to remain young and we're not going to go to college and we're going to do this stuff, we should really be good at what we do. Like on the first album, I said, I'm not really a singer, I'm just a vocalist, but now I say I'm a singer because I have paid attention to how one sings. And everyone else in the band, now, each of our musicians is pretty spot on.

■ Share Your Ideas

Most of your songs need to reach a certain level of maturity before you can record them. You need to hear them over and over and over again. Rehearse, gig, entertain or bore your friends—writing a song is all about making it interpretable to many sets of ears.

Play your music; play it for everybody you know. Appreciate the feedback. The bulk of your songs will not be great after the first pass. Ask your friends for help and direction. You may get some weird responses, but some will be very helpful. Matthew will tell you, "Connect with the dark side of the force, Luke. You're too in touch with your feminine side." Doug might comment, "You need to add backbeat." Diana will say it needs some brio. Lois will tell you that the melody needs more balance.

Maybe you don't want the opinion of every Tom, Dick, and Diana, but do play your songs for people who know something about music and might have something constructive to say. Play for the people whose opinion you respect.

Pay particular attention to the feedback you get regarding song structure; remember, the melodies are key.

🔆 COMMIT IT TO MEMORY: *A strong melody is quintessential to a great song.*

Production should be competent. It is actually not all that consequential, because if your music is picked up by a label, inevitably your Artist & Repertoire contact (the person who signs you) will want to bring in more ears to spice up your music and make it work with the current sound.

"Worry about the songs, not the execution," confirms Kathy Callahan, senior director of western regional sales at BMG Music. "You will probably end up changing it when the A&R people get their hands on your record. If a label is going to put your album out, the A&R people will always have a theme of how they'd like to make things sound. If they're really interested in the songs, they like to bring in their own producers."

A good song is all about melody, but what does it sound like? That's an arbitrary decision. All music sounds different. Everyone in the industry has a different opinion on what a single sounds like. One thing people do agree on is that good songs have something that you remember—a riff, a hook, a line, a chorus.

Producer Chuck Plotkin, who has worked with people like Bruce Springsteen, says that there's a guideline for writing a popular hit song. You write forty songs, four of them make the cutting board, and one of them may be a hit. So, you need to write forty songs before you get to your single, if you're shooting for singles.

Keep in mind, forty songs doesn't mean, We're jamming today, this is cool, I should remember this—and a song is born. A good music session does not a great song make, most of the time. Remember, good tunes survive the test of time; Aerosmith's "Dream On" sounds as good now as it did in 1974. If you go to play your newly composed tune again and you can't remember it, then maybe it's not worth remembering. It takes time, a lot of time, to write an album's worth of good tunes.

"Some of these songs go back to the *Dog* album; Alice in Chains didn't want to use them," observes Alice in Chains guitarist Jerry Cantrell about the material for his first solo effort, *Boggy Depot*. "That's okay with me, they had that right. I was writing lots of songs in the time we had off, because I'd known that I wanted to do this record for a long time."

For some people, it's easy to write a song. There's a certain rhythm to it; that rhythm flows into verses and choruses, hills and valleys. There's a unified theme that runs through it—like a river through the countryside. There's a consistency to their writing style which naturally yields a consistency in their music. Other people compose sporadically, when the urge hits them.

What works totally depends on the type of music you're making. Sure, radio friendly pop and rock is about tightly constructed, catchy tunes, but if you're doing ambient, world music, new age, jazz, classical, or jungle, there aren't any singles, per se. Radio stations that indulge in formats beyond Top 40 will play what they want to play off of the album. If you feed them a single, these radio stations will most likely reject it and play another track from the album.

Once your music is purchased, you have no idea what's going to happen to your tunes. Be prepared. Get your songs together; make sure that they are strong; make sure that they work. When you've got a whole lot of them that work well together, maybe then you're ready to do a CD.

When Are You Ready?

How do you know when you're ready to do a CD? You're ready to do a CD when you're not struggling to find songs. Think about doing an album when you have more good songs than you need for recording a CD, so you're not trying to fit in two or three last songs just to get the CD done. A lot of people are in a rush to get the project done, and if they would have waited six months, they would have had better songs.

Making a record is clearly a question of material—you have to have the songs. For example, way back in the mid-nineties when Hanson went into the studio to record their first major album, they had already written two hundred songs.

"We wrote two albums, *Load* and *Reload*, at the same time, and all the songs were recorded at the same time," offers Metallica drummer Lars Ulrich. "There was really no debate about what was going to be on one and what was going to be on two, because we culled those songs down from more than fifty pieces we had written. Six months into recording the project we realized we had enough strong material for two albums. We decided that the songs that were going to be on the first *Load* record were the songs that were the furthest along. We chose the songs that had finished lyrics and completed solos. The thirteen songs that are on the *Reload* release were written and recorded at the same time, but they needed more work—mostly vocals and guitar overdubs."

Define the Term "Album"

What is an album? A very easy question, and yet a very difficult one. An album is a set of songs, sure . . . but it's much more than that. An album defines your musical sensibilities at this moment in history. You're about to create something that will live on forever. It's a pretty weighty responsibility if you think about it.

"What gives an album its uniqueness is where it is at in the scheme of your music-making career," notes Oded Noy, a Java developer and musician who has done a number of solo projects. "Each song is an experience in time, but the whole album together is an experience in time within itself; it has to tell a certain story."

An album is a set of songs that work together to make a united whole. It needs to have a style. Take groups like Nelly, Linkin Park, Pearl Jam, and Counting Crows—they each have their own unique style. Pearl Jam is renowned for angry and angst-driven rock. Counting Crows lean toward mellow-tempo, melancholy melodies. Counting Crows don't venture into a lot of other areas. There's a distinct style to their music; they don't try and do a reggae song or a hard rock song and a pop song. They are who they are; they don't try to be all things to all people.

A Unified Whole

Not only do your songs have to be good; they have to be unified. You need to know the focus of the CD, and what the CD should be about. A CD can have anywhere from eight to fifteen songs. Keep in mind that some songs probably don't translate well from one medium to another. As a composer, when you write a song, you sit with your instrument and play the song the way you would hear the song. Taking the song from an intimate composition to a popular-style listening arrangement is another thing altogether.

What is popular music? Vangelis, Space, Prodigy, Pink Floyd, Enya, the Wallflowers—all of them can fall into the realm of popular music. If people listen to it and it's popular, then it's a pop song.

"You have to let the music flow, let the music take on a life of its own," observes guitar god Edward Van Halen.

Figure you need ten good songs to think about making a record. Once you have ten songs, the goal is to write four more songs that make sense and work with the rest.

When you're writing an album, each song is only a portion of the larger opus. Look at the big picture—imagine this big body of work in your head before you record your album.

The Feel of the Music

There are two types of musicians: (1) People who play out a lot, and (2) People who stay home and get technical.

The musician who gigs has a band that plays and plays and plays, modifying and refining the song as they go along. Playing a tune for an audience and shaping it according to audience reaction is how they prepare to record in a studio.

Technical types want to be in a studio recording music; they want to be engineers. Musicians who go the studio route rack up credits quickly. Get a job at a busy studio, and within a few years you have a résumé of three hundred albums you've worked on.

In a band, the producer just tends to evolve out of the situation. One guy has a good set of ears, so he steps into the role. As a growing musician, at some point you may well cross the line and become a musician/engineer/producer. It's a natural progression. Over the years, as you go through the ranks of the music industry, you naturally evolve from one role into another. And when you pick up something new, it's quite possible that you leave another part of yourself behind.

"I tried to write, but I was expected to be the engineer because I was good at that," observes Oded Noy about his seven years of playing with the same guys. He has worked on more than ten albums, but is currently creating his first solo project. "I didn't write any music, but I learned a lot about music by producing. That was okay. I always knew how to play; now it's time to figure out what it is I want my music to sound like."

Your band needs a technical guy, particularly if it's on a budget. If you are the technical one, when you go into the studio to record, you will be wearing two hats, that of a musician and that of an engineer/producer. You need to evolve into this cool species. You learn how to make your music sound exactly the way you envision it in your head. You become an engineer/producer by just doing it.

Being a musician and a producer means being accomplished enough in both fields to make the two meet and compliment each other. It takes maturity to figure out and create your band's image in the studio; it requires the same sort of contemplation as figuring out when you have enough material to make an album.

Keep in mind: If you're a prolific writer, you're producing material. You're not going to want to do the rock star thing forever, so think about publishing. That way, after you get tired of being in a band, you can still stay in the music business by producing for other bands, by giving them your songs. You'll be able to live off the publishing long after you've lost the taste for hanging out with bands. If you get publishing royalties on everything that you've worked on, you eventually end up making a living on it before any one songwriter does.

■ Ozzy Osbourne: The Theme of an Album

When Ozzy Osbourne, the godfather of heavy metal and husband of talk show hostess Sharon Osbourne, was working on his 2001 release, *Down to Earth*, we talked about how to create the theme of an album.

You've been recording for more than thirty years. How do you keep fresh?
OZZY OSBOURNE: The album cover is me in a military coat walking through a forest, and it's foggy and it changes a little bit and in the end there's a series of photographs. The album sleeve has this invisible alien weird thing. I looked at the artwork and I thought to myself, "What am I going to call this release?"

I was thinking of all kinds of sci-fi names, and I suddenly sat down and said, "Okay, where did it all begin for me? Black Sabbath." Then I said, "Was there anything before that?" I realized, well, yeah, we were called "Earth." So I started singing "Down to Earth," and I said, that's it, *Down to Earth*. The front cover looks like an alien come down to earth, and it's always down to earth when I started playing music; and I like to think of myself as a down-to-earth kind of guy. Then people were saying there was a Rainbow album called *Down to Earth*, there was a movie called *Down to Earth*. So what?

The songs on Down to Earth—*what are they about, and what do they mean to you?*
OO: Whatever I think about it, why should I spoil someone's fantasy? Some of them are pretty straightforward, like "Dreamer." It's like an Ozzy version of the John Lennon song, "Imagine." "Gets Me Through" is pretty straightforward. "Junkie" is straightforward. It's about heroin and how disgusting it is. But there are other songs where you can make your own mind up of what they're about, so you leave a bit of an enigma to it. Not like I was walking down the road and a pot of paint fell on my head, so I decided to go, "The sky is blue on my head today." In the past, when I heard songs that I really liked, I used to wonder what the composer must have been thinking about . . . Once on a Frank Zappa album, he sang a song about dental floss, and I was thinking I knew what it was all about—it was all about cocaine. So when I met Frank Zappa, I said, "You know that song "Dental Floss"? Was it about cocaine?"

Zappa said, "No."

So I asked, "What was it about?"

Zappa said, "Dental floss."

And I went, "Ohhhh. . . ." And I thought that I really like what I imagined the song to be about instead.

It took you four years to get this album out. . . .
OO: It didn't take me four years to record the album; I did it in small spurts. The Ozzfest always throws a kind of spanner in the works because I have to stop being creative and go back on the road and do a Sabbath tour, and so on and so forth. On the Ozzfest tour, between performing with Black Sabbath and my band, I was doing two shows at one gig —that was killer. Then I did a tour with Black Sabbath, then I did the Ozzfest with my own band, and in between I was trying to find out whether Black Sabbath and I could do an album together. And meanwhile I'm trying to get a solo album out.

I must confess, had it not been for producer Tim Palmer, this album would never have been made. He was so patient with me. Tim did a lot of constructive work on the album; I didn't push the buttons. He'd just say, "We'll sing this, and we'll try this and we'll try that." He was really a producer in the truest sense of the word; even though you can wear two hats at the same time, you're not going to get the same effects. Some people can have two bands at the same time; I don't know how they do that. How can you do two different projects without sounding similar on each one?

■ Steve Addabbo: Producer Talk

Steve Addabbo, a producer with his own studio, Shelter Island Sound in New York City, established his niche by finding artists like Suzanne Vega and Shawn Colvin early in their careers. He nurtured these artists along, working on their early recordings and helping to establish them as successful artists with successful careers in music.

What turns you on to an artist?
STEVE ADDABBO: With Suzanne Vega, there was a uniqueness to her guitar style and her voice that I was drawn to; I thought there was a different point of view about lyric writing. The songs seemed to be very fresh, very new at that point—1983, 1984. With Shawn Colvin, there was this incredible emotional voice that you had to be fairly deaf not to get. There was an attitude there and a longing in her voice, and I just connected with it immediately.

How many artists do you get to see? What made you choose these two?
SA: A lot of artists come by. People are constantly looking to have you get them a record deal or work with them and help them develop their music. There's a constant flow—four to five serious demos every week. A lot of unsolicited material comes through, and it's hard to get the time to even listen to it. Most of the demos I listen to come from word of mouth, people I know, that kind of thing.

Do most producers find their own acts and develop them?
SA: There are all different types of producers. Some producers work with established artists, Bonnie Raitt and people of that caliber. There's guys like me who have made their way finding new stuff and bringing it to the label. Everyone dreams of finding a new phenomenon, developing it and having it hit.

What's the difference between recording an artist and recording a band?
SA: I enjoy working with self-contained bands. There you're trying to capture a vibe between people who have been working together. With someone like

Suzanne Vega or Shawn Colvin—where you're putting people into the studio around her—it's interesting because you have more choice. Suzanne is very much a solo artist, and you add stuff around her. You can say, I hear a trumpet player on that song; then you hire a drummer for something else. It's a free-flowing thing, and it's certainly more expensive because you're paying the musician union scale.

A self-contained band will pretty much do whatever they have to do to get the record done.

■ Budgeting the Project

When it comes to budgeting your album, there are two areas to take into consideration—time and money. You might think that you have all the time in the world to do an album, but you don't.

"We like to have the stuff written before we go into the studio, because then we can work on musicality and dynamics and things like that instead of being forced to write in the studio," notes Mark Janowski of Sister Hazel, a platinum act on Universal Records. "We've only sold a million records; it's not like we've sold eight million records and have all the money in the world."

An easy way to budget the project is to figure out approximately how many hours it will take to do each song. A bit of advice: be safe; overestimate so you won't go over budget and spend more money than you actually have. Allocate money for your engineering, your studio time, and your musicians.

"We spent a relatively short time in the studio recording *Mr. Funny Face*," notes Steve Summers of Sprung Monkey. "It was probably a little over three weeks total, one of the weeks being preproduction. We went in for a week, then came back for two weeks."

If your musicians are not really good in the studio, it can take a long time to lay down a track, particularly for the drummer. The drummer is key because he lays down the beat. Sometimes you have drummers that play well live, yet they can't keep rhythm when they go into the studio. Situations like this cause a lot of problems and can cause the budget to skyrocket. When you're calculating, be generous. Figure how long it takes to lay down a drum track . . . and keep in mind, it can take all day to lay down a drum track.

Another frequent problem with recording is singers who can't sing on pitch. Sure, they sound great live, and are very dynamic to look at, but the studio is a whole different thing.

🌂 **A BIT OF ADVICE:** *Be safe; overestimate so you won't go over budget and spend more money than you actually have.*

Variables, such as band members who are unable to adapt to the environment, can run up the cost. But they're not the only expenses; there are dozens of others, as well as numerous unforeseen variables. For instance, what happens if you don't like the way the music sounds after you've mixed it? Don't be harsh and jump to conclusions right away. If you're not thrilled with the sound, leave it standing for a day with all the dials up. Then, come back to it and reanalyze how you feel about the mix.

You'll inevitably have some unforeseen expense when you create your album. Take your time and enjoy each step—that way you'll most likely end up with a product that you're proud to have created.

■ Preproduction: Live versus Studio

"Playing live or recording in the studio are kind of one and the same, because we play live in the studio," notes Edward Van Halen. "It blows my mind when you walk into a session and there's one guy playing and you're like, 'You guys don't even play together? Aren't you a band?' We play together, but I'm in the control room, Al is in the drum room, bass is usually direct."

How much preproduction do you have to do? If you're Van Halen and you have a studio in your home compound, you don't have to worry much about preproduction; you just go in and jam. If you're a regular band and you're paying for every moment, think a bit more.

Playing live is different than recording, though both processes can be equally enjoyable.

"They're both really special experiences," notes Stone Temple Pilots bass player Rob DeLeo. "Being able to interpret your music in a studio is a thing in its own. Live performance is really best because you have people reacting to your work, giving you feedback. Live is just a better way to interpret your art."

If you haven't had a lot of experience in the studio, you'll find the original composition takes on a completely different tone in the recording studio. You need to know how it's going to sound. Songs that sound good live sometimes don't sound good on tape. The production values are different.

If you're a live band, test the songs out first in performance. See how they sound; see how the audience reacts. Then preproduce the song on a little eight-track; listen and see what works. Then try the song again. Go back and forth. You can make changes before you go into the studio. Sometimes the song has just been written, and you haven't really lived with it long enough to make a good recording. You just play it a few times, get a response and make some changes.

■ Goals for This Project

"When we all walk out of the studio, we're happy amongst ourselves," notes Edward Van Halen. "If we touch somebody else, mission accomplished."

If you've been around the music industry for any length of time, you know that the first time you do something it's the luck of the draw. It is whatever it is—you never know if you're going to turn out to be Alanis Morissette, Hootie and the Blowfish, Lode, or Polara. For many musicians, the goal is the incentive to do a second album.

"I want to get my music across to enough people so that it totally inspires me to do a second album," observes Oded Noy. "It would truly please me for people to listen to *Dance of Love*. In that respect, my goals are more about composition and production."

What your goals are really depends upon who you are. Some artists are born with a voice, something they need to say. Other musicians are nineteen-year-old guys who just want to get chicks, be really famous, and make lots of money. You've got to decide.

If you're making a record, you want it to do something. If your first album doesn't do anything besides sit on the shelf, the second album is going to be really hard to create. If you want to make albums, you need people to be able to hear and buy them. Your goal should be simple: Generate enough momentum with this album so there's no question that the next album will follow.

Of course, there are exceptions. The easy-listening artist Yanni did four albums before he sold any records. He had four albums that shipped less than fifty thousand units before he met actress Linda Grey, who got him connected. Yanni went on *Oprah*, secured a public broadcasting special, and became what seemed like an "overnight success." Ironically, Yanni would have been considered a flop in most businesses, but he kept working at it and ended up having huge success.

A lot of success in the music business has to do with finding the right people who will stay dedicated to you. When you create your team, choose people who will be with you for the long haul. When you make your album deal, try to make a deal that's for more than one album—that way, you have a chance to develop as an artist.

■ Billy Howerdel: Guitarist for A Perfect Circle

A Perfect Circle is the arc of the alt-metal art rock style popularized by its core influence, Tool. Formed by Tool vocalist Maynard James Keenan and former Tool guitar tech Billy Howerdel, A Perfect Circle is less dark and more melodic and ambient. Both Tool and A Perfect Circle have sold millions of albums and are highly regarded by fans and musicians.

Fill us in. How did A Perfect Circle come into being?
BILLY HOWERDEL: I remember meeting Maynard in 1992. I was working for Fishbone and Tool was opening for Fishbone. We became friends. When I bumped into Maynard in '95, I was looking for a place to live and he had an extra room, so we became roommates. I was continuing to work on music. I'd saved up enough money to pay rent for a year, and I wanted to focus on writing songs. Maynard heard them and said, "I can hear myself singing on them," and that's how A Perfect Circle came about.

Maynard has two successful bands—Tool and A Perfect Circle. Is it difficult to wait for him when he's working with Tool?
BH: I wait because I knew that going into it. Maynard always claims it's like having two children. You don't treat one better than the other. You give equal duty to each. In the meantime, I'll sit and write the songs. I'll work on stuff forever and they're waiting around for Maynard to get done.

How does A Perfect Circle's songwriting process work? Do you write the music and then let Maynard add the lyrics at a later date?
BH: I'll give Maynard a song, he either likes it or doesn't, and we go from there. On the second record, I had a lot more critiquing, which is why Maynard is credited as executive producer on the record. He made the executive decisions on how he wanted the record to sound. I don't know if he had a clear picture of what he wanted it to sound like, but rather, what he didn't want it to sound like. From there, we kind of took it bit by bit. The whole project was about six months of concentrated work, which spread over two-and-a-half years for me. But it's okay, because as long as I'm willing to wait, Maynard is willing to do another record.

CHAPTER TWO

Getting Started: Who and What You Need to Know

Music is an unspoken language that's felt more than it's

understood, and I love that. It's like, before there was a

God, people looked at the sunset and thought it was God,

because it was such a phenomenal sight. I like how songs

affect people the way a sunset or holding a child would. It's

a wonderful thing to have in your memory. And every time

you sing it, it evokes the same feelings you had the first time

you heard it. The creator—or Jesus or Yahweh or Buddha

or Allah—is still a creative force, and those who create, I

think, are closest to what spirituality means.

—Steven Tyler, Aerosmith

So, you've decided to do an album. Congratulations—may you follow in the footsteps of Aerosmith and Britney Spears, sell many millions of copies, and experience mass acceptance of your music beyond your wildest fantasies. Now that we've gotten the praise and accolades out of the way, it's time to get down to business—how are you going to make your album?

You've obviously figured out the time parameters for creating something like this; now it's time to tackle the other details. Whose help do you need? How much is it going to cost? You have to tackle all these quandaries before you get down to the actual process of making music.

■ Smells Like Money

Every daddy with the desire has found some way to afford doing a record. You can, too. You don't necessarily have to pocket the whole project, but be prepared to put in some up-front money so you have something to present to the people with fat checkbooks.

If you've got the product, getting money is all in the presentation. Act like a winner and people will treat you as such. Step one is to figure out which people you will need to help you record your album. Step two is surround yourself with a good team.

☀ **COMMIT IT TO MEMORY:** *Don't act needy.*

Sure, the five figures you need to properly do an album would be a blessing and a godsend that could possibly change your life, but desperation scares secure people away. Be strong. Your energy will make them aware of the fact that they are investing in a good product with a healthy potential for return. Keep in mind that finance people are not about art so much as they are about money. Talk to them in dollar signs, not chord structures. There is a business to having a successful band. You need to be aware of the rules of this game to truly succeed.

■ Choosing Your Lawyer

If you can be like that artist they once called Prince and do all the creative aspects of making and marketing a record yourself, then more power to you. Even if you don't need help recording (and that would make you extremely special, indeed), you need people on the outside working on your behalf.

Say you plan to raise money to record your disc. That's great, but when someone gives you a check for $10,000, what are you going to do? Say thanks and walk away? Don't think so. You need somebody to help you negotiate your album, write up an agreement, book your gigs, help with your equipment, and act as if they're on your side.

"You might want to do it all yourself, but it's so hard to do absolutely everything yourself," notes Carl Bell, guitarist and songwriter for Fuel, a band that has gone from releasing their own records to having a successful career with the Sony subsidiary label, 550 Music. (Fuel share their success story later in the chapter.) "It's all very political. If you don't go through the proper channels, the powers that be can nix the whole thing for you and not let you get the proper gigs. We've been very fortunate in meeting a lot of good people who have really been supportive."

You don't need to start with a lot of people. One technical person and a business guy or two working on your behalf is a great starting team. You grow from there. When an artist is fully loaded with all the people on her team and payroll, she's going to have a record company, a publishing company, a manager, an agent, a business manager (that's really an accounting company), a lawyer, and sometimes a road manager and/or a personal manager.

None of these people are difficult to find. When they're hungry and building clientele, they're hanging out in the clubs every night looking for you. Representatives of every aspect of that industry are out combing the clubs for new acts, listening to solicited tapes, and trying to find the next big things.

There are many arguments for many different people: managers, booking agents, lawyers. While we were writing this book, we spoke with a lot of musicians and learned that the first person most bands choose to ally with is an attorney.

As a poor, starving musician, you probably can't afford the $250-per-hour fee lawyers like to charge. The way to get around that is to make a deal. A lot of people will ask for a percentage and a modest retainer. If you're a band, be reluctant to give more than $1,000 or $1,500 to someone. Truly successful attorneys don't necessarily need or want your money. If the lawyer you're working with is desperate for your money, be afraid, be very afraid.

Of course, you also know that if you're going to give your attorney money, you must check him out very thoroughly to make sure that he is indeed a legitimate, successful lawyer and not a fast-talking hustler looking for a quick buck.

Be aware that there are a lot of scam-artist lawyers out there. Some attorneys make a business of doing nothing but taking fees to mail out letters and tapes. People at the companies know that these guys don't screen the tapes, and that they'll shop anyone who walks in and pays them a fee. Sign with one of these clowns and your career will be almost guaranteed to go nowhere. Your tape will be worse off than if you were just sending it out yourself and getting a nice rejection letter that says: "We don't take tapes unless it is through a lawyer or a manager."

If your attorney believes in you, he'll most likely work for a minimal up-front percentage of gross, or points, on your album. You're not going to get charity; give him some incentive, some motivation to work on your behalf. It's $1,000 or $1,500 well invested. That way you've got someone who knows the business looking out for you, and you don't have to pay him anything until you get a deal. Making albums is like playing the lottery—you never know when you will hit a million. It's very tempting, and attorneys like easy money.

"Lawyers might work on hourly, they might work on percentage," observes entertainment industry attorney Michael Leventhal, whose firm, the Law Offices of Michael Leventhal, is located in Santa Monica, California. "It's more likely a percentage on everything the artist makes less certain types of deductions. What types of deductions? For example, if the artist is going to get $250,000 to record the album, and all of that is actually going to go into production, the lawyer and the manager probably won't take a part of that money, because the artist is never actually going to see that money."

When choosing an attorney, make sure the person you select is someone who knows how the business works. Your buddy the personal injury lawyer may not be the best choice, but the friend of a friend is always a good place to start.

"Bands find me a lot of different ways," notes Michael. "Some bands find me by word of mouth or over the Internet."

You may be able to find an attorney at your shows. An aggressive music attorney will also be doing a lot of networking, going to clubs, checking out talent, searching for bands—acting very much like a talent scout.

Word of mouth is another good way to find an attorney. Oftentimes a label, publisher, manager, or the first person to discover your band will pass you along to their favorite attorney.

"I pick my clients on a bunch of different criteria. I don't take a lot of young bands, although I like to take a few because it's exciting to watch a young band happen," states Donald Passman, who negotiated a $70 million deal for Janet Jackson, and an $80 million deal for R.E.M. "I have to like them and feel like they've got a passion for what they do. It will be based on either a manager or a record company I know who says this person has really got some talent. Or sometimes they come in with five or six companies chasing them, and I get a sense that there is something there."

Unless you win the cosmic lottery, you're probably not going to get Donald Passman at stage one of your career, but there are plenty of capable attorneys out there.

Talk to your lawyer. Can you see eye to eye on things? Your legal representative is as important as a band member. Make sure you choose wisely.

"A lawyer is very important to your project. There are a lot of rights to be protected," declares Michael. "Legal representation for your album isn't simply about getting the most money for your client. It's about protecting the client's rights, making sure that he's not entering into a deal that will ultimately kill his career. It's about determining which are the good labels. Some attorneys do a lot of shopping of deals, and they will be the ones to help the artist to find the right label."

■ Know Your Rights

Lawyers are important because there are a lot of different rights to protect, and a lot of advice to be given. Most artists don't really understand what the issues are. Legal representation is not about getting you the most money—it's about guaranteeing your career. The average lifespan of an artist's career is about that of an NFL quarterback—careers don't last very long. If you make a deal that screws you and puts you on the shelf for seven years—which is how long a typical record contract has you bound to a label—by the time you get out of that and are able to make music again, your time may have passed and your potential market may have already graduated into the working world.

George Michael is a good example of getting caught up in a bad contract while his career was flying. He had a six-year battle with his record label, Columbia. When the label was bought by the Japanese conglomerate Sony in 1989, George felt he was not getting adequate representation and promotion. It took him six years and $14 million to get out of his deal. He survived to release *Older* on DreamWorks in 1996. George Michael was one of the very lucky ones. Only the really exceptional artists manage to survive the various trends and establish themselves as serious artists.

You need a lawyer. You can't allow yourself to get into a situation where you miss your window of opportunity because you're in a dispute with your record label.

■ What Rights Are You Protecting?

Inalienable rights—life, liberty, and the pursuit of happiness. There are a variety of rights that come along with a record deal. Some need to be transferred; some need to be retained. The first two rights that need to be addressed are the *underlying composition* rights for any song that the artist may write, and the rights to the *sound recording*.

🔆 **COMMIT IT TO MEMORY:** *One recorded song has two sets of copyrights that must be protected.*

When you hear a song, you're listening to two different copyrights at the same time. You're listening to the copyright of the song itself, and you're listening to the copyright in a recording of the song.

When you enter into a record deal, you're really talking about the rights of the sound recording; you're not really talking about the right of the underlying composition. We will address the underlying composition rights, but these are not the rights you are transferring to the record company. In a standard, major-label recording deal, the label pays for recording, and the record label owns the copyright to the sound recording. The underlying composition rights are in conjunction with your publishing company.

The distinction between underlying composition rights and sound recording rights can clearly be exemplified by the song, "I Heard It Through the Grapevine," written by Norman Whitfield and Barrett Strong.

Marvin Gaye went into the studio and recorded the song—that's a sound recording. Aretha Franklin recorded her classic interpretation—that's another sound recording. Gladys Knight and the Pips did a version of "I Heard It Through the Grapevine"—there's a third sound recording—then, Creedence Clearwater Revival did a fourth version. And therein lies the distinction between sound recordings and underlying composition. Norman Whitfield and Barrett Strong are the writers on the song; those writers own the publishing rights. The songwriter gets paid when Creedence Clearwater Revival, Aretha Franklin, or Gladys Knight sells albums with a version of "I Heard It Through the Grapevine."

■ Royalties

Record royalties are dividends that the record company pays to the recording artist from the sale of the album. The "mechanical license" (right to use a musical composition) is one of the main areas of publishing income, and it's paid for through the sale of the album. How much you're going to get is totally dependent on how many albums you sell. If "I Heard It Through the Grapevine" is on your record, for every album that you sell, Norman Whitfield and Barrett Strong get to divide 6.6 cents.

Sure, 6.6 cents doesn't sound like a heck of a lot of money, but let's crunch some numbers. When Dolly Parton wrote the song, "I Will Always Love You," back in the sixties, she did fairly well on the publishing. Along comes the movie *The Bodyguard,* and the Whitney Houston version of "I Will Always Love You" on the soundtrack. Whitney Houston's version sold 12 million albums. Dolly's probably got a deal where she's making 3 to 4 cents on per record, which comes to $400,000. Not bad for a song she wrote thirty years earlier.

■ Saving Your Rights

In the wild, early days of recorded music, artists sold all their rights. There are classic old songs like "Crossroads," written by old blues artists, that were sold to some big-time record company guy for $25. Twenty-five dollars—that's all they ever got for a song that half the world still hears once a week. Blues artists like Willie Dixon, Robert Johnson, and Muddy Waters were broke bluesmen in the old South. They made music, they were poor, and the song hawkers paid them $25 for a song. The song hawker then turned around and made up to several million dollars off of their songs.

Such is the case with the Kingsmen's version of the song "Louie Louie," a classic tune that made lots of money and yet the Kingsmen haven't received any royalties for at least thirty years—and they should, a federal appeals court has ruled. The band, who recorded the hit version of the rock standard in 1963, signed a contract in 1968 that was supposed to provide them with 9 percent of the profits or licensing fees from the record. They never got a cent.

In 1993, the Kingsmen, some of whom are still on tour, sued Gusto Records and GML, who held the rights to the recording. A federal judge rescinded the contract, granted the musicians the right to all royalties from the time they sued, and held the companies in contempt when they refused to surrender the master recording (*Peterson* v. *Highland Music*).

"I'm thrilled for the band that they're finally going to get what is due to them," said Jeanette Bazis, a lawyer for the five members of the group who filed the suit.

Recent sources of royalties include the movie *Mr. Holland's Opus*, the television show *3rd Rock from the Sun*, Coca-Cola commercials, and compilation albums. Total royalties due since 1993 are in the hundreds of thousands of dollars.

"Louie Louie" was written by rhythm-and-blues artist Richard Berry as a Jamaican love song in 1955. Since then, the tune has been recorded more than a thousand times. The hit version, by the Kingsmen in 1963, featured Jack Ely's almost-incomprehensible lead vocal—shouted into a microphone twelve feet above his head in a primitive studio—and the song's signature three-chord, ten-strum guitar rhythm.

Rumors on every high school campus in the country that the lyrics were obscene prompted a federal investigation, which concluded that the words were unintelligible at any speed. Berry's actual lyrics, sung by Ely, were a sailor's lament to a bartender named Louie about his lost love, and contained not a hint of impropriety.

Berry sold the rights to all his songs for $750 in 1956, but got $2 million in royalties for "Louie Louie" thirty years later, with the help of an artists'-rights group. The Kingsmen's contract was supposed to give them a percentage of the profits from their version, which has been included in various revival records and films over the years.

U.S. District Judge William Keller of Los Angeles ruled in the Kingsmen's favor. The court said it was undisputed that "the Kingsmen have never received a single penny of the considerable royalties that 'Louie Louie' has produced over the past thirty years." It was also undisputed that the companies sued by the band "have breached their agreement repeatedly."

When you're making music, be very, very wary. There are a lot of sharks that know musicians are not business-savvy. People are always getting taken. That's why you need someone who can watch out for your best interests, leaving you free to make your music.

Those are classic music scams, but they're certainly not the only ones. If you're doing an indie record deal, be sure to get a knowing mind to read over your contract. Indie labels are infamous for offering hungry artists bad contracts. In a legalese language laden with *hereto* and *forthwith*, the contract, when stripped down to its basic elements, reads something along the lines of, "We, the record company, are giving you $5,000 up front, and we're giving you this percentage on the back end." It looks really good on page two, but it's the back of the contract you have to be careful of—the part of the document that really starts giving you a headache because there's so much information to absorb.

Somewhere on page seven, this independent label contract might just transfer all of your underlying composition publishing rights to the record label.

 WARNING: *Be very, very careful with your contracts; one little paragraph and you've given away all your rights—or signed yourself into some other nightmare.*

■ Case Study: Robert Williams

Robert Williams has been playing drums since he was eight. He's had various bands and released albums on major labels like Arista and Epic, in addition to several smaller releases. These days, he has a day job as director of sales and marketing for Demeter Amplification. He was recently working with the surf band the Vultures, when they got an offer from a small label called Statute Records. Here is his recollection of the experience:

My most recent album is a surf album I did with the Vultures. We did it on the cheap. I work with Demeter Amplification, and we have a full recording studio on the premises. I was talking to Jim Demeter, our company founder, and he said, "Oh, you can do it here. Do it on ADAT." We had really good microphones and really good equipment to work with. We used an ADAT as our medium to record.

We recorded on ADAT because David Waldroop, one of the guys in the band, said he'd get us a record deal with Statute Records. It was decided that we would foot the bill for recording, and then hand the master tape over to Statute, and they would do the distribution. I called my lawyer, and he helped us negotiate the deal.

We finished the Vultures album, and when we contacted Statute Records with the product, they told us they wanted $600 from us to defer some of the costs to set up for duplication and distribution. They're a record company. We're the artist. Here is the product; distribute it. That was the deal. We told them that they could take the $600 out of the royalties of the record. They said no to that idea.

We looked deeper into the scenario and researched the reputation of the record company. Turns out Statute Records has a real dubious reputation of doing this sort of thing to bands—taking their material, tying it up in a legal muddle, and never releasing it.

■ Publishing Longevity

In the long run, when you break music profits down to who gets what for how long, publishing is the longer lasting deal. Your album may sell for a while, but if you write a classic song, you can clean up time and time again. Take the David Bowie song, "The Man Who Sold the World"—Bowie's version was a hit single in England in the sixties. Thirty years later, "The Man Who Sold the World" was a Top Ten hit by Nirvana, and David Bowie made another bundle on the same song. Publishing royalties are evergreen; they continue to generate income for decades. If you can write songs, do yourself a favor: get a publishing deal. Your grandchildren will thank you.

■ Oh, and One Other Right

Publicity rights are another set of record company rights you'll need to transfer. You need to give the record label permission to use your name and image for advertising on the album. If you don't give them those rights, they can't legally promote your record. And you want them to do that.

■ After Lawyers Come Managers

Managers can be very good things. Good managers are like parents. They take care of you, nurture you, and look out for your best interests. They're the ones who will support you emotionally through it all. They will see that you get to your gig on time when the bus breaks down, and will deny to the media that you were arrested for having sex with a minor. Bad managers—and there are many—will steal you blind and get you so weighed down in court battles that you no longer have time to make music.

You need a manager when you get too popular to take care of yourself, but you've got to make sure that he's going to take care of you and not steal you blind and cheat you out of a career.

"When our manager, Ed Leffler, was around, his attitude was, do everything that's right for the individual and the band as a whole," notes musician Sammy Hagar about his days with Van Halen, before Ed Leffler passed away and Sammy subsequently got the boot from Van Halen. "All of a sudden a new manager comes in and it's, like, to hell with Sammy Hagar."

If you choose to take on a manager, find someone who can really execute your vision. Is this the person you want to represent you? Can he walk into a record company or MTV and perpetrate your vision? Will he help you be the best musician you can be, or will he just leech off of you and hold you down?

☼ **COMMIT IT TO MEMORY:** *Surround yourself with people who truly understand where you are as an artist.*

"A manager can be a very good thing," notes Kathy Callahan of BMG Music. "A manager knows the boundaries and the direction of where this whole musical thing you're making is going. The manager should be the visionary who can do that for the record company. He decides how often the artist should go on tour. There are positives and negatives to management from a record label point of view. The manager can be your best friend or be your worst enemy."

If you've got a deal, your manager is the one whose responsibility it is to stay on the label's case and get it motivated in your direction—among other things. Your manager is a necessary voice inside the record company to keep the label on their toes. Keep in mind that a big record label may be working two dozen other acts in addition to yours. It's hard for the label to devote time to all its artists. Since the record company is distracted by so many other projects, your manager needs to be strong to keep the label focused on your act.

You are what is important to your manager, not the other twenty acts that are going for radio that week. He should be working you, getting your name out there to the right people as often as he possibly can.

"I speak to managers about getting artists to do interviews, dinners, meet-and-greets—we're trying to get the artist into the consciousness of the consumer," explains Kathy.

If you get to a record label and have no manager, the record company may perceive you as directionless, and there's a likelihood that you'll get lost in the shuffle. If you just start happening and you get a deal, your lawyer can fill in for you. But it's a very weak presentation when a band represents themselves to a major record label.

"They seem to not know where they want to go, what they want to do. The information flow is not nearly what it ought to be," notes Kathy. "If somebody has a good manager, it makes the job a lot easier. It's a good thing to have a manager, especially someone who knows what they want the artist to do and has a vision about where the artist is going."

A connected manager is the best possible thing of all. Somebody who actually has connections is a great thing. Experience has a lot of value.

■ David Krebs: A Manager's Point of View

David Krebs is president of the band management firm Krebs Communications. In his career, David has done management work with the likes of Aerosmith, AC/DC, Ted Nugent, Chumbawumba, Michael Bolton, the Trans Siberian Orchestra, and Richie Sambora, among others. This is his take on things:

What does a manager do for a band?
DAVID KREBS: A manager is like a coach. He makes sure that all the elements are working as close to 100 percent as possible—from the record company to the public relations company, to the agent, to the band's crew, to the band. It's a manager's job to make sure elements are working together.

What makes for a great manager?
DK: Passion for the music.

How do you decide which bands to handle?
DK: It's music that I'm into. It's hard to manage if you're not into the music. Management is not like a label, where you have to satisfy all sorts of tastes. I have to satisfy my tastes in order to get motivated.

How do you get a band signed?
DK: By somebody being smart enough at a label to make the deal. It takes a lot of sending around tapes and showcasing and what have you.

If a band has several labels to choose from, who should they sign with?
DK: That's not easy to answer. It's a balancing of who's most passionate about a band; what the label roster looks like. There are too many intangibles to briefly explain who to go with.

How do you negotiate a deal; how do you know what a band's worth?
DK: You don't; it's all guesswork. It depends what label it is. It depends how successful the band is, how great the group is. There are a lot of factors. Look for somebody who's definitely going to go forward with the second record, notwithstanding the failure of the first.

If you've got more than one label bidding, are you able to drive up the price?
DK: To some degree.

As a manager, what is your relationship with the label?
DK: A cheerleader for the band. You've got to be reasonably optimistic without being the one that overhypes. A lot of elements have to be measured—each band is different—but you've got to play up the band's strengths and minimize their weaknesses. I look a lot for longevity, because if you look at the bands I've found and launched, they're still here, some from the seventies. Between Aerosmith, AC/DC, and Michael Bolton, they've all had long careers.

Longevity is important. The music business is moving toward the one hit wonder phenomenon, and that is definitely going to undermine the bottom line of these major conglomerates. You go to these radio shows, like the Z-100 Christmas show, and you get ten bands for fifteen minutes each. Ultimately, the promoter could call up and say, Send us the singer, we have the backing band for everybody. The business has become that generic.

It's become a very singles-oriented market?
DK: The record companies are making tremendous errors by doing that. Major errors. It's a long-term negative reverberation. They're treating these artists much more like candy bars than artists. They're branding, short-term. There's no mystique anymore, so it's hard to build a fan base. There's way too much music available for free on television; why should I go see you?

How do you build a band's mystique?
DK: By implementing the philosophy that less is more. Easier said than done. It's much harder to maintain mystique, because it's the essence of music television to explore nooks and crannies, and the more you put stars under the microscope, the more you create the feeling of familiarity breeds contempt, which totally undermines the idea of fandom and mystique.

What advice would you give to a band that's trying to get a deal?
DK: Once you stop making music, you're no longer in the game. It took Chumbawumba fifteen years to break, so there's always hope. You have to believe in yourself, which is a major ingredient. There are too many people out there who can occupy these slots.

■ Management's Role

The purpose of management changes from the presigned to the signed band. You already know that lots of young bands often have friends as their managers—the roadies turned reps who do everything. They're there to help out and have all the best intentions. Any knucklehead can be a manager, but those guys rarely cut it when a major label comes along and a band gets its deal. Sure, they do one part of the job—babysit the act. Your buddy-turned-manager should take care of the band's personal and professional matters so the members can concentrate on their art and their performance. Thing is, your friend has no more access to the inside of the music industry than you do. He's just as young and naïve as the rest of the band.

Usually, the inexperienced manager will be blown out for somebody who can bring some juice to the scene. He needs to add something to the family that's trying to develop this act. For example, when David Krebs signed on to bring Chumbawumba to the United States, he was able to generate offers from both Atlantic and Universal Records. Universal Records was chosen because, according to Krebs, "Atlantic got tied down with censorship issues from their legal department. It looked like at Universal that wouldn't be a problem."

Your buddy probably can't get you offers from two major labels. He most likely won't mature with your band, but keep him around anyway. When your group gets to the majors, there's usually a place for rookie managers somewhere else in your organization.

Of course, there's always the success story of the rookie who makes it— the one who stands out from the crowd. In this case, it would be Steve Stewart of Stone Temple Pilots. He was as green as grass when the group first got signed, but he learned. Steve was a hard worker and a good learner, and he remained Stone Temple Pilots' manager through three multiplatinum records—a rare feat.

If you're going to reach for the best managers, think of someone like Q Prime Management. With a roster that includes the likes of Metallica, Smashing Pumpkins, and Hole, Cliff Bernstein and Peter Mench are not only great business managers, they're creative managers as well. These guys are so good, they liaison with the record company, usurping the powers of the A&R department and serving as the band's main form of representation. (FYI: *A&R* stands for "artist and repertoire"—these are the guys who get ahold of your tape and sign you to a record deal. Keep reading for more info.)

Once your act breaks, you don't necessarily need to continue to have strong A&R representation. That's true with several of the Q Prime acts. Metallica hasn't had A&R representation in ten years. Smashing Pumpkins' A&R guy, Mark Williams, decided to go off and form a record label of his own. Q Prime stepped in and solidified the record company relationship. Hole also no longer has A&R representation. These acts are all well represented because of their managers' rapport with the record company. Their managers will not let them flounder just because their A&R contact is gone. A strong manager will help a band maintain its direction.

Managers that don't have leverage get trampled by record companies. A head of marketing will stick a fork in a manager's long-term desires to tour or make an expensive video, and if the band doesn't have a manager who's willing to argue on their behalf, they have no recourse. The group gets swept under the rug in a heartbeat unless they've got a manager with pull.

🔆 **KEEP IN MIND:** *The music business is all about leverage; it's all about who you know. It's an incredibly fickle business.*

■ **Your A&R Contact**

A band gets signed to a record label through A&R—the artist and repertoire department. The person who signs you to your record label deal is your liaison with the record company. If you need something, you go to him. He talks to everyone else at the label. The philosophy of the record label is: If they perceive that you're going to make money, they will spend money on you.

"Basically, our job is to take the vision of an artist and bring it to the consumer," observes Abbey Konowitch, executive vice president at MCA Records. "What that means in reality is you've got to get it on the radio. If you make a video, you have to make the right video which captures the right image for the artist. Then you get that video exposed in some way. You work with creative services so they can visually present your record to the marketplace. You come up with sales campaigns, retail campaigns, advertising, and the look of the point-of-purchase displays, and you have to make all of that work for the consumer. It's not easy. It's not easy on a lot of levels."

Being a successful recording artist is a lot of work. You need as many allies as you can get working on your behalf.

"We have a lot of great people working on our team," confirms Linkin Park guitarist Brad Delson. "From our manager, Rob McDermott at Andy Gould Management, to our record company, Warner Bros., to our attorney and our business manager, there is really a whole team of people around helping us to run our business."

■ Who Gets Paid What

You didn't think all these people working on your project were working for free, did you? Nahhh—not by a long shot. Your attorney will take 5 percent, or will just expect his bill to be paid; it depends upon the deal you have worked out. The big money will go to your manager; he'll probably take 10–20 percent of your gross earnings right off the top. And if they're good, they deserve it. Your booking agent, the guy who books your concerts, may take 10 percent or more from the gigs that he's generated.

Your band probably doesn't have much of anything in its early phases. But these people believe in you; they want to see profits off the back end. If you get famous, they'll take income that's generated off the record deal. When that income is on the way to the artist, it first stops at the accountant. He'll dole out proper payment to the members of the team, even though your accountant is not personally a part of your deal with the record company. If you don't have a business manager, sometimes your lawyer or your manager will give the record and publishing company a letter of "Direction of Payment." This letter, signed by the group, indicates that the artist has directed the record label to pay specific members of the team directly out of that check, as opposed to having the money go to the artist and having the act pay the bills. A lawyer's letter of direction to the record label might say: when you're getting ready to write that check for $100,000 to your act instead of writing $100,000 to the artist, write $95,000 to the artist and $5,000 to me, subject to the artist's approval.

■ Copyrighting Your Material

Before you go giving your first tape away, remember to copyright your material. It's not a big deal, really. A couple of forms, twenty dollars, and all the songs on your album are protected from plagiarism.

If you're beyond the do-it-all-yourself phase, someone else will probably do your copyrighting for you. If your band has a record label, the record company's going to handle the copyrighting of the sound recordings. If you sign to a publishing company, the publishing company will take care of registering the underlying content. If your band is unsigned, oftentimes, a lawyer will do it, but you can do it yourself. Copyrighting is not that complicated a process.

"Copyrighting has actually become a loss leader at a law firm," notes Michael Leventhal. "It's just filling out forms; I can't charge them my hourly rate to fill out a form. And it costs $20 to send the form in."

The truth about copyrights is that the moment you create the work and fix it in tangible form, meaning you write the lead sheet or you record it on a tape, there is a copyright that has been created that you own. That has already happened, but for record-keeping purposes and political reasons, you should always file your copyrights, because if you're creating a work of art, you should own the rights to it. In the United States, you maintain those rights by copyrighting your material.

As always, there are times when people forget about copyrighting. When the copyright is in question, court battles may ensue. A common lawsuit results when a lesser-known artist claims that his material was stolen or imitated by a higher-profile act. One such case goes to trial every few years, and most of the claims are totally frivolous—the artists who are being sued would have never had the opportunity to hear the song that the plaintiff claims is similar.

Take industrial artist Trent Reznor and his project, Nine Inch Nails, for instance. His recording career was totally hampered in 1997, when Mark Nicholas Onofrio, from Houston, Texas, filed a complaint in a Los Angeles federal court against Reznor. Onofrio claimed that Reznor used five of his songs on the 1994 album, *The Downward Spiral*, and also declared that the song "Burn" on the *Natural Born Killers* soundtrack is incredibly similar to another track he had sent to Reznor.

This whole lawsuit falls into the murky gray area of cyberspace. Onofrio claims that he met Reznor in a chat room in the summer of 1993. (Haven't all chat frequenters met Golda Meir, Weiland, or Reznor in some remote part of the Web at three in the morning?) Onofrio claims he asked Reznor if he would listen to some of his work, to which Reznor allegedly gave a positive reply via e-mail and supplied his address. Onofrio claims he then FedExed a demo to Reznor's house.

When *The Downward Spiral* was released in 1994, Onofrio noticed that five tracks on the album were based on four songs from the self-produced *Elephant Man* collection that he allegedly sent to Reznor. The lawsuit claims that the Nine Inch Nails songs "Closer" and "Mr. Self-Destruct" are "strikingly similar" to the Onofrio-penned "Voice." "March of Pigs" is allegedly ripped off from Onofrio's "Nothing," while "Hurt" is supposed to be derived from Onofrio's "Real." "The Downward Spiral" is hypothetically taken from the tune "Dinner with Jeff." Onofrio also claims that one of Reznor's contributions to the *Natural Born Killers* soundtrack, "Burn," is "strikingly similar" to his tune titled "This Hell."

Onofrio's lawsuit seeks unspecified damages for copyright infringement and seeks injunctions against the further distribution of *Downward Spiral* and *Natural Born Killers*, both the movie and the soundtrack. The complaint names Reznor, Nine Inch Nails, Interscope Records (Reznor's record label), Warner Bros. (the movie studio behind *Natural Born Killers*), and others. Onofrio is indeed taking on the system. But the system has yet to react. No hearings have been scheduled, and the whole experience has made Reznor unwilling and unable to work on creating his own music. Thus, he's been producing others. His work on Marilyn Manson's *Antichrist Superstar* proved to be a phenomenal success. Reznor has also remixed David Bowie's tune, "I'm Afraid of Americans," and produced the *2 Voyeurs* album for Rob Halford.

"I would still take precautions," notes attorney Donald Passman, who has handled such prestigious clients as R.E.M., Janet Jackson, Bryan Adams, Tina Turner, Quincy Jones, Green Day, and Bonnie Raitt. "If you can't afford to copyright a song—and it's probably not worth the expense until you're actually going to exploit it—at least mail it to yourself in an envelope and put it away."

Mailing a song to yourself establishes the date on which you created a song. That's all it does, but it might work. Filing the copyright form is a sure way of protecting your work, but it certainly isn't the only way.

Form PA

Detach and read these instructions before completing this form.
Make sure all applicable spaces have been filled in before you return this form.

BASIC INFORMATION

When to Use This Form: Use Form PA for registration of published or unpublished works of the performing arts. This class includes works prepared for the purpose of being "performed" directly before an audience or indirectly "by means of any device or process." Works of the performing arts include: (1) musical works, including any accompanying words; (2) dramatic works, including any accompanying music; (3) pantomimes and choreographic works; and (4) motion pictures and other audiovisual works.

Deposit to Accompany Application: An application for copyright registration must be accompanied by a deposit consisting of copies or phonorecords representing the entire work for which registration is made. The following are the general deposit requirements as set forth in the statute:
Unpublished Work: Deposit one complete copy (or phonorecord).
Published Work: Deposit two complete copies (or one phonorecord) of the best edition.
Work First Published Outside the United States: Deposit one complete copy (or phonorecord) of the first foreign edition.
Contribution to a Collective Work: Deposit one complete copy (or phonorecord) of the best edition of the collective work.
Motion Pictures: Deposit *both* of the following: (1) a separate written description of the contents of the motion picture; and (2) for a published work, one complete copy of the best edition of the motion picture; or, for an unpublished work, one complete copy of the motion picture or identifying material. Identifying material may be either an audiorecording of the entire soundtrack or one frame enlargement or similar visual print from each 10-minute segment.

The Copyright Notice: Before March 1, 1989, the use of copyright notice was mandatory on all published works, and any work first published before that date should have carried a notice. For works first published on and after March 1, 1989, use of the copyright notice is optional. For more information about copyright notice, see Circular 3, "Copyright Notice."

For Further Information: To speak to an information specialist, call (202) 707-3000 (TTY: (202) 707-6737). Recorded information is available 24 hours a day. Order forms and other publications from the address in space 9 or call the Forms and Publications Hotline at (202) 707-9100. Most circulars (but not forms) are available via fax. Call (202) 707-2600 from a touchtone phone. Access and download circulars, forms, and other information from the Copyright Office website at *www.copyright.gov.*

LINE-BY-LINE INSTRUCTIONS

Please type or print using black ink. The form is used to produce the certificate.

1 SPACE 1: Title

Title of This Work: Every work submitted for copyright registration must be given a title to identify that particular work. If the copies or phonorecords of the work bear a title (or an identifying phrase that could serve as a title), transcribe that wording *completely* and *exactly* on the application. Indexing of the registration and future identification of the work will depend on the information you give here. If the work you are registering is an entire "collective work" (such as a collection of plays or songs), give the overall title of the collection. If you are registering one or more individual contributions to a collective work, give the title of each contribution, followed by the title of the collection. For an unpublished collection, you may give the titles of the individual works after the collection title.

Previous or Alternative Titles: Complete this space if there are any additional titles for the work under which someone searching for the registration might be likely to look, or under which a document pertaining to the work might be recorded.

Nature of This Work: Briefly describe the general nature or character of the work being registered for copyright. Examples: "Music"; "Song Lyrics"; "Words and Music"; "Drama"; "Musical Play"; "Choreography"; "Pantomime"; "Motion Picture"; "Audiovisual Work."

2 SPACE 2: Author(s)

General Instructions: After reading these instructions, decide who are the "authors" of this work for copyright purposes. Then, unless the work is a "collective work," give the requested information about every "author" who contributed any appreciable amount of copyrightable matter to this version of the work. If you need further space, request additional Continuation Sheets. In the case of a collective work such as a songbook or a collection of plays, give information about the author of the collective work as a whole.

Name of Author: The fullest form of the author's name should be given. Unless the work was "made for hire," the individual who actually created the work is its "author." In the case of a work made for hire, the statute provides that "the employer or other person for whom the work was prepared is considered the author."

What is a "Work Made for Hire"? A "work made for hire" is defined as: (1) "a work prepared by an employee within the scope of his or her employment"; or (2) "a work specially ordered or commissioned for use as a contribution to a collective work, as a part of a motion picture or other audiovisual work, as a translation, as a

supplementary work, as a compilation, as an instructional text, as a test, as answer material for a test, or as an atlas, if the parties expressly agree in a written instrument signed by them that the work shall be considered a work made for hire." If you have checked "Yes" to indicate that the work was "made for hire," you must give the full legal name of the employer (or other person for whom the work was prepared). You may also include the name of the employee along with the name of the employer (for example: "Elster Music Co., employer for hire of John Ferguson").

"Anonymous" or "Pseudonymous" Work: An author's contribution to a work is "anonymous" if that author is not identified on the copies or phonorecords of the work. An author's contribution to a work is "pseudonymous" if that author is identified on the copies or phonorecords under a fictitious name. If the work is "anonymous" you may: (1) leave the line blank; or (2) state "anonymous" on the line; or (3) reveal the author's identity. If the work is "pseudonymous" you may: (1) leave the line blank; or (2) give the pseudonym and identify it as such (example: "Huntley Haverstock, pseudonym"); or (3) reveal the author's name, making clear which is the real name and which is the pseudonym (for example: "Judith Barton, whose pseudonym is Madeline Elster"). However, the citizenship or domicile of the author **must** be given in all cases.

Dates of Birth and Death: If the author is dead, the statute requires that the year of death be included in the application unless the work is anonymous or pseudonymous. The author's birth date is optional, but is useful as a form of identification. Leave this space blank if the author's contribution was a "work made for hire."

Author's Nationality or Domicile: Give the country of which the author is a citizen, or the country in which the author is domiciled. Nationality or domicile **must** be given in all cases.

Nature of Authorship: Give a brief general statement of the nature of this particular author's contribution to the work. Examples: "Words"; "Coauthor of Music"; "Words and Music"; "Arrangement"; "Coauthor of Book and Lyrics"; "Dramatization"; "Screen Play"; "Compilation and English Translation"; "Editorial Revisions."

SPACE 3: Creation and Publication

General Instructions: Do not confuse "creation" with "publication." Every application for copyright registration must state "the year in which creation of the work was completed." Give the date and nation of first publication only if the work has been published.

Creation: Under the statute, a work is "created" when it is fixed in a copy or phonorecord for the first time. Where a work has been prepared over a period of time, the part of the work existing in fixed form on a particular date constitutes the created work on that date. The date you give here should be the year in which the author completed the particular version for which registration is now being sought, even if other versions exist or if further changes or additions are planned.

Publication: The statute defines "publication" as "the distribution of copies or phonorecords of a work to the public by sale or other transfer of ownership, or by rental, lease, or lending"; a work is also "published" if there has been an "offering to distribute copies or phonorecords to a group of persons for purposes of further distribution, public performance, or public display." Give the full date (month, day, year) when, and the country where, publication first occurred. If first publication took place simultaneously in the United States and other countries, it is sufficient to state "U.S.A."

SPACE 4: Claimant(s)

Name(s) and Address(es) of Copyright Claimant(s): Give the name(s) and address(es) of the copyright claimant(s) in this work even if the claimant is the same as the author. Copyright in a work belongs initially to the author of the work (including, in the case of a work made for hire, the employer or other person for whom the work was prepared). The copyright claimant is either the author of the work or a person or organization to whom the copyright initially belonging to the author has been transferred.

Transfer: The statute provides that, if the copyright claimant is not the author, the application for registration must contain "a brief statement of how the claimant obtained ownership of the copyright." If any copyright claimant named in space 4 is not an author named in space 2, give a brief statement explaining how the claimant(s) obtained ownership of the copyright. Examples: "By written contract"; "Transfer of all rights by author"; "Assignment"; "By will." Do not attach transfer documents or other attachments or riders.

SPACE 5: Previous Registration

General Instructions: The questions in space 5 are intended to show whether an earlier registration has been made for this work and, if so, whether there is any basis for a new registration. As a general rule, only one basic copyright registration can be made for the same version of a particular work.

Same Version: If this version is substantially the same as the work covered by a previous registration, a second registration is not generally possible unless: (1) the work has been registered in unpublished form and a second registration is now being sought to cover this first published edition; or (2) someone other than the author is identified as copyright claimant in the earlier registration, and the author is now seeking registration in his or her own name. If either of these two exceptions applies, check the appropriate box and give the earlier registration number and date. Otherwise, do not submit Form PA; instead, write the Copyright

Office for information about supplementary registration or recordation of transfers of copyright ownership.

Changed Version: If the work has been changed and you are now seeking registration to cover the additions or revisions, check the last box in space 5, give the earlier registration number and date, and complete both parts of space 6 in accordance with the instructions below.

Previous Registration Number and Date: If more than one previous registration has been made for the work, give the number and date of the latest registration.

SPACE 6: Derivative Work or Compilation

General Instructions: Complete space 6 if this work is a "changed version," "compilation," or "derivative work," and if it incorporates one or more earlier works that have already been published or registered for copyright or that have fallen into the public domain. A "compilation" is defined as "a work formed by the collection and assembling of preexisting materials or of data that are selected, coordinated, or arranged in such a way that the resulting work as a whole constitutes an original work of authorship." A "derivative work" is "a work based on one or more preexisting works." Examples of derivative works include musical arrangements, dramatizations, translations, abridgments, condensations, motion picture versions, or "any other form in which a work may be recast, transformed, or adapted." Derivative works also include works "consisting of editorial revisions, annotations, or other modifications" if these changes, as a whole, represent an original work of authorship.

Preexisting Material (space 6a): Complete this space **and** space 6b for derivative works. In this space identify the preexisting work that has been recast, transformed, or adapted. For example, the preexisting material might be: "French version of Hugo's 'Le Roi s'amuse'." Do not complete this space for compilations.

Material Added to This Work (space 6b): Give a brief, general statement of the additional new material covered by the copyright claim for which registration is sought. In the case of a derivative work, identify this new material. Examples: "Arrangement for piano and orchestra"; "Dramatization for television"; "New film version"; "Revisions throughout; Act III completely new." If the work is a compilation, give a brief, general statement describing both the material that has been compiled **and** the compilation itself. Example: "Compilation of 19th Century Military Songs."

SPACE 7, 8, 9: Fee, Correspondence, Certification, Return Address

Deposit Account: If you maintain a Deposit Account in the Copyright Office, identify it in space 7a. Otherwise, leave the space blank and send the fee of $30 with your application and deposit.

Correspondence (space 7b): This space should contain the name, address, area code, telephone number, fax number, and email address (if available) of the person to be consulted if correspondence about this application becomes necessary.

Certification (space 8): The application cannot be accepted unless it bears the date and the **handwritten signature** of the author or other copyright claimant, or of the owner of exclusive right(s), or of the duly authorized agent of the author, claimant, or owner of exclusive right(s).

Address for Return of Certificate (space 9): The address box must be completed legibly since the certificate will be returned in a window envelope.

MORE INFORMATION

How to Register a Recorded Work: If the musical or dramatic work that you are registering has been recorded (as a tape, disk, or cassette), you may choose either copyright application Form PA (Performing Arts) or Form SR (Sound Recordings), depending on the purpose of the registration.

Form PA should be used to register the underlying musical composition or dramatic work. Form SR has been developed specifically to register a "sound recording" as defined by the Copyright Act—a work resulting from the "fixation of a series of sounds," separate and distinct from the underlying musical or dramatic work. Form SR should be used when the copyright claim is limited to the sound recording itself. (In one instance, Form SR may also be used to file for a copyright registration for both kinds of works—see (4) below.) Therefore:

(1) File Form PA if you are seeking to register the musical or dramatic work, not the "sound recording," even though what you deposit for copyright purposes may be in the form of a phonorecord.

(2) File Form PA if you are seeking to register the audio portion of an audiovisual work, such as a motion picture soundtrack; these are considered integral parts of the audiovisual work.

(3) File Form SR if you are seeking to register the "sound recording" itself, that is, the work that results from the fixation of a series of musical, spoken, or other sounds, but not the underlying musical or dramatic work.

(4) File Form SR if you are the copyright claimant for both the underlying musical or dramatic work and the sound recording, *and* you prefer to register both on the same form.

(5) File both forms PA and SR if the copyright claimant for the underlying work and sound recording differ, or you prefer to have separate registration for them.

"Copies" and "Phonorecords": To register for copyright, you are required to deposit "copies" or "phonorecords." These are defined as follows:

Musical compositions may be embodied (fixed) in "copies," objects from which a work can be read or visually perceived, directly or with the aid of a machine or device, such as manuscripts, books, sheet music, film, and videotape. They may also be fixed in "phonorecords," objects embodying fixations of sounds, such as tapes and phonograph disks, commonly known as phonograph records. For example, a song (the work to be registered) can be reproduced in sheet music ("copies") or phonograph records ("phonorecords"), or both.

Copyright Office fees are subject to change.
For current fees, check the Copyright Office
website at *www.copyright.gov*, write the Copyright Office, or call (202) 707-3000.

Form PA
For a Work of Performing Arts
UNITED STATES COPYRIGHT OFFICE

REGISTRATION NUMBER

_____

PA   PAU

EFFECTIVE DATE OF REGISTRATION

_____

Month   Day   Year

DO NOT WRITE ABOVE THIS LINE. IF YOU NEED MORE SPACE, USE A SEPARATE CONTINUATION SHEET.

1

TITLE OF THIS WORK ▼

PREVIOUS OR ALTERNATIVE TITLES ▼

NATURE OF THIS WORK ▼ See instructions

2 a

NAME OF AUTHOR ▼

DATES OF BIRTH AND DEATH
Year Born ▼   Year Died ▼

Was this contribution to the work a "work made for hire"?
☐ Yes
☐ No

AUTHOR'S NATIONALITY OR DOMICILE
Name of Country
OR { Citizen of _____
Domiciled in _____

WAS THIS AUTHOR'S CONTRIBUTION TO THE WORK
Anonymous? ☐ Yes ☐ No
Pseudonymous? ☐ Yes ☐ No

If the answer to either of these questions is "Yes," see detailed instructions.

NATURE OF AUTHORSHIP   Briefly describe nature of material created by this author in which copyright is claimed. ▼

NOTE

Under the law, the "author" of a "work made for hire" is generally the employer, not the employee (see instructions). For any part of this work that was "made for hire" check "Yes" in the space provided, give the employer (or other person for whom the work was prepared) as "Author" of that part, and leave the space for dates of birth and death blank.

b

NAME OF AUTHOR ▼

DATES OF BIRTH AND DEATH
Year Born ▼   Year Died ▼

Was this contribution to the work a "work made for hire"?
☐ Yes
☐ No

AUTHOR'S NATIONALITY OR DOMICILE
Name of Country
OR { Citizen of _____
Domiciled in _____

WAS THIS AUTHOR'S CONTRIBUTION TO THE WORK
Anonymous? ☐ Yes ☐ No
Pseudonymous? ☐ Yes ☐ No

If the answer to either of these questions is "Yes," see detailed instructions.

NATURE OF AUTHORSHIP   Briefly describe nature of material created by this author in which copyright is claimed. ▼

c

NAME OF AUTHOR ▼

DATES OF BIRTH AND DEATH
Year Born ▼   Year Died ▼

Was this contribution to the work a "work made for hire"?
☐ Yes
☐ No

AUTHOR'S NATIONALITY OR DOMICILE
Name of Country
OR { Citizen of _____
Domiciled in _____

WAS THIS AUTHOR'S CONTRIBUTION TO THE WORK
Anonymous? ☐ Yes ☐ No
Pseudonymous? ☐ Yes ☐ No

If the answer to either of these questions is "Yes," see detailed instructions.

NATURE OF AUTHORSHIP   Briefly describe nature of material created by this author in which copyright is claimed. ▼

3 a

YEAR IN WHICH CREATION OF THIS WORK WAS COMPLETED
This information must be given Year in all cases.

b DATE AND NATION OF FIRST PUBLICATION OF THIS PARTICULAR WORK
Complete this information ONLY if this work has been published.
Month _____ Day _____ Year _____
Nation

4

COPYRIGHT CLAIMANT(S) Name and address must be given even if the claimant is the same as the author given in space 2. ▼

See instructions before completing this space.

TRANSFER If the claimant(s) named here in space 4 is (are) different from the author(s) named in space 2, give a brief statement of how the claimant(s) obtained ownership of the copyright. ▼

DO NOT WRITE HERE / OFFICE USE ONLY

APPLICATION RECEIVED

ONE DEPOSIT RECEIVED

TWO DEPOSITS RECEIVED

FUNDS RECEIVED

MORE ON BACK ▶ • Complete all applicable spaces (numbers 5-9) on the reverse side of this page.
• See detailed instructions.   • Sign the form at line 8.

DO NOT WRITE HERE
Page 1 of _____ pages

EXAMINED BY	FORM PA
CHECKED BY	
☐ CORRESPONDENCE Yes	FOR COPYRIGHT OFFICE USE ONLY

DO NOT WRITE ABOVE THIS LINE. IF YOU NEED MORE SPACE, USE A SEPARATE CONTINUATION SHEET.

PREVIOUS REGISTRATION Has registration for this work, or for an earlier version of this work, already been made in the Copyright Office?

☐ **Yes** ☐ **No** If your answer is "Yes," why is another registration being sought? (Check appropriate box.) ▼ If your answer is No, do **not** check box A, B, or C.

a. ☐ This is the first published edition of a work previously registered in unpublished form.

b. ☐ This is the first application submitted by this author as copyright claimant.

c. ☐ This is a changed version of the work, as shown by space 6 on this application.

If your answer is "Yes," give: **Previous Registration Number** ▼   **Year of Registration** ▼

5

DERIVATIVE WORK OR COMPILATION Complete both space 6a and 6b for a derivative work; complete only 6b for a compilation.

Preexisting Material Identify any preexisting work or works that this work is based on or incorporates. ▼

a

6

Material Added to This Work Give a brief, general statement of the material that has been added to this work and in which copyright is claimed. ▼

b

See instructions before completing this space.

DEPOSIT ACCOUNT If the registration fee is to be charged to a Deposit Account established in the Copyright Office, give name and number of Account.

Name ▼   **Account Number** ▼

a

7

CORRESPONDENCE Give name and address to which correspondence about this application should be sent. Name/Address/Apt/City/State/ZIP ▼

b

Area code and daytime telephone number   (   )   Fax number   (   )

Email

CERTIFICATION* I, the undersigned, hereby certify that I am the

Check only one ▶
☐ author
☐ other copyright claimant
☐ owner of exclusive right(s)
☐ authorized agent of _____

Name of author or other copyright claimant, or owner of exclusive right(s) ▲

of the work identified in this application and that the statements made by me in this application are correct to the best of my knowledge.

8

Typed or printed name and date ▼ If this application gives a date of publication in space 3, do not sign and submit it before that date.

Date _____

Handwritten signature (X) ▼

☞   x _____

Certificate will be mailed in window envelope to this address:	Name ▼
	Number/Street/Apt ▼
	City/State/ZIP ▼

YOU MUST:
• Complete all necessary spaces
• Sign your application in space 8

SEND ALL 3 ELEMENTS IN THE SAME PACKAGE:
1. Application form
2. Nonrefundable filing fee in check or money order payable to *Register of Copyrights*
3. Deposit material

MAIL TO:
Library of Congress
Copyright Office
101 Independence Avenue, S.E.
Washington, D.C. 20559-6000

Fees are subject to change. For current fees, check the Copyright Office website at www.copyright.gov, or call write the Copyright Office, or call (202) 707-3000.

9

*17 U.S.C. § 506(e): Any person who knowingly makes a false representation of a material fact in the application for copyright registration provided for by section 409, or in any written statement filed in connection with the application, shall be fined not more than $2,500.

Rev: June 2002—20,000   Web Rev: June 2002   ♻ Printed on recycled paper

U.S. Government Printing Office: 2000-461-113/20,021

"People are under the mistaken impression that a song is not copyrighted until they send it to the Library of Congress, when, actually, it's officially copyrighted when it hits some form of medium, be that a recorded version or a written version," notes Mr. Passman. "You need to register the copyright at that point."

■ How to Copyright

You can copyright an album's worth of songs by filling out Form PA and sending it to the Register of Copyrights in Washington, D.C. You don't even need to send a tape; you can send music charts and lyrics.

■ Fuel: A Homemade Success

Fuel is a homemade success story. Their immaculate, muscular, impassioned rhythms and sturdy hooks walloped a region of our country and won Fuel a major label deal with Sony subsidiary 550 Music. Now Fuel is taking on America.

Brett Scallions (vocals, guitar), Carl Bell (guitar), Jeff Abercrombie (bass), and Kevin Miller (drums) established themselves in an area that was accessible to touring. They moved from Tennessee to central Pennsylvania. They toured extensively through New York, Philadelphia, Pittsburgh, Baltimore, and Washington, D.C., and built a strong local following. Their regional popularity led to a major label record deal for their second album, *Sunburn*. They're very satisfied, proud musicians, and would like to share their story with you. . . .

So, how long did it take for the band to make Sunburn, *your third collection of songs, but your first major label album?*
CARL BELL: Approximately six years.

Your first venture was a self-titled tape. Then you recorded your own album, Porcelain. *How did you know that you were ready to make an album?*
BRETT SCALLIONS: We had a nice collage of songs.

CB: We always wanted to record our own stuff, so we would take whatever money we'd make from gigs and buy our own recording equipment. We bought some ADATs and stuff, so we had recording equipment sitting around. The *Porcelain* CD, as well as the *Fuel* tape, were self-recorded in clubs. We'd go in before we played a show, set up the band, and actually record a song during rehearsal. Then we'd go back and mix it on the same recording console that we used for the gig that night.

Porcelain grew out of that experience. It wasn't that we made the decision that we're going to make a record now. The way we did the recording process took us a long time to get it all together.

How long did it take you to get your music together?
BS: A year, year and a half.
CB: We did our first tape in '94, and *Porcelain* in '96, and *Sunburn* in '98, so it took us a couple of years to get it all together. Obviously, with *Porcelain*, we were working at the same time, so we just had to do it as we were able. Finding the time was as hard as finding the money.

The songs that you had on your tape—did those make it onto the album?
BS: No. That tape was basically a tape of us trying to find ourselves.

Does Porcelain *have a theme?*
CB: The songs started to be a little more refined and a little more focused than on our tape. It was our second time through; we were a little more comfortable and had more of an idea of what we wanted to do. The third time around was even easier.

You sold over ten thousand copies of Porcelain *without any specific form of distribution; how did you do it?*
BS: We sold it at shows and also local music stores in our area, Harrisburg, Pennsylvania.
CB: We distributed it out of the trunk of our car; we went around to the music stores delivering albums.
JEFF ABERCROMBIE: A couple of chains of stores like the Wall picked it up.

You guys are originally from Kenton, Tennessee. Why did you move to Harrisburg, Pennsylvania? For your career?
BS: Harrisburg worked out for us. It was a short drive to markets like Philadelphia, Pittsburgh, New York, Baltimore, and Washington, D.C., where we began building a loyal following. The fan base here has been really overwhelming. They've supported us from day one, and it just grew and grew.

How did you promote yourselves?
BS: The radio stations were really, really responsive to the CD once we got it out. They started playing a couple of tracks off it, and that really spawned the labels getting interested in us. We played live shows all the time, we hauled

our own PA system, our own backline, our own lights, everything. We'd just go out there and make it happen the best we could. Get someplace to play and just do it. We were determined to keep on persevering until it happened.

How did it happen?
CB: Once we started getting great support from the fan base in Harrisburg, we got great support from the radio stations there. Once the radio stations started playing a lot of us, word of mouth started going around to the industry that there was a song being played, and this band Fuel was hot. We created a lot of word of mouth inside the music industry.

So, it was a combination of playing live and getting radio airplay that broke you?
CB: It was definitely a combination. It takes a lot of different avenues to make it all come together. It's a whole mix of things.

How did you get a major label deal?
BS: Our agent, Mike Krebs at ICM, had a genuine interest in the band before we even started to get label attention. He liked us a lot and said, "Hey, I want to work with you guys." We said, "Yeah, sure." A couple of hours later, he called us up and said, "Hey, you guys want to open for Silverchair?" The next thing you know, we're in front of four thousand screaming kids. He booked some key shows for us and invited people out.

Was it the Silverchair gig that got you signed?
BS: That was a good start. We had a lot of label people who did come out to see the show, and that was their first time.
CB: That was the first time 550, the label that we're signed to, ever saw us.
BS: A label rep sent out his assistant to check us out.
JA: Also, the radio stations were calling into the record companies, saying, Hey, you know, we want you guys to hear this! And they would even send them the CD. Local radio was really supportive of what we did.
CB: We were very lucky. We met some great people at radio stations in Harrisburg.

How did you finally get signed?
BS: Our manager started making calls, and we set up a few showcases in New York City and invited people out.

How did you get the money for the showcases?

CB: We had a band fund. You need to ration the money very carefully, and keep a band fund going that will get you gigs and get you to places that you need to play.

BS: We had to give away a lot of CDs, but we were selling our CDs at the same time, so we were getting some money back from the sales of the CD. The CD was done totally on our own, so we didn't have to pay anyone anything. We didn't have to pay to play, either.

JA: It was funny—the last time we played CBGB in New York, it was a packed house, and they actually paid us to play. They were like, You were the first band who actually got paid to play at CBGB. Wow. It was cool. Our agent was so happy, he asked if he could be the one who collected the money. That was a landmark day.

BS: When we signed our contract, that was really cool, too. We had just gotten off the stage. We had done a big show with Tonic and the Verve Pipe at Millersville University, in front of three thousand people. As soon as we walked off the stage, we went back into our dressing room and signed the contract.

When did you bring on a lawyer?

JA: It wasn't until our deal with 550 that we bought in a lawyer. Our management took care of it before that. It's great that we have such wonderful management, David Levin. They've been managing Live, so they know the ins and outs, and it makes a lot of difference.

Now you've got a major label deal. What's the difference between recording an album on a major label and creating an indie release?

JA: Obviously, you get a bigger budget for your record. You have all this input and all these other talented people around you.

CB: If Sony distributes your record, it sure carries a heck of a lot more weight than you doing it out of your trunk. You're hooked up to major national distribution. We can now concentrate on our music. But we had to get to where we are. You've got to have contacts to make contacts. When you're doing it all yourself, it's just a lot of time and a lot of distractions from your music.

You didn't use a producer or an engineer on Porcelain. *What was it like to have the luxury of Steve Haigler's extra ears on* Sunburn?

JA: It's really nice to have someone there who knows all the tricks. When it comes down to mike placements and everything like that, it's always neat to sit back and watch the guys who have been there and done it for years and years and years and years. It's like, Wow! Okay, if you put the microphone a little further out on the speaker you get that kind of a tone.

How does your more recent album, Sunburn, *differ from* Porcelain, *your first record?*
CB: It's got different songs on it.
BS: We refined our music somewhat and tried to take it to the next level. Our goal was to make *Sunburn* a much bigger and better thing.
CB: We like the melody, we like to rock, we're really into the lyric side of things. The music has to be engaging and passionate; it just can't be wallpaper in the background. We're very conscious about melodies, and we like to have engaging lyrics, but we're not afraid to rock.

What would you like to accomplish with Sunburn?
CB: Just have people hear the music and if they like it they pass it on, spread it to the world.
JA: Have it touch somebody.

If you were going to share some advice as to how you got to where you are, what would it be?
CB: Work hard. Nothing in this business is easy. Nothing. We've been working really, really hard for a long time and are totally dedicated to making it happen, to the point of risking it all. We hauled our own PA system.
JA: Our life consisted of driving to the gig, setting it up, playing our show, breaking down the PA, driving back home. Then doing it all again the next day and just on and on. We persevered.

Have you made it?
CB: We've always said that making it is having roadies. We've hauled our equipment so long, if I could just look over my shoulder and see somebody packing my gear one night, I'd be, like, All right!

CHAPTER THREE

Raising Money

When I was going to UCLA, I thought, Any day now, I'm

going to get a record contract. I didn't worry about what

kind of job I would have because I was going to be a big

rock star. I'm now of the belief that you have to go out and

meet people and let them know who you are so you can

make it happen.

—Fletcher Beasley, musician and producer

If you build it, they will come. Start building your dream. A lot of musicians hell-bent on making a record begin their careers by self-financing an album through credit cards and in whatever way, shape, or form they can concoct to raise some extra income. Absolutely! Find a way to get something decent down on tape, but make it a work in progress. Demonstrate that you want to be the next U2 or Tchaikovsky. Show interest to get interest. If what you're working on is good, you'll find backers.

"Bands will get family money, money they raise themselves, favors from existing studio people—wherever they can get it," observes Lonn Friend, former vice president of A&R West Coast for Arista Records.

"Maybe they engineer and get some free studio time; they can work in the middle of the night and not interrupt the studio's daily process. Cut a couple of tracks that way. Find an independent benefactor that will throw in a few thousand dollars with the commitment that if they do get a deal, there will be an override for that individual down the road."

To get to point B, getting money to make an album, you have to start at point A, recording an album. To win people, you have to have something to show them. The more effort you put into making it happen, the more likely it is to happen.

"Initially, I got outright loans with a payback percentage rate," explains Tom Viscount of Viscount. "I paid those people off with money from people who wanted to invest. After the beginning of the project, people could see if they liked it. That's when the money really started to build."

Start somewhere, even if it's small. Get the ball rolling. A hot project always gathers momentum. If you believe in yourself, others will believe in you.

■ Live Helps

If you're a band that gigs, you'll learn that finding financing for an album is easier if you're recording music and playing out at the same time. Kill two birds with one stone—invite financiers to your shows.

Tom Viscount is one of the myriad of performers who secured funding for his CD, *My Name Is Nobody,* by inviting potential investors to see him play.

"People came to my shows. They heard the gigs. They liked what I did, and we were in business," Tom recalls. "I had about $20,000–$25,000 given to me to cover recording costs to get the CD done; the vast majority of those people came to see me perform live. If they liked it, they wanted in. I took a buy-in from people who were familiar with and liked the music. I didn't get a lot of offers from people who hadn't heard the music."

■ People Who Can Help You

Finance people are people that you know. If you know people in business making good money, oftentimes, they want to be involved in something creative—be patrons of the arts, so to speak. Approach them, give them an earful about what's going on, and they either can get excited about it or not.

"We put out two albums before we were signed," reveals Matt Devine of Kill Hannah. The band got a deal with Atlantic Records in 2003, eight years after their beginning. "We just borrowed and borrowed. We were, like, $40,000 in debt. We borrowed from lawyers, parents, financiers, whoever."

Gifts of album contributions come in packages of all shapes and sizes, wrapped in a rainbow of ribbons. Your album sleeve may feature shots from a photographer that has taken pictures of you. The photographer might want to get involved just to have the ego stroke of seeing her work on a CD. Maybe you know someone who is a creative director who might get off on doing the artwork for you. Your friend the writer can do the album sleeve and bio. Your buddy the big-time marketing man can teach you ways to get your word out there.

"Viscount is truly just Tom Viscount and his writing partner. We have rotating bandmates—talented session guys from Los Angeles that sit in with me. They played on the CD for next to nothing," notes Tom. "The guy who produced it for us did it for next to nothing. We got a lot of favors. But that's buy-in; they all get a piece of the pie."

To get people to give you time and money to make your album, you have to figure out how to get people to like it. That comes back to the material: the songs have to be good. Whatever you demo, make it seem like you put some time and money into it. This is your art that you're presenting to the world; take pride in your effort.

"If someone hands me a tape, I look at the packaging," notes Lonn Friend. "If they put some work into a presentation, then I'd pop it on in the car and listen to one song."

Another really great aspect about investing in your project yourself is that you get to keep a higher percentage of any profits because there's less buy-in from other people. If you truly believe you're going to be a big star, this is a great way to go about making your music and keeping the largest part of your proceeds. It's how Ani DiFranco went about her career.

■ The Ani DiFranco Story

Ani DiFranco blends many forms of contemporary music into a sound that's completely her own. She takes edgy punk and melds it with mellow folk sensibilities, simultaneously sounding like jazz, blues, and pop. Her lyrics are political, yet personal. She makes good, competitive music—but that's not what makes her so interesting. Ani DiFranco is extremely pertinent because of her approach to business. Since 1990, Ani has released eight albums on her own label, Righteous Babe Records, out of Buffalo, New York.

Her career started out like everyone else's. Ani's first "release" was a demo cassette she recorded to help secure gigs. She also sold tapes out of the trunk of her car and from the stage after the gig.

When Ani tried to shop a deal, the major labels didn't show much interest.

She thought about signing with an independent label, but the idea of retaining complete control of her music and finances appealed to her too strongly to ignore. She formed her own label, Righteous Babe Records. Her label currently employs six people, and DiFranco has sold nearly four hundred thousand albums.

■ More Creative Funding Ideas

David Bowie sold stock in himself. In February, 1997, Bowie raised $55 million by selling bonds backed by his first twenty-five albums. Motown songwriters Brian Holland, Lamont Dozier, and Eddie Holland followed suit with their own $30 million offering. Then, Rod Stewart received a $15.4 million securitized loan from Nomura Capital backed by revenues from his catalog.

Selling stock in artists has become the new trend. According to the *Wall Street Journal* Interactive Edition (February 10, 1998), the securities unit of Prudential Insurance Company of America has provided in the neighborhood of $200 million in financing to a new company, CAK Universal Credit Corporation, which plans to make loans to musicians and other artists backed by income from future sales of their works. The company is headed by Charles Koppelman, former chairman of EMI Capitol Music Group, and is based in New York. In the meantime, Crosby, Stills & Nash, the Rolling Stones, Elton John, and other platinum-selling acts are now weighing similar deals.

To create diversified investment portfolios for their old age, mature rockers are leveraging their steadiest source of income—recording and songwriting royalties. These artists have decided that selling securities now beats waiting for that monthly royalty check, because it allows them to cash out and invest money elsewhere.

It's a great idea. Find a way to modify the selling-stock-in-yourself concept and make it work for you. How's this for a concept? Investment bankers package years' worth of cash flow—in this case, expected earnings from royalties—into debt securities that are pitched to private investors. The proceeds from the sale (minus bankers' fees) go to the artist; the investors are repaid as the royalties roll in.

Do it on a small scale. What these megastars are leveraging are very large catalogs that generate steady sales. Investment bankers say such catalogs should be valued at more than $10 million to attract sufficient investor interest.

What is your vision for your catalog of work? Do you want to put it up for collateral? Mr. Koppelman's company lends money specifically to the owners of songs, movies, books, and other intellectual property, allowing them, according to Koppelman, "to cash in on their assets without cashing out of their assets." CAK Universal Credit is already sitting on applications for at least $150 million of loans from various musicians.

There's a great business plan there. How can you make it work for you?

■ Lawyers, Guns, and Money

Having power people on your side can most definitely be a big help. Lawyers and managers want you to make money, so they're going to do their best to help you find those greenbacks. Unless you're incredibly special, they're probably not going to whip out their checkbook and ask you how much you want. But they're businessmen, and a good businessman is an expert at playing with other people's money.

A well-connected lawyer will usually hook you up with a record label or publishing company. If he's a really perfect lawyer, he'll supply the best-of-all-worlds scenario and have a record label sign you first, because a record company is going to sign you for a decent amount of money.

When you've got a record deal, your lawyer will then approach a publishing company. A publishing company can best be described as a giant collection agency that collects the royalties on your song. It will give you a nice healthy advance on your album.

Once you get the first deal, the rest tends to fall into place. Because you have a record deal, the publishing company knows that you will eventually release an album. A good lawyer will go to a publishing company and say, Sign Emoticon and give them a big, fat advance, because you know they've got a record coming out. Within a year, you can start to recoup your money.

If a record label is not interested enough in signing you right now—and your group, Emoticon, is desperate for cash—your legal guy may lure the publishing company into a smaller deal. Publishing companies like to sign acts before they get too big: that way, they spend less money. An unsigned artist will always get the smaller deal.

"If you look like you're sitting on top of a hot enough catalog of publishing, they will give you an advance," notes veteran songwriter David Javelosa. "But be advised, those deals are few and far between these days. Not much of anyone is getting major publishing or writer advances, but they are getting other perks."

"The theory of a publishing company in the nineties is to act more like a bank than anything else," observes Lonn Friend. "They will give an act money, although they don't incur any of the nut to market and promote that act which a major label has to incur. So, they're throwing anywhere from $10,000–$200,000 at a band that's got a record deal in the hopes that the band gets them a hit and they recoup big mechanical royalties. Unsigned acts that get the attention of a publisher will be given development money so they can make that demo or that record."

If you're an unsigned act and the record labels aren't biting, but you've got good, solid songs, a publisher may take a chance on you. They'll give you a smaller advance, basically enough to help you get your record made.

"When we did the deal with Poshboy Records, we negotiated for as much publishing money as possible," recalls David. "Poshboy had enough acts where they could generate a stream of income from one of the publishing associations."

Publishers can be very beneficial to young artists. A lot of publishers have their own studios, so they'll just bring you in and set you up with things like studio musicians and producers. They'll help you develop your craft. If you're one of those really lucky musical acts, your publisher may work with you until you're ready for a record label, and they will help you shop the labels, as well.

Once you're an established band, publishing advances can become extremely lucrative. It could easily be a six-figure advance if you're already charting on the Billboard Top 100. Even if you're not with a major label and you've got a handful of records out on an indie label, you can still get a four- or five-figure advance.

■ Royalties

BMI and ASCAP are companies that license music. They acquire the rights from writers and publishers for their music. In turn, these companies grant licenses for their entire repertoire to places that use music: TV, radio, hotels, nightclubs, amusements parks—any of the hundreds of thousands of establishments where music is publicly performed. ASCAP and BMI collect the license fees from these users of music and distribute that money to the writers and publishers.

To put it quite simply, BMI and ASCAP are the organizations that make sure you're paid when your music is played in all the places that it's impossible for you to monitor yourself. ASCAP was founded by writers and publishers, and is still run by writers and publishers to this day. BMI is run by broadcasters.

"The biggest difference between ASCAP and BMI is that I believe that we are more hands-on," notes Cheryl Dickerson, senior director of writer/

publisher relations at BMI. "We try to cater to our writers and take care of all their needs. We don't pass them around from one department to another; we try to keep them with one person at the company. BMI tends to be a little more hands-on, but we both do the same job. We collect money and distribute it to the writers and publishers."

You're eligible to become an ASCAP or BMI writer if you've written a musical composition alone, or if you've collaborated with other writers, and if that work is either ready to be commercially published or recorded or otherwise likely to be performed somewhere.

If you're playing a lot and you're showing up on charts, you get checks for clumps of money. If you've got a million-seller that's all over the airwaves—heavy rotation nationwide—you can easily make a million dollars off of an album just because of the structure that's in place.

"Before our album *For Never & Ever* was released, we basically got pocket change," notes Kill Hannah's Matt Devine. "We had some songs used on MTV, and a couple of other things but the money was nothing substantial."

Publishing is actually split up into two sections. They call it a 200 percent system. One hundred percent goes to the artist who wrote the tune; the other 100 percent goes to the publisher. If you're independent, you own the publishing as well; if not, there's an "industrial clause" (stating that the mechanical rights belong to the publishing company) in your contract, so somebody owns half of what you do. As the songwriter, you can negotiate for a section of the publishing. Do this; otherwise, half of what you own will go to someone else.

Here's something to take note of in your search for extra cash to make your record: If you look like you're sitting on top of a hot enough catalog of publishing, ASCAP or BMI might give you an advance, although publishing and writing advances are few and far between these days.

■ Pitching Your Demo

Okay . . . so you've done everything you need to do to get to this juncture—you've started making a record. Great, now you've got something, but you've got to get people to listen to it.

Find a way to get your music to the right people. Look on recent record albums; bands always list their A&R contacts. Finding them is easy; they're probably in New York or Los Angeles. Have the most outspoken member of your band make phone calls to A&R guys and hype them a little bit so they expect to get your demo. Find a way to make your stuff stand out, because A&R people get so much stuff, and a lot of stuff is terrible. Their ears get saturated. They've got to have a reason to want to hear your stuff—so give it to them.

"Uggh! It's a hard thing to pitch your demo; it's a numbers game," notes Lonn Friend. "A&R gets so many projects. I advise initially going for the small label that doesn't have a lot of acts."

It's important to find a label that really likes your music. If it's small, who cares? Oftentimes, if you get to a small, independent label, that's the new A&R for the major labels. The small company might be the one that pushes you, and all of a sudden, you're on a major label through a small label that got bought out by a larger company.

Show them your media kit—clips of the magazines you've been involved with. Let them know that you're actually being played on a college radio station.

"There certainly is a level of dollars that people are willing to give," declares Kathy Callahan, senior director of western regional sales at BMG Music. "With each act the record company is asking themselves, How much are we going to spend recording this record?"

The basic criteria to deciding how much a record company is willing to put up to do a record is return on investment. What does the label think it will be able to get out of the investment on the back end? Other questions the executives will ask themselves are: Historically, how much does it cost to make an album like this? How much studio time do we need? How many musicians do we need? There are a lot of different aspects to funding an album.

■ Media

There's money in getting media attention. One really good way to get people interested in your project—both as financiers and consumers—is to show them that other people approve of what you do. Get the media involved. Call the local press; invite them down to a show. Do whatever you can to collect a scrapbook of other people's opinions of your band.

Talk to the media; they don't bite. Go through your local publications and identify all the record reviewers, and send them your record. Follow up with a phone call—act interested, like you care. You may find commercial radio to be a brick wall, but try college radio; KUSF in San Francisco, KXLU in L.A., and others, are pretty open-minded.

There are college radio stations all over that will play songs from unsigned bands. You can get a list of these stations, pitch your song to them, and maybe, if you're lucky, they'll put it in the midnight rotation. Get people to talk about you; at the very least, it will help you sell tickets to your shows.

"When we first started out as Los Microwaves, we would book clubs in cities that had scenes, fanzines and college radio stations—places where we were actually able to identify the market on our own," shares David Javelosa. "It absolutely helped us to sell singles."

You also never know who's going to be thumbing through a local weekly or monthly checking out the bands.

"Consumer press, I pay mind to if acts are getting written about in a fanzine," declares Lonn Friend. "Industry press is nothing but a spin vehicle, and it generally doesn't sway my opinion. It helps a group get attention, but it also brings out all the lemmings. It creates heat where sometimes there shouldn't be any heat, driving the price of a band up to a level where it should not necessarily be."

■ Points

When you make an album, the royalties you make on a record are calculated by points. The point system is essentially music industry terminology for a percentage of an album.

The standard contracts in the nineties are universal when it comes to sharing points. On a contract, you're usually going to get from twelve to fourteen points on your record. Some indie labels, who often get the coolest music, don't have a lot of money to spend to record or sign, so they up the royalty rate to upwards of twenty points to do the deal with that act.

"The gross on the record is subject to a lot of different definitions, and by the time you're done with things like packaging, and all sorts of other different expenses from the calculations, 14 percent can be a whole lot less than you'd think," observes music industry attorney Michael Leventhal. "Your royalty rate is based on a certain number, and that number is generally the suggested retail list price, less all sorts of deductions."

For example, packaging deductions can be anywhere from 10 to 25 percent of the entire amount.

"All sorts of other things can come into play during the length of a sixty-page contract," notes Michael. "They give it to you in one paragraph, and they take it away for the next fifty-nine pages."

With most labels, points are calculated on suggested retail price, i.e., 14 percent of $16.98 or thereabouts; but be wary, because it's not always that way. Some labels—Sony is one of them—calculate your percentage on the wholesale price. Under that scenario, let's say, the band Smarty Boots is drawing twice the amount of points on half the amount of money—for example, 28 percent of $8.49. If Smarty Boots were going to make a 14-point deal with

Warner Bros. on the suggested retail price, they might get 28 points on the wholesale price with Sony. Neither one is better; it's nothing more than another way to confuse people. If the label changed, it would wreak havoc in the accounting department.

☼ **COMMIT IT TO MEMORY:** *Watch for added expenses thaat the record label will charge against royalties.*

Here's the next thing to watch out for: you'd think with 14 points, you'd get 14 percent of $16.98. Such is not the case. You have to watch for added expenses. The record company will shave off money for expenses they would otherwise be paying for.

"Record companies are like one big bank; you just get money when you need it, you recoup it when you can; if not, you don't. I don't know what band sees royalty checks," observes Joe Daniels, half of the gold-selling Island Records band Local H. "Take a group like the Smashing Pumpkins—they sold 7 million records [*Mellon Collie and the Infinite Sadness*]. When they did the next record [*Adore*], they probably asked the record label for a $14 million advance. Maybe the record label said, 'No, we'll give you $7 million, because you sold 7 million records. Then we'll give you another million—$8 million.' That's how it works; they're not really giving royalty checks. Anyway, imagine all the money the record company had to spend on advertising, radio play, MTV play, all that stuff, in order to sell your 7 million records. They had to spend a lot of money to make that money. So, it just goes in a circle."

Pressing and packaging are one of those added expenses you have to watch out for. In theory, this expense is what it actually costs to create and press the disc, put the paperwork in, and package it in a jewel box, but they're usually building in an additional bit of profit, as well. How do we know this? Pure logic.

In the old days, you had a 10 percent packaging charge on vinyl albums. When tapes came in the charge was upped to 20 percent. The idea was that the manufacturers had to tool up to generate cassette tapes. Same thing happened when the market turned toward CDs in the early eighties—the packaging charge went up to 25 percent. Crunch the numbers. The reality is, it's cheaper to generate packaging for CDs than it is for vinyl albums. It's just a way to shave off money from what they might owe you. So, when you start at $17.98, you just lop off 25 percent from your calculations before you apply your 14 percent.

■ Who Gets Points

And you thought all those juicy profit points were for your group. Wrong! Other people are cutting into that pie. The producer usually gets two to four points, depending on the power of the producer and the power of the artist.

"Typically, a producer will get 3 percent of retail," confirms George Drakoulias, the staff producer and A&R executive for American Recordings. "Top producers can get 4 percent, but almost never more than that. Sometimes a producer will have to settle for 2 percent, but rarely less than that."

That price is prorated per track, so if you use several different producers, they'll each get a percentage based on how many tracks on the album they produced.

Other people get a piece of the pie, as well. Sometimes, an engineer may get half a point. Your A&R guy will get a point, but he's still your friend. He doesn't take that from the artist's share; his profit on you is calculated from the record company's percentage.

■ Financing Points

Points are like Las Vegas gambling chips, and are given to people who are part of your team. Figure points are really a percentage of the album's gross sales. People who finance your album expect points in return. In other words, you've sold stock to finance your business—the making of your album—and your investors will want their dividends in the form of points. Who gets what is all negotiable, depending upon how desperate you are and how much money they contributed to your project.

When reimbursing investors for their contributions to your project, one usually uses a system where they get a certain percent of the first CD and a different percent of the second CD. Some people have been foolish enough to give a lot of it away. They had no money and they were desperate, so they gave 50 percent of the project away. How you bargain will depend on what your situation is.

How you should structure your record career totally depends upon your objectives. If Pumping Red is trying to sell a million records, they're never going to do it by self-releasing and distributing their own album. They will have to find investors and reimburse them with points. If they're trying to break the act in Boston, they can probably do it by themselves, without giving away shares of the project. If Pumping Red wants to get a radio station in Houston to play the record, and use that to help them get a buzz started and get signed by a major label, they can go that route. There are many paths to take in financing and producing a record. It's rare that a band creates a record and makes it a hit all by itself, but you never know.

▇ Sister Hazel's Success Story

When Universal Records picked up Gainesville, Florida, band Sister Hazel their album was selling as big as the Wallflowers' album was selling in that market at that time. People were buying it because they heard it on the radio and they liked the record. The record company figured that if Sister Hazel could be a hit in Gainesville, it could be a hit anywhere. Sister Hazel has since gone platinum. Their first single, "All for You," from the album . . . *Somewhere More Familiar,* was top ten at three different formats of radio. We had the opportunity to speak with drummer Mark Janowski about how Sister Hazel broke.

How did Sister Hazel get a major label deal?
MARK JANOWSKI: We were a pretty huge independent band that was touring and doing well in six to twelve states, primarily in the Southeast. At first there was a cassette made, a demo cassette used to get gigs. So many people really liked the songs on the cassette that we recorded a few of them for a CD. Our CD became a real popular seller in the South. We kept touring around the South, and selling this CD. In May of 1996, we went into the studio to record the album . . . *Somewhere More Familiar,* which was released nationally in 1997. But it was first recorded as an independent album.

What made . . . Somewhere More Familiar *work?*
MJ: We spent eight months on the road singing the songs that were going to be on the album. They were pretty tight, and a lot of people already knew all the songs. We went into the studio and basically financed the whole thing by ourselves.

We came up with a huge campaign of how we were going to get ourselves signed. We did a full merchandising catalog based on what bands like Dave Matthews, Phish, and Widespread Panic had done—it was a ten-page full-color catalog that actually went into the disc. So, we had this huge promotional catalog that went into the CD. We also did the rest of the artwork for the disc.

Once the record and package were done, we spent quite a bit of money buying spots on the radio promoting the record, as well as putting up posters that we designed to promote ourselves.

How did you get distribution for your independently released album?

MJ: Our management team, Split Nickel Entertainment in Atlanta, owns Timeless Records. They were working with a distribution company and were able to get distribution through them, and the distribution company was able to get it into the major chains and the mom-and-pop and one-stop stores. We bought some end-capping [product placement] in some places—when you can actually see the CD notched in the bins on the front of the aisles. That was a wise investment. When you walk into the record store and you see the CD right in front of you instead of having to go to the shelf, it's more visible.

We also had one person who was totally working on radio and press. All they did every day was call up radio stations and let them know what was going on.

It's really hard to do, to get a station to play your independent album. It was really a lot of work, that and calling all the press people and trying to get them to write stories about Sister Hazel, so we'd come into the cities and we'd have an article. We'd also buy ads promoting our shows, and we put up a Web site.

Also, to help promote the music, we made a four-song sample CD of the four songs we thought were strongest on the album. We sent that out to radio stations six to eight weeks before the album was going to be released. That way, they already had songs to spin on the radio.

We used that four-song CD as a marketing tool. We'd go into college-area cities where we were trying to build a following and give out a whole bunch of these four-song samplers. Those samplers had a telephone number on them, so people could call the local radio stations and request the songs. The sticker also said where you could buy the CD, so we ended up using that as a marketing tool.

How did you figure out how to market your product?

MJ: A lot of it we made up ourselves. We had a plan of what we wanted to do, we knew what the end goal was, so we just came up with ways that we thought would put us in a better situation. First and primarily, we've been a touring band, so we wanted to keep our touring base and keep growing in concentric circles away from the South. As soon as we could play one city and draw a good amount of people, we knew we could then go to the next city further away.

How did you get on the radio?

MJ: We had two stations in Florida. On one of them, we were the number one song for 1996 as an independent band. That helped a huge amount. We also had SoundScan track our CD sales in the store, so with the SoundScan, the crowd numbers we were drawing at shows, and the press, we were creating a huge buzz.

How early on did you pick up management?

MJ: We picked up management a year before we got signed. We decided to get management because you can't do everything yourself. The main thing for Sister Hazel as a band is to go out there and play good music every night.

We were very involved at the indie stage, but there's only so much you can do from the road. We knew Annie Levine at Front Row management from Gainesville. She had a great grasp of the club scene in the South, so she became our first manager. Front Row was doing everything: personal management and booking the band. They could take us so far. As we progressed, there came the time when we needed to switch the booking to someone else and gain some other services. Front Row stayed with us as our personal management, and then we signed up with Steve Epstein and Roger Stemmel from Split Nickel. That got our album distribution with Autonomous, so that was a huge leap for us. In addition to being able to book us well in the South, Split Nickel was able to hook us up with some other bands around the country.

We had eight months with both teams in place before the album was released.

How did having two management teams in place help build your following?

MJ: We already had three cities where our shows had more than a thousand people in attendance. Split Nickel booked us in some other places and really pounded them hard. By the time . . . *Somewhere More Familiar* came out, we had six cities that were really strong, plus a couple of other places that were starting to build. So we really laid a lot of groundwork building other markets before the album came out.

Split Nickel also hooked us up with an attorney four months before the album came out independently. At that point, we took the plan we formulated in our head to our attorney and figured out how we were going to utilize what was happening for us as a tool that he could take to the record companies and let other people know about us.

The only way the labels would have known what was going on with us was if they had people doing research. We wanted to make sure the labels knew, so we forced the hand of everything that was happening. Our attorney sent out faxes of what we accomplished every month to the record labels and publishing companies, and at some point, they took notice. If you're selling CDs and you're on the radio, and you're doing this as an independent band, they're going to take notice.

When did the record labels finally call on you?
MJ: In approximately three months, ten thousand copies of . . . *Somewhere More Familiar* were SoundScanned. *White Copy,* the original Sister Hazel CD, was at about ten thousand, also. Then we had several labels calling us. Universal Records won the bid and rereleased . . . *Somewhere More Familiar* at the start of 1998, because that was doing so well.

All these things were happening together, and that was the key for us getting noticed.

You're from northern Florida. Did being from off the beaten path make it difficult to get access to the record companies?
MJ: Hootie and the Blowfish were the first thing to explode from the South in a long time, and it really opened people's eyes and ears to what was happening in this part of the country. Then, Dave Matthews, who's from Virginia, came along and the labels really started to look to the South. Now, there's Sister Hazel, there's Creed, there's Matchbox 20, Less Than Jake, Mighty Joe Plumb, Marilyn Manson . . . there's a lot going on. Everyone's trying to compare it to Seattle, but in Florida, there's no trend like grunge; every band sounds totally different. Sister Hazel doesn't sound anything like Seven Mary Three or Creed, and those bands don't sound anything like Matchbox 20 or Less Than Jake or For Squirrels. Everyone sounds completely different. It was hard to try and get record people out and to know who you are in Florida, but these bands have really started to open doors for a lot of other bands.

Once you got signed to a major label deal, did you feel like you were on easy street?
MJ: Even after you get signed you still have to be majorly involved with your career. Too many people take it for granted that once you get a deal, you don't have to do anything anymore, that you let the record company steer you. We're very heavily involved in our career, because that's exactly what it is, our career. We want to do what we want to do.

Universal has been awesome in that respect. From the beginning, they plugged into what we were doing, the grassroots thing in the South. When we came out with our record, Universal had people going to some of the bigger shows of bands that were similar to us—like Counting Crows and Blues Traveler—and handing out our four-song sampler just to get people turned on to Sister Hazel. Universal was listening to what we were doing. They just kept plugging into our ideas and running with them.

What you need to do is have a vision of what you want and what you want to do, and do it. Don't expect things to be done for you; then, you have no control over that situation, and if something goes bad, you have no one to blame but yourself.

If you knew three years ago that you'd be where you are today, would you be satisfied?
MJ: We couldn't be happier. We're still doing exactly what we want to do, and that's make music in front of people, have them enjoy what we're doing and sing along to our songs. We've accomplished our goal of making a career out of the music industry. Not that many people are fortunate enough to do what they want to do and make a living at it. For us, just being able to do that is a great accomplishment.

Where would you like to be three years from now?
MJ: We want to do everything that we're doing now, but just bring it to a wider audience. Right now, we have a really large fan base—we appeal to from, like, eight to fifty year olds because there's something in our music for everyone. Our core fan base is definitely our college crowd, but now radio has spurred on the under-eighteen crowd. They're bringing stuff home to their parents, who are listening to it and saying, Wow, this is something that my child likes that I can actually listen to. That's a unique situation, and a great feeling that we can appeal to so many people. That's why our album went platinum.

Is having a vision important?
MJ: The worst thing to do is to go into a deal and let the record label lead you in different directions because you don't have a vision of what you want to do. We were doing the same circuit for years in the South and playing all these shows and touring and getting a really strong fan base—we had a plan, and the record companies took notice of that.

Nowadays, it's different in the music business than it was in the eighties. You don't have arena shows. You have bands that are multiplatinum playing in these two to three-thousand-seat theaters. Music is still really popular today, but sports has taken over the entertainment dollar in America, so you don't have this huge push behind the entertainment field.

Also, radio is definitely different. Ten years ago, radio would pick a band that they thought was really good—those that had pretty good albums, but never had really huge songs, like .38 Special. Radio stayed behind the band and finally got them some hits. Nowadays it's all about songs; you have to write really good hit songs to get on the radio. You can have a really great band that doesn't have any hit songs—Widespread Panic and Phish are perfect examples—and they don't get any radio airplay.

The more things that you can have to back up your career, the stronger it's going to be. There's room out there for all kinds of music. If you have your own plan and vision put together, you can do anything you want to do.

What advice would you give to bands looking for a record deal?
MJ: It's important to put together a story like we did. Have a following in several areas, have people coming to your shows, and be determined. Have some kind of management working for you; build a really strong team so that when you try to find a deal, you have a good attorney and a good manager. Then, once you get the deal, you'll have a plan and a concept.

As a breaking act, the more things you have in your corner, the better off you're going to be. If you were selling CDs on your own and good things were happening, then you took it to a label and it didn't work, you would still have something to fall back on.

No matter what happened to Sister Hazel, whether we got a record deal or not, we were going to continue to go out there and make music because that's what we wanted to do. We knew we could do it. Bands like Fisher Wife still do it. They don't have songs on the radio, and they still get huge numbers of people at their shows. If you can do that and make music and keep recording, then you should be totally content, because you've got a career making music.

CHAPTER FOUR

Getting the Album Deal

Some people want to succeed so badly that they'll let

common sense go out the door. They'll make business

decisions that, under normal circumstances, they might not

make. I try to warn people that a bad record deal can be

worse than no deal at all.

—Mike Sistad, manager of A&R, Arista Records, Nashville

"To succeed in the mainstream, a band needs a record label," declares former Arista A&R Vice President Lonn Friend. "There's no way to get marketed or distributed properly on a national level if a band doesn't have a record label. Sure, on a local level, they can do it, even on a regional level, but not on a national or an international level. You need to have a network to grow beyond the local level, and you will develop that, if you have the goods."

Getting a major label deal means getting seen, which means you have to put yourself in the proper situation. If you're in a small town and you know you have a really cool band, invite the media to your shows. Promote your performance like you do your demo: invite the local press out to your concerts; get the local radio station out; put them on your guest list. When these VIPs finally do show up, have the guy at the door who checks off the names on the list call you; introduce yourself, and give this person who can help you a copy of your disc. Be personable; make friends. The music business is all about who you know, so know as many people as you can.

"Creating a buzz is important. You'll need to have some kind of story for an A&R person to notice you," notes Laura Cohen, former manager of publicity for Virgin Records. "If an A&R guy hears about you—without you telling him—then that's great. You couldn't have it any better way."

■ Attracting a Major Label

As the number of major labels shrinks annually, the possibilities of getting a major label deal become a surreal concept. According to Lonn Friend, major album deals are a very rare commodity indeed. "A number of universal occurrences have to take place for a band to get a record deal," he proffers.

Fortunately, there are lots of independent labels out there that are nearly as powerful as the majors. They offer many of the same benefits—if you're lucky enough to score a deal with them. Getting a record deal with a major or a well-heeled independent label is a long and involved process. First, you have to get a demo tape to an A&R person at a record label. The A&R person's job is to sign bands, so if you want a deal, you have to go to him. Let's say you succeed in getting your tape into his hands. This is not the time to breathe a sigh of relief; remember, the music industry is all about connections. Your tape needs to be brought to the A&R person's attention by some sort of recommendation.

"New music comes from various places," notes Cheryl Dickerson, senior director of writer/publisher relations at BMI. "Oftentimes the artists are recommended by the producers who actually developed the acts. Sometimes they come from entertainment attorneys that represent these acts or shop deals for them. It could be from the manager of the group, or through publishers, who often have writers signed to them who are artists themselves."

If you send in an unsolicited sampler, figure your album is one of forty to one hundred that come into the A&R department each week. Somebody—an intern or a secretary, perhaps—will listen to it. If the listeners like your music, they'll mention your album at their weekly meetings, where trusted ears reveal what they've found that's cool. This process can work, but it's certainly not the easiest way to get your music into the right hands.

"I usually listen to stuff people I know send me first, or if someone recommends something," notes American Recordings' George Drakoulias. "But I go through a phase where I'll say, Okay, the next few days I'm going to try to get through as many tapes as I can. We don't send them back. They'll know if we like the music."

Ironically, American Recordings has never signed a band off of an unsolicited tape. "I've heard a couple of things that I've followed up and gotten stuff back, and realized that whatever the one thing was that I liked was probably a mistake," offers George. "Like, they had a good idea and didn't know what the idea was. I haven't really gotten too many interesting things out of the mail, although Rick [Rubin, president of American, cofounder of Def Jam] got LL Cool J out of the mail. He came in and listened to it and called him up the next day, so you never know."

■ Demo Format

Tape and/or CD? What format will you put this out on? Of course, you, the musician, are going to say, Everything and anything. Yeah, sure, a CD; yeah, sure, a cassette. Absolutely on the Internet; maybe even MIDI, so we can have a MIDI plug-in; that way, people can download the whole five-minute song. It's mainly a question of finances. If you're a band just starting out, you'll most probably do a tape, because you can't afford anything more. Record companies are hip to that; tapes are okay, but we've become a CD world. Everybody in the music business has a CD player. They also find it a lot easier to pop in a CD and peruse the music from track to track than to fast-forward and rewind a tape.

Record companies like CDs because they have less guesswork. They know the product they're getting and can judge your whole album concept. Pass along a CD, and the record company has the whole package in their hands; they can see what they're going to be selling and make an accurate assessment as to whether or not this agrees with their corporate vision.

■ You Never Know

There's no way of knowing what makes an A&R executive's ears perk up. What makes him want to sign an act is an elusive quality, something indefinable, but something he definitely knows when he hears the music.

"It's hard to put your finger on what it is that makes you want to sign a band," confirms Chris Douridas, an A&R executive from DreamWorks. "It's like asking what you look for in a mate, or why you love the people that you love. How can you describe that? It's just something that makes your senses come alive, and you respond to the artistry of it in a way that you don't very often."

A true A&R person won't sign a band based on marketing potential or the potential hit quotient. They sign music that they love. If they hear your demo and love it, you're going to know. The first thing they're going to do is call the contact number on your demo.

☀ **COMMIT IT TO MEMORY:** *Be sure everything you submit to a record company has the contact name and number clearly printed on the product and the packaging.*

When an A&R person likes what you do, the first thing they're going to do is research you. They're going to call whatever phone numbers come with your package. After the A&R person finds you, they're going to want to meet you and spend some time getting into your head.

"Discovering a band is the start of a relationship," confirms Chris Douridas. "You want to get to know as much about the person as you can. Once you investigate further and find out that not only is this what I think it is, it's much more, then you're on the right track. It's very exciting."

If he absolutely loves you, the next thing an A&R person is going to do is crunch some numbers to see if the amount of money that the label has to put into the band is worth the investment. The numbers he's going to be looking at have nothing to do with how much the band needs. Production costs of an album are puny, maybe $100,000, whereas the marketing of a record can go into the million-dollar range. Advances can also go that high, which is why bidding wars are not always in a band's best interest.

If you get a really key A&R person, he's not going to be so concerned about whether or not you recoup the record company's investment on the first album, because he's making a commitment to you; he's behind your artistry and viability for the long haul.

"The great thing about DreamWorks Records is they take things at their own pace. They don't have to get a hit out of the box on anything they sign," confirms Chris Douridas. "They're looking at the long term. The Eels had a number one alternative radio hit, but that only sells a certain amount of records. We saw their first release as a success. If you look at it worldwide, it was definitely a gold record. We're not in a hurry. DreamWorks can work with an artist over the three or four records that it needs to hit."

■ Getting to A&R

There are ways to call attention to your record, but walking up to an A&R guy in a club is definitely not the way to do it. Lonn says he listens to about one in five tapes handed to him. "I look at the packaging; if it's really lame, I don't listen to it. If it looks like they put some work into a presentation, then I'd pop it in the car and listen to one song. Nine out of ten times I'd either toss it out the window or I'd take it to work the next day and have the staff go through the system and then just send it back."

There is a way to circumvent this random and painful rejection process. Have your tape handed to an A&R person by somebody who has a personal relationship within the music industry. This is where good representation really comes into play, and this is why you need to have a good lawyer or a good manager.

It was heritage, hearsay, and a good network that got Deadsy settled in with Elementree Records. Deadsy visionary Elijah Blue Allman (the only son of cross-cultural musical luminaries Cher and Greg Allman) needed to be with a label that could relate to him, which is why he chose Korn's record label, Elementree.

"It's tactical to have somebody on your side with the industry political resources, artistic vision, and taste that Jon Davis has. [Davis is the frontman for multiplatinum rockers Korn and a cofounder of Elementree Records.] Jon is another champion in our corner—something that has obviously proven to be extremely valuable. We were on a huge arena rock tour before we even had our album out. We were on Family Values. Those are the benefits of that relationship. Deadsy is such a specific vision—it's so different that people may shy away and be afraid, so we need someone like Jon Davis, who can champion our cause."

If you're determined to get a record deal, gird your loins and be prepared to go in and do battle. If you can't get the deal yourself, you may need to get someone to do it for you. There are a lot of ways to do that—agents, managers, and A&R people. A music rep is anyone with contacts.

■ Mike Sistad: Choosing What to Sign

Mike Sistad is manager of A&R for Arista Records Nashville. It's his job to find and develop country artists for Arista.

How do you find artists?
MIKE SISTAD: We accept artist packages on a limited basis, usually from people that we know. We have producers who bring projects to us. We also

go out and look for artists. There are all the little feelers that you can put out there. Maybe somebody who is excited about something will give us a call and get us to take a listen to it. In the end, we still have to decide if it's for us or not. Unfortunately, we can't sign everything. Sometimes, we actually see artists and acts that we believe will get signed somewhere in town, and that's not reason enough for us to sign them. If we don't feel like we're in a position to really follow through on it, then it's not advantageous for either party if we sign them. We just have to let it go.

What advice would you give to an aspiring country songwriter?

MS: The thing I love about Nashville is that it's a songwriter's town. It's great to be a part of that community and learn. The songwriters who come here and are really serious about it get so much support from the songwriting community. The flipside of that is that sometimes you get caught in the formula that some people are scared of, where everyone is writing the same radio-formula-type songs. That uniqueness of writing from wherever you are in the country might get lost, because all of a sudden, you are piled together with everybody else who is trying to get radio success.

For country music, is one way better than another?

MS: There is not any one right way of writing a great song. You get structures and things you can learn from technical books about writing songs. All that is great. Songwriting is like learning to play an instrument. You have to learn the technical stuff first. At some point, you will become good enough at the basic craft, so that when the inspiration comes, you can put something on paper and make it work in a way that is commercially acceptable and also something that everyone would love to buy and own.

There are always those universal themes that everyone is trying to write about.

The miraculous thing that everyone is trying to do is to say it in a different way, or in a very visual way, or a very conversational way that everyone can relate to on a personal level. You have to follow through on your inspiration and maybe write a hundred songs to get that one that is special. You've got to work at it.

■ Another Way to Get to the Right People

To get a record deal, you need someone who's connected. If you're weak on contacts in the music industry, and if you're not from a big city, an easy way that's available to everybody is a service called Taxi. This is an independent

A&R vehicle, founded by Michael Laskow, based in Los Angeles. Taxi is an A&R connection for unsigned bands to get their music to major labels, publishers, and film and TV music supervisors. The cost for a year's membership to Taxi is $299.95, a very reasonable price for A&R access.

Once you join, you get a twice-monthly list of "Who's Looking For What." This is your big chance. When you see a listing of what someone is looking for that sounds like it's appropriate for your music, you send your tape to Taxi labeled with the corresponding listing number. Taxi will then screen the tape, and, if appropriate, they will be your A&R contact, putting your tape in the hands of the label that requested the type of music you play.

The beauty of Taxi is that your tape will be sent directly to the person who asked for it. It will be sent as solicited material, and definitely given attention. Taxi will notify you which company it was sent to. If the company is interested, they'll contact you directly.

They also offer developmental feedback. If your tape is not forwarded to that listing, you will be sent a written critique that will tell you why the tape was not forwarded, and what you can do to improve it. Or you can just submit it again the next time you find a listing that interests you. The nice thing is that you can submit as much material as you like throughout your membership year. Taxi is a source that's worth looking into. Check out their Web site at *www.taxi.com*.

■ Major Labels

Besides funding the recording of an album, record labels are really, really good at marketing, sales, and distribution. If a major label gets behind you, they're going to work your record.

"Record companies promote all of their artists, although some artists are priorities," states former Virgin Records publicist Laura Cohen. "You work a record until it's over. You're working as a whole company, so you work a band until it's no longer on the agenda at meetings. For a smaller band, you find that you put out a single or two and there's absolutely no radio response; you'll work at press for maybe six months and then you just know when it's over because everybody's moved on; it's not on the agenda."

If the major label marketing machine gets behind you, people have heard of you. Your record is in all the stores because it got on the radio, because your record label used its vast resources and relationships to get your music to the right people. Your newfound fans will want to go into the record store to get your album, and voilà—your record's there. The label is there to help fund your tour. It will make sure that anywhere you go, the consumer knows your name and your face, and your music is present in the record store. So if potential fans get the urge to go buy a record, it is definitely there waiting for them.

It is the label's business to be on the spot. If the record label screws up when Accelerator comes to town on a tour, and a bunch of Accelerator fans go into the local Blockbuster Music, Tower Records, or wherever to buy Accelerator's new album and the record is not on the shelves, chances are they're going to buy something else. Next week, after Accelerator's already passed through town and the momentum has died down, they're not going to be buying that album. It's a missed opportunity that can really damage Accelerator's sales figures.

■ Phish Tales

Phish started in Vermont, and is now being heralded as the next Grateful Dead. They have created a massive following of tie-dyed, freethinking fans who follow them from summer festival to summer festival, dancing their way through Phish's long and varied sets. In a few years' time, Phish should follow in the Dead's footsteps by consistently being the highest-grossing touring band.

Phish first came together during the autumn semester of 1983, when guitarist Trey Anastasio, then a student at the University of Vermont, posted flyers looking for musicians to start a band. Drummer Jon Fishman, bassist Mike Gordon, and another guitarist ripped off the phone number and made the call. Keyboardist Page McConnell came into the band two years later, when Page persuaded Trey and Jon to transfer from the University of Vermont and join him at Goddard College.

Their first poster promoted their gigs as "Phish playing the music of the Grateful Dead." Indeed, their following has grown in a similar manner. Phish began by playing regular gigs at Nectar's in Burlington, and, eventually, expanded around New England, where they developed a strong local following. In April 1988, Phish won first place in a battle of the bands at the Front in Burlington. Soon thereafter, all four members were full-time musicians with no other day jobs, and were playing their first gigs west of the Mississippi. Phish was out there doing it, and people were passing along the Phish vibe.

Fans spread the word that Phish was one of the most exciting and innovative new bands around—each night was a different blend of classical rock, jazz, funk, folk, and blues.

John Paluska was one of those that heard the word early on. In 1988, when he was a junior at Amherst College in Massachusetts, he saw Phish while away on a ski weekend. He called the band the next day and booked them for an all-campus party at Humphries House. It was Phish's highest-paying gig and their first professional out-of-state gig. John got the word out around the campus and the party turned out to be his favorite Amherst party ever. John was so fond of the band that he continued booking gigs at Amherst and Hampshire colleges and at Northampton clubs.

Eventually, John formed Dionysian Productions with Ben Hunter, a.k.a. Junta. As a Boston University student, Ben had rented out Molly's for a Phish gig in November of 1988—it became their first sold-out show.

Phish spent a decade making albums and going on the road, oblivious to the music industry. They let fans record shows and trade tapes, much like the Grateful Dead did twenty years before. They were able to sell out clubs from coast to coast before they even had a record contract because their live performances were so unique.

Phish won over their audience with extended jams, quick song shifts, improvisation, and audience participation. An elaborate Web presence, supported in great part by their fans, added to the buzz.

Phish broke in a big way in 1994 with *Hoist* and is now being promoted as the Grateful Dead of this generation. They now play shows in stadiums and large amphitheaters, sometimes for more than seventy thousand fans. In 1995, Phish was number fifteen on *Pollstar* magazine's "Top 50 Grossing Acts" of the year.

■ Small-Town Benefits

See, there are ways of getting attention and getting a record deal besides moving to New York or Los Angeles and playing a showcase to forty-five different A&R guys. Be creative about it, and take advantage of the assets your environment has to offer you.

"Wherever you are, stay where you are—don't come to Los Angeles and don't go to New York," advises American Recordings' George Drakoulias. "Wherever you're from, you should stay there and play as much as you can, do some kind of residency, maybe. If you excite people, people will start talking about it. Someone will hear about it. Otherwise, I think it's forced—it's not natural."

Look at it this way: there's less competition in a small town, and that's a good thing. You can be a really great band, but if you're in New York, there are five thousand other bands playing every night. You may never get the opportunity to play with groups who can spread the word about you because they're too busy spreading the word about other people.

If you're in a smaller town—a B market or a C market—you can get major label attention through a regional rep at the distribution company, or by a local promotion rep who's working records and goes out on the town and sees local gigs. The northern Florida band Sister Hazel got their major label shot through a regional promotion guy at BMG Music. Another band from that area, Limp Bizkit, got a major label deal with Interscope and a lot of exposure thanks to the hardcore group Korn.

Korn was good enough to get Limp Bizkit visibility because they took them out regionally. Limp Bizkit is also a hardcore band—the second coming of Korn, so to speak. Somebody got their tape to Korn; Korn liked them, and gave Limp Bizkit a break.

■ Finding Your Reps

If you're a band in a small town like Logan, Utah, or Carroll, Iowa, you need to contact your regional reps. You can find out who they are and how to get to them by calling up the big distribution companies like EMD, Warner Bros., UNI/Polygram, BMG, and Sony, and asking where the nearest regional office is in your area. If you're in Preston, Idaho, ask if they have an office in Boise. If you're in Indian Springs, Georgia, ask about Atlanta. Do your homework; pound the pavement. Nobody is going to make this happen but you.

When you call these people, be nice, be sincere, and be professional. Rehearse your conversation before you make the call. If you telephone a record company and say, Duhh, hey . . . I've got a band and I want to, uhhh, uhhh, get my tape to you guys, they'll inevitably give you a curt answer. These people are busy, and you're taking time away from their work. Appreciate what they can do for you. Perhaps you want to say something along the lines of: Hi! My name is Robert Williams, and I'm from the band Trainwreck Ghost. We're based out of Ten Mile, Tennessee. We're looking to get some exposure, and I was interested in contacting your nearest regional rep to invite them to our show. Do you have a regional rep in Knoxville?

Make sure you're well-spoken and sincere. Most people are so inundated with work that they don't want to hear from you; they don't have time to talk to you. There's no science to this, and no rules. Anything can happen; you just have to believe.

And if something does happen, think about the team you choose. If you're working with a bunch of small-town guys who've never done a deal with a major label or publisher, think twice before signing your life away with them. It is wiser for a band or artist to go to someone who is in the game on a daily basis and who knows who the players are and how they like to play.

■ What You Have to Believe

As an artist, you have to believe that you're writing music that says something. You're creating lyrics and phrases that come from your heart. Using clichés, being derivative, and not having something worthwhile to share with other people won't work.

The music industry personnel you're trying to reach are professionals. They hear new music every day. They're given tapes and CDs all the time. Don't play anything for anybody if you don't think it's the best thing that you have to offer at that point in your development. Don't give anybody a tape that you don't think is the best you can do. And when you hand out that tape, if you don't think that the first song on that tape is the best song that you have, then you don't have a chance of getting the second track heard, because industry reps and A&R people have the attention span of amoebae.

Have faith. Believe. Remember: if it's meant to happen, it will happen. Somehow, you will be seen; you will get the opportunity. Whether the opportunity leads to success or frustration depends upon the aligning of the planets and many different things happening in unison.

"Nobody but you can tell you what to shoot for with your career," observes Kathy Callahan. "If what you want is a career of making albums for mainstream America, which translates into the mainstream of the world, you have to be careful how you go about that. There are not a whole lot of people who get discovered by selling records out of the back of the car; it just doesn't happen that way. You need to find somebody who believes in what you're doing and who will stay with you and will get you to a place where you'll get more than one record made."

You may not get signed out of your car, but if you are selling records regionally in a record store, no doubt, the major labels are going to notice you.

■ From Radio to Major Label Deal: Hootie and the Blowfish

All of the major label A&R executives had essentially passed on Hootie and the Blowfish when they first sent their demo around. It was said that they were just another bar band. A research assistant for Doug Morris, who was then running Atlantic Records, was researching which independent bands were selling. She kept coming up with this band named Hootie and the Blowfish that was selling fifty to one hundred pieces in virtually every store in the Carolinas.

When the retail sheets were brought to Doug Morris, he said, "What is this band Hootie and the Blowfish?"

A&R said, "Oh, it's a bar band, and we passed on them." Doug essentially said, "Well, get someone to un-pass right away, because this is the real deal."

When a Hootie record in the Carolinas was outperforming other records that were national hits at the time, the decision to sign the band became a no-brainer.

When the time is right, and all the stars are aligned, you'll get your deal.

■ Semisonic: A Curious Success Story

Semisonic writes pretty tunes that are simultaneously gutsy, erotic, and intimate. Dan Wilson, John Munson, and Jacob Slichter received heavy praise from critics when they were working on their 1998 MCA Records release, *Feeling Strangely Fine*. The band used a rather unique approach to recording when they went into Minneapolis' Seedy Underbelly Studios: they had sixty songs and no professionally recorded demos. Creative force Dan Wilson is a unique guy with a refreshing attitude toward making music.

How does a band from Minneapolis get signed to MCA?
DAN WILSON: We made some demo tapes that were extremely developed and perfected of the songs "Delicious," "If I Run," "Brand New Baby," and "F.N.T." We had made a bunch of demos, but this particular one started making the rounds and seemed to catch.

How much time, effort, and money did you put into those demos?
DW: It was done in the basement on an eight-track cassette player. If you use it right, the sound quality is really slamming because it really compresses the low end and makes it very intense sounding. I don't think we spent a lot of time or money. We probably spent two days on each song, maybe three. So, two weeks, total, but we'd been playing a lot of shows, so we really knew how to rock, and there were a lot of hooks. I think everyone thought, here's Semisonic, the band with the hooks from hell.

Did you ever think about putting the songs on your tape on CD?
DW: Because it was recorded onto cassette as a master medium, I always felt like it wouldn't sound snappy enough on a CD. It just didn't have enough level, it was too murky; you could never really turn it up loud enough to make a really loud, great-sounding CD. I'd always assumed we'd rerecord those songs. Turned out not to be the case; we only added to them.

When you had your demo tape, did you get radio airplay off of it? Did you have to work at that?

DW: We got airplay at home in Minneapolis. Our tapes sounded good; people just wanted to play the songs. Oddly, our album *Great Divide* didn't get much airplay at all.

How did you get your tapes around?
DW: We knew several different A&R people and lawyers. It was one of those tapes that people started copying for their friends. Finally, we got the tape to an attorney who helped us decide between several labels.

Why did you choose to go with MCA?
DW: Hans Haedelt, our A&R guy, is just a super-convincing guy.

Did you get a deal you were satisfied with?
DW: Yes. We wanted to make CDs. I'd say we did about as well as you'd ever want to do. None of us were able to buy new cars, but we were able to up-date some of our gear and get a new drum set and pay for a rehearsal space for half a year.

Were you able to quit your day jobs?
DW: We'd been doing so many shows that we didn't have day jobs. We lived in Minneapolis, where you don't have to pay to play. We were touring around and playing in places like Fargo, Chicago, Milwaukee, and Madison, and making a living.

How did your first album, Great Divide, *sell?*
DW: It really didn't get played that much; it ended up selling maybe sixty thousand copies.

How do you promote yourself? Does Semisonic have a marketing strategy?
DW: We play shows, and make sure that we get information to people via e-mail. We make sure there are ways for people to find out about us on the Web, and we make sure we send posters to the club two weeks before the show.

If I had to explain our approach, it would be that we had clarity about who we wanted to speak to with our music. Some people might want to reach the coolest people in town, but they might not make the coolest music; they might just make good music. You have to be honest with yourself and try to reach people who like good music, rather than cool music.

Minneapolis is a very cool-oriented town, and I'm not a cool-oriented guy. That makes it easy to create a marketing strategy; you just bypass the cool people. I'm not going to try and play to the coolest bar; I'm not going to try and get written up in the coolest underground 'zines and the weekly paper. I'm going to get the guy from the daily paper on the phone and convince him to come to the show. It's normal people that I want to come see the show, because I know that we're not the coolest band around. I know that we rock and we make great songs. That's a marketing strategy, because I know that I'm not fooling myself who it's for.

Semisonic's objective with our music is to move people. I know we're a rock band, but we're not really violent and abrasive; we're kind of feminine and into seductive, juicy grooves. We want to be honest about who we are. That makes it easier to reach the person that would be the ideal listener for our music. We're looking for ways to play in front of people that want to hear the juicy groove and ways to play in front of people who don't need an expression of violence and hate in their lives. So, if that's a marketing strategy, then we totally have that. It's just knowing yourself.

We've always had some kind of plan, although sometimes, the plan is just to proceed and see what happens. That is totally how we did it with the new album, *Feeling Strangely Fine*.

How did your recording process change for your second album?
DW: With the album, *Feeling Strangely Fine*, we made every recording into its own first stab. Recording this album was like chopping bits together and trying different things. Like, on "Completely Pleased," I sang it once. We had the guitars and the singing and the drum machine, and then there was no need to do any more singing. It was sort of like one take, but then we added some bass, and then added the drums a little bit at a time. It wasn't really in one take, but very few parts were recorded again and again.

Recording Feeling Strangely Fine *sounds like a pretty simple process. How long were you in the studio?*
DW: Oh, many months. We had between fifty and sixty songs, and, because we didn't have any demos of them, we had to try them all and see how they sounded. Whatever was promising on that day, we would work on. There were lots of days where the entire day's work was thrown away. I really wanted to do it in that way, where the plan was wildly up in the air. Like, nobody heard the song "Secret Smile" until we were in the studio. I played it for the band one afternoon as a surprise. Everyone jumped on their instrument, and said, Let's try this, and we captured a real immediacy with the music.

Do you know when you have a great song?
DW: Yes, sure. Usually the things that I work hardest on turn out to suck. Most great songs, you can tell that they're great because they just pop out really quickly.

When you hear yourself on the radio, does that excite you?
DW: No, because it sounds just like the record. It's just as though you're listening to the cassette in the car; it's just more compressed. I've got to admit, when I heard someone talking about the song afterwards, that was a little bit exciting. After hearing the song "Closing Time," when you hear the deejay say, Yeah, I always know who I want to take me home, but she never does want to go home with me, that's kind of cool, because he's actually responding to what you're doing.

What role has the Internet played in your evolution?
DW: It's been huge. We have a really, really involved, intelligent Internet fan group. They communicate with each other a lot, and they're really vocal. If we come into town and play a show that isn't so great, they totally tell us. We get tons of e-mail about stuff—like, a hundred a day. It's hard to keep up; you can't send everyone a response. You have to answer general questions by referring people to the Web site, and then really great, specific questions, you try to get somebody in the band or somebody who works the Web site to help them find the information they need.

To me, the Web is about making information available to people if they want it. And it's assuming that anybody who's on the Internet—young or old—is going to be smart enough to figure it out. You just put stuff out there as much as you can. Don't put too much emphasis on giving it a personal touch, because you can't. You're going to miss most people if you try to get personal and shake everybody's hand, but at least let the fans know that you care about them and that you want to provide information, or let them know who to contact.

The Web has been really wonderful for us. We do these radio shows around the country, and we'll make sure that our fans from the Internet will win tickets to these radio shows, so there's always a good vibe because there are always some diehards in the group.

So, your Web fans get to check out your radio performances?
DW: Yeah. It makes it better for us, because there are people there who really know what we're about—not just contest winners, but bona fide fans.

CHAPTER FIVE

Going the Indie Route

As an artist, it was no longer possible for me to work for major labels. There was no way to get around this fact of copyright ownership, which I had always understood to be my property. You can make a case for the royalty rates which majors pay. You cannot make a case for record companies owning the phonographic copyrights. So, the only alternative at that point is to form an independent record label, which is the last thing any player wishes to do—only necessity will take you to that point. Most young artists say, "I'm not interested in doing my own label," and I say, "Well, I sympathize, because I hate it myself quite substantially." But anyone can be their own record label as long as they can print up at least ten cassettes and sell them at shows, and then perhaps 500 CDs and sell those at shows.

—Robert Fripp, solo artist

Let's say the majors decide to pass on your music. That's okay. There aren't many major labels left, anyway. Never fear—in the new millennium, musicians increasingly are turning to independent record labels, or starting their own labels, and bypassing the media conglomerates. There are so many niche markets where your music might be appropriate and would be well cared for and properly distributed.

"In the future, I foresee a million artists on the Web and 500,000 labels," notes Chuck D, founder of the multiplatinum rap band Public Enemy and founder of Rapstation.com. "Everybody's going to be looking for different ways of exposure, and my whole thing is, let's create an avenue for exposure so people can link up into a situation that can help them. The genre needs servicing and organization."

By some estimates, there are now 10,000 independent record companies. Jim Olsen cofounded Signature Sounds in 1995 and runs it out of his colonial farmhouse in Massachusetts. An industry veteran, he says major record labels don't nurture acts like they did in the 1960s and 1970s. If Bruce Springsteen were an emerging artist on a major label today, Olsen says, he wouldn't have a chance because he didn't get any radio play until his third album. Will the White Stripes and Eminem have careers like Bruce Springsteen or Aerosmith? Depends on their major label support. Since MTV took hold, the major labels have been investing in singles, not building careers by focusing on long-term album sales.

"They dump hundreds of thousands of dollars into an act and then hope it hits big. If it doesn't, they drop the artist—who's still on the hook for huge recording and touring costs," observes Olsen.

Truth be told, the odds of hitting it big are quite small. Of the more than 27,000 CDs released in 2002, only 404 sold more than 100,000 copies. About 25,000 sold fewer than 1,000 copies.

An independent label such as Signature Sounds can offer an artist the opportunity to build a following while putting their artistic stamp on all aspects of their production— from the recording to the CD cover art. Signature's roster includes an eclectic array of artists, such as Richard Shindell, who has toured with Joan Baez, Amy Rigby, and Josh Ritter, who won ASCAP's Sammy Cahn Award for the most promising young lyricist.

Signature estimates they spend $10,000 recording an album, and a big-selling album is 25,000 copies. "Most of the time we're in the black at 8,000," Olsen declared.

Independent labels, comfortably referred to as "indies," may be more sympathetic to what you're trying to do and may help you get there. You won't be shipping fifty thousand units—you may be shipping two thousand units—but your margins are different. Not to mention the way artists are treated. Indies may give you the support you need, believe in what you're doing, and see the niche for it. They will get the music to your audience, and you may may end up making more of a profit than you might expect.

"In 1998, we did the *He Got Game* soundtrack, which was a major movie, and not to say that we don't need the money, but $10 million or $5 million or $1 million has got some strings on it. And you have to ask yourself, 'Can we do this? Can we pay our bills? Can we go around and tour if we make a record with no strings attached to it? And we can build another business template for people to follow and say, is this cool for me?'" Chuck D says.

"Leaving our label, Def Jam, and going out on our own was a fight, but Public Enemy is built to be the ugly ship in the water that breaks the iceberg so the pretty ships sail behind us," he continues. "There's nothing like being able to make a road, and you know that somebody else paves that road to be able to go to their success. That's our measure of success—can we build a road? I'm very happy with that road. And if I had to put in the business-savvy, moneymaking head, it's always out there; you just have to find different ways to get it."

■ Success Story: Mary Gauthier

Mary Gauthier did a bluesy storytelling album called *Filth and Fire* for Signature Sounds. Gauthier, who ran a successful restaurant in Boston before turning to songwriting, paid for the recording of *Filth and Fire* out of her own pocket. Her songs caught on, and *Filth and Fire* ended up as one of several independent releases on a *New York Times* list of the best of 2002. Mary's deal has her owning the recording she paid for, and licensing the music to Signature Sounds. She has pocketed money on every sale.

"I'm an entrepreneur," she says. "I'm an owner of a small business. I never wanted a chain of restaurants, and I don't want some corporate entity telling me how to look, what to wear, and where to play. I won't be a wildly famous household name. I never really wanted to be, so that's no loss. I'll sell fewer records than someone being pushed by a big, huge publicity machine, but I make more than enough to maintain a life. I'm in it for the long run. I think the big record companies are in it for a quick flash."

Most small-label artists pay $6 or $7 for a CD from their record company and sell it for $15 at shows or on their Web sites. Gauthier has elaborated on that procedure. She pays Signature only for the manufacturing cost of the CD—about a buck.

■ Finding the Right Label

Making dance music? Rock group U2 recently started an underground dance label called Kitchen Records, named after their Dublin club. Frontman Bono and his friend Reggie Mannuel are overseeing the label's A&R duties. More club labels? Try Perfecto, Kinetic, Logic, Champion, Ultra, FFRR, Subliminal, Strictly Rhythm, Work, or Nervous.

Producer Glen Ballard started his own record label, Java Records, based in Los Angeles. A&R responsibilities are handled by Amos Newman, who is actively looking for new talent. Try Quinlan Road for country, Righteous Babe for folk. There are labels galore, with practically every name you can think of—Lava, Wind-Up, No Limit, Bad Boy, Republic, Heavyweight, Noo Trybe, NPG, Emperor Jones, Mute, Bingo, Southern, Caroline, Mud, Arf! Arf!—and the list goes on and on.

Figure out who your audience is, then approach the appropriate labels. Does your music interest several crowds? Does it appeal to ambient, techno, and the Deadhead crowd? To the college kids of today, and the trippers and the boppers? Making music is not really about appealing to people of one age group and musical taste anymore. Figure out your market—where should people listen to your music? Is it car music, relaxation music, or exercise music? Maybe it's great massage music or yoga music.

"Independent labels don't have as much marketing muscle as the majors, but if the band is an alternative act, it needs to be discovered outside the mainstream," observes Lonn Friend. "An independent label will have a better affinity for how to market a unique act. A lot of times a band will either stay with an indie or sign with an indie over a major label, even if they have the attention of the major."

■ Roger Stein: An Indie Opinion

Roger Stein is president of Iguana Records, one of the multitude of independent labels that are rising out of the decentralization of power in the music industry.

What's an independent label's place in the music market today?
ROGER STEIN: I'm the one writing the checks. If I see a band and want to sign them, I don't have to deal with internal politics. I don't have to get four different people who have to come see the band and be enthusiastic about the project. I have the flexibility to go out, see a band, sign it, develop it, and get it moving instead of letting it sit around for a while.

The other good thing is the tendency for independents to be a lot closer to the street level, musically. Majors are big corporations. They have lots of people; they have projections they have to work on; they have numbers; they have requirements.

What are the benefits of an independent label?
RS: Artists are hip to the idea that independence can be really cool and mean positive things. We're not putting out sixty records this quarter, so there's not a lot of internal competition. Some of the majors are working many projects each quarter, so there's automatically internal competition. If you've got the Sheryl Crow record and the Patti Griffin record coming out, and you're a new female artist that's coming out at the same time, you have a problem. We don't have issues like that.

Artists know that they're going to get more time and attention. We can't afford to sink a lot of money and effort into a band, then bail on it after a record. We're probably going to be in it for a little while; otherwise, I wouldn't sign it. I wouldn't want to work with it if I didn't expect to stick with it.

Do indie labels ever do joint ventures with a major?
RS: Joint ventures can work really well. Interscope has done quite a number of those. Bush and No Doubt were both joint ventures with Trauma Records. Nine Inch Nails is a collaboration with Trent Reznor's label, Nothing Records. A number of Interscope releases, with the notable exception of the Wallflowers, are on Nothing/Interscope.

Most independents do a lot more ground-level micro marketing. Major labels don't necessarily do that well, so they wind up hiring outside companies to do that.

The other thing about an independent or an independent joint venture is that it gives the artist a lot more autonomy and a lot more creative input into what's going on. When we did that joint venture with Interscope, we came to them with a finished record, a whole package. They liked that because it was a lot less for them to deal with, and they had a finished record. All they had to do was press it, distribute it, market it, and promote it.

If you think about it from the artist's point of view, it's better having an independent label, as well as a major, on your side. You have the independent to help you focus on working the album, in addition to a major spending more money on the project.

When bands come to you for a deal, do they have finished product, or do they have demos?
RS: I've seen bands that have nothing on tape, and I've seen bands that have a finished record. It seems that most bands these days are putting something

on CD—even if it's a demo—because they think it looks more like the end product. That can backfire to the extent that the people who have some creative vision will view it as though it's finished already and therefore may not like it or want to deal with it. On the other hand, if it's great, then it's that much easier. I'm just signing a band now that came in with a finished record. All we're doing is repackaging it and putting the record out. That's rare.

What kind of deal do you generally offer your bands?
RS: There's a huge range. On the lowest level of interest, it could be: Hey, there's something cool going on here; they don't know anyone; they don't know any labels; no one will really come after them; we can get them for whatever we want. There are a lot of issues—in terms of imaging, in terms of developing the music—that affect the price. If they're a young band, it would be a developmental or a production thing. Here's a couple of thousand dollars; let's try and direct what you're doing a little bit better, and let's work on it over the course of six months—let's cut a couple of tracks and see how it goes. If it works, we do a more full-blown regular record deal. If it doesn't, you've got some great-sounding demos, and see you later. That's the lowest level of a deal.

The highest level of a deal is when a band comes in with a finished record that's already been paid for. For example, we did a deal where another label had already screwed up the project because they didn't know what they were doing with it. The band got a huge amount of radio airplay, but had no records in stores. The distribution wasn't very good. So we stepped in and took over the project. That's been the most expensive project I've gotten into, but I don't want to talk about dollars and deals.

The first and most important thing is that the album has to be a great record, and it has to be able to compete on a national level. Given that, obviously, we're willing to spend some real money making our records. In terms of cash to bands, we're not paying several hundred thousand dollar advances to artists, but we're helping to keep them alive and doing stuff over a period of time while we're working the record.

■ Finding Independent Labels

The way to find the indies is to get out there, press the flesh, and do your homework. An easy way to find labels that may be appropriate for your music is to go to music conventions, walk the floor, and see who is selling what. Two big music conventions are NAMM in Los Angeles in January and CMJ in New York in November. If you find one or two contacts in ten thousand people, it's a golden opportunity.

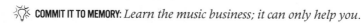 **COMMIT IT TO MEMORY:** *Learn the music business; it can only help you.*

Another way to find out what kind of music the labels are doing is to go to the record store and look at product. See what labels are releasing albums similar to yours, and track those people down. These indie labels may be in strange places—Emmaus, Pennsylvania; Smyrna, Tennessee; Burlington, Vermont. There's a lot of stuff that happens underground away from the major cities. Another way to find talent is to look under labels in any of the music industry handbooks. A little research will give you a thousand connections.

■ Round Two: Pitching to A&R

If the planets are aligned on your behalf, the people who are paid real money will listen to your music and offer their well-paid opinions. To get your album this far is quite an accomplishment—it means that the CD has gone through a tremendous clearing process, merely because of the sheer volume of material that's come into the record company. Figure one out of a hundred demos get this far.

"Say something gets my attention; the next step is to call the representatives and start to do some research on this band," notes Lonn.

You should be prepared for the moment the A&R guy calls the contact number on your tape. Have a small bio put together—a couple of paragraphs on what the band is all about, where you've come from, and what you've done. Keep it short, but tell as much about the band as possible. Perhaps you want to model it after this brief bio on Alanis Morissette . . .

Alanis Morissette opened the door for Girl Power with her honest, biting views on life, love and relationships. Metaphorically, Alanis stripped naked, showed her heart, and won acclaim beyond her wildest fantasies.

"The most ironic thing was that the moment that I let go and stopped wanting celebrity status was the moment that I got more of it than I'd ever gotten in my life," reveals Alanis. "I can't forget that moment, which led me into this fulfilled place."

Years of therapy and writing have helped Alanis channel the anger out of her system. While she may have been a finicky and cranky kid, she's totally got it together as she enters adulthood. "Anger is a cowardly expression of pain," declares Alanis, who uses her songs to channel her pain *and* her anger. The world can relate. Chart riding anthems like "You Oughta Know" and "Ironic" share a vulnerability many of us are familiar with.

The Ottawa-born feminist's first album, 1994's *Jagged Little Pill,* could have been interpreted as the whining of a poor little rich girl. Instead, the disc became quite the event. The album was accepted and adopted globally. By the time Alanis finished her world tour, *Jagged Little Pill* had sold some 26 million copies worldwide, making it one of the biggest-selling albums ever by a female performer.

■ Selling Yourself

If and when you're contacted by an A&R rep, he's going to want to know about your past, where your fan base is, where you came from, what other material you have, and if you're performing live anywhere. Different genres of music make money in different ways, but if you're playing rock music, you've got to sell yourself live.

"Rock and roll is all about live performance; it's not about if some producer can magically put together loops and vocals onto a track," observes Lonn Friend. "You need to see the artists perform live. You need to know if they convey a certain sense of real, original talent. Is the frontman powerful? Does the guitarist stand apart from the average riff player? Is there some synergy of band members onstage?"

A band worthy of a record deal will have a certain innate ability to transcend all the bad music that's out there. Inevitably, in the eyes of an A&R guy, your band is going to be young and fresh—even if you've been gigging together for a decade. Every A&R guy wants to sign an act that will develop like Elton John—something he will be benefiting from thirty years after it's been signed. But signing a band is all about finding it early in its development.

If an A&R person came to see you and you blew him away, the next step would depend upon what record company he's with. If he's someone like Capitol Records' Perry Watts-Russell, who has signed Meredith Brooks, Everclear, and the Dandy Warhols, or one of Geffen's very talented suite of A&R vice presidents, like Tim Sullivan, Wendy Goldstein, or Craig Coburn, he can sign at will. If he works with any number of other record companies, he just moves on to the next step, passing the tape along to the president of the record company.

Lonn found that being in A&R can be very frustrating, because his label didn't really understand rock and roll, and he was not given the opportunity for unilateral signing. Lonn was able to sign the little-known band the

Bogmen, but he was forced to pass on more profitable groups like the Eels, Goodness, and For Squirrels because people just didn't understand.

"The problem with Arista's rock department is the people who are paid to sign rock oftentimes have to answer to people who have no clue of what rock is," observes Lonn.

■ Step Three: The Big Players

If your music has made it this far, be impressed, be very impressed. Now you get to work with the big players. Your tape goes to the president of the company so he can evaluate the music with his respected minions. If the CEO likes your music enough to see your group play, your record company will set up a showcase. This means a free trip to New York or Los Angeles for your band, and definitely something to tell the grandkids. If a label wants you, you'll go to it to showcase, because the very powerful executives generally won't go that many places to see a band.

For those who need to know, a showcase is a private concert, one without an audience. A showcase can take place on a soundstage, at a private studio, or in a club. As opposed to doing an entire show, the band is expected to perform a twenty- to thirty-minute set of its strongest material for the executives of a record company.

Playing a showcase has its pluses and minuses. The pluses are that the label gets a real good look at you, the artist. Granted, you're under pressure to deliver, but if you can deliver great music in that kind of suffocating environment, then you probably have the goods to be a recording act on a major label—to record, to tour, and to develop into a subsequent star act. Sounds very glamorous, doesn't it?

The downside of showcases is that you are put under a microscope for suit-clad individuals. "They don't feel the energy of the audience, they can't play off of their fan base, and, therefore, it's ofttimes an empty performance experience," notes Lonn. "If you're a label executive, you have to put them in a vacuum and analyze what you're hearing and how they perform."

When executives showcase a band, they scrutinize it as if the band members are performing in a vacuum, as you would an album. You may have spent years doing the Fuel thing and building up a local or regional fan base, but all the fans in the universe are no good to you in a showcase situation. You don't get to use your audience to an advantage when you're vying for a record deal because it's industry belief that the sheer energy of a dedicated audience will sway a less-than-capable A&R individual's opinion.

It's a slightly flawed perspective because your band did something to develop that audience base. But since the music business is a slightly flawed business, all you can do is roll with the punches.

"To get our deal, we were relentless," notes Kill Hannah vocalist Matt Devine. "I don't know how many showcases we played in Chicago—maybe twenty or thirty performances set up by specific labels. We had been selling out the Metro, which holds 1,200, and we were doing it on our own shows without label support. We were selling out our performances and we still weren't getting a deal. It was the greatest struggle ever."

Kill Hannah was in Chicago, whereas the major labels are centered around New York and Los Angeles. You can always choose a local independent label, but Kill Hannah wanted a major label touring budget, so they held out. While waiting out their dreams, they learned that scoring a deal off the coasts takes longer because it's more of an effort for the executives to see you.

"Being in Chicago made it just a complete bitch to convince anyone in New York or L.A. to buy a $200 ticket and miss their squash game that weekend," he concludes.

■ Securing the Deal

Okay, the record executives have seen your act, and it's changed their life—they want to sign you. A number of scenarios can now take place. If you're a hot act and there's a buzz on about you—i.e., you're getting great local press and getting written up in industry trades—you're in for more money. Figure if you're hot, more than one record company is going to want you, and it may turn into a bidding war.

This is, again, a point where good representation makes all the difference. If there's competition, a competent band representative will work on spinning the price up due to either real or perceived competition. "You have to be diligent about finding out what the smoke and mirrors really mean," advises Lonn. "Otherwise a record company is apt to overpay for an act that, if there was no competition, it could get for $75,000."

Don't be swayed by all the money and romancing that will come toward you if there's competition. Your future ultimately depends upon how you, as the artist, and your rep feel together. You need to decide which label is going to work best for you, who understands you, can work your record, and can get it on the radio.

When presented with a variety of offers, major label veteran country rocker Jason Ringenberg chose an indie label. For the record, Ringenberg founded country/hard rock band Jason and the Scorchers, who rolled out of Nashville in 1981 with a infectious cover of Bob Dylan's "Absolutely Sweet Marie." They were fairly popular and critically praised through the first part of the '80s. Recently, when presented with label choices, Jason chose the indie label Yep Roc, a rising North Carolina label. The reasons for his choice were twofold: economic and artistic. When Jason and the Scorchers were signed to EMI in the '80s, they had a couple of international hits, yet they never made any money.

"Major labels create the illusion that you are the band that's going to be the next big thing, when, in reality, only one in 10,000 bands becomes the next big thing. The other 9,999 owe a whole bunch of money to somebody."

It's now twenty years later and Jason knows his balance sheet. He oversaw the recording of his solo effort, *All Over Creation,* and licensed it to Yep Roc domestically and to other companies overseas. It's approaching 20,000 copies sold.

"I'm making a living with my music and that's what's important to me," he says.

■ Decision Making

If you've got a variety of offers, who should you sign with? Depends. Depends upon relationships. Depends upon the genre of music you're making. Different record companies excel in specific areas of music. Labels like Interscope and Maverick have a lot of rock music, and therefore they have a lot of leverage to get your rock band played. They can use that leverage to get videos on MTV and songs on the radio. You know: hey, play my new band, and I'll give you an exclusive on the latest from our multiplatinum act. A label like Arista can get any ethnic song on any radio format because they have hot R&B stars like LaFace, P. Diddy, and Whitney Houston, which gives them tremendous leverage. Can Arista get an unknown rock band like the Bogmen on the radio? Historically, no, because one genre's leverage and power does not transcend the other genres.

Keep your eyes open when you sign. Very few companies have power in all formats—Atlantic is one exception, Columbia is another. From Mariah Carey to Alice in Chains, Columbia is a full-service company. Arista is a very conservative company; they don't sign a lot of acts and don't have unilateral power at radio. But Arista is a financially responsible company; they generally will not sign acts unless they are willing to develop them.

The opposite end of the spectrum is Warner Bros. Records, which follows the throw-them-against-the-wall-and-see-what-sticks philosophy. Warner Bros. may release a hundred albums a year, and seventy-five of them won't sell more than two thousand copies. But they take a lot of chances, and throw a lot of stuff out there.

If you're going the indie route, you have plenty of options. Choose a label that can properly market your music and doesn't tie up your rights, allowing you to continue to market and sell your music to various other formats and compilations.

■ Money

Believe it or not, your big deal may pay only $75,000, including recording costs. That's all Hootie and the Blowfish started out with, but by 1996, their debut album, *Cracked Rear View*, had sold more than 13 million copies, and they had earned tens of millions dollars in royalties. But $75,000 was all Hootie got to sign to Atlantic Records. If you sign to an indie, expect a lot less.

Money wasn't so minimal a decade ago. When Robert Williams got signed with the Pop in 1977, the five band members were given $10,000 apiece, as well as recording expenses. So, their deal was close to $140,000. In 1990, Nirvana got signed for half a million dollars, but they had the major buzz happening.

These days, nobody's paying a lot, because most artists are selling moderate amounts of records. Fewer albums sold means less profit.

🔆 **COMMIT IT TO MEMORY:** *A band is always playing a numbers game.*

Even when you get signed, you're still battling the odds. An A&R rep gets many projects, and sometimes a label signs too many acts. Virgin Records has thirty acts they're still trying to release. Just because you get signed to a label doesn't mean you're going to become a successful band with an album out. If your A&R contact leaves the label before your album is released, there's a good chance your album may never see the light of day. The upside is if they've given you an advance, you can keep the money.

Early in his career, British pop star Nick Lowe was the house producer for the seminal indie punk label, Stiff Records. Since then, Nick has spent a couple of decades on major labels. He is currently signed with indie Yep Roc. "At this point in Nick's career, he doesn't want to have anybody telling him what he has to do," explains Glenn Dicker, cofounder of Yep Roc. "He wants to work with people who are not doing it purely for the business side of things, but are music people and believe in what his vision is."

■ Your Own Record Label

Okay, let's say everybody—both indies and majors—decides to pass on your project, or you want to retain complete control over your music and maximize your potential profits; go the same route as Ani DiFranco or the Pernice Brothers and start your own record label.

The best thing about making your own record is that if it sells, you own a bigger percentage of your product. If you have the finances and the songs, and you do the CD by yourself, you benefit in two ways:

- You have control over the recording process.
- You can make considerably more money off of your project.

"Whether a band goes for a deal or releases music on their own label really depends upon the band and the attitude," notes attorney Michael Leventhal. "What do you want? If you want to be a megastar, then go with the major label. If you want to be like Ani DiFranco and run your own life, if you're happy selling moderate amounts of albums by owning your own franchise and directing your future, then you do it yourself."

Ani DiFranco is a good example. She was unusual in her day, but now her story is being heard more often. She put out records on her own label, Righteous Babe Records, got distributed, toured heavily, and her reputation grew.

You don't get the marketing muscle or the distribution machine when you do it yourself, but you own your own life. It's working for Ani; by now, she is making good money. She has made close to $3.5 million off of recent albums. Ani has around two dozen albums out—and she's in control of her own life. So, whether you go with a major, an indie, or go it on your own totally depends upon what your goals are.

The Pernice Brothers explored all routes. They released two albums with renowned independent label Sub Pop (a Seattle-based label who signed great acts like Nirvana, Hole, and Mudhoney). The majors didn't come knocking at their door, so they explored other options. Being with Sub Pop gave Joe Pernice, the songwriter behind the iridescent pop of the Pernice Brothers, an idea of how the business works. So for the Pernice Brothers' third album, *Yours, Mine & Ours*, they left Sub Pop and started their own record company—Ashmont Records. Now totally independent, Pernice was motivated to promote his album; he made 300 calls to record stores asking them to stock *Yours, Mine & Ours* before it was released in the summer of 2003. The disc sold more copies in just five weeks than any before it.

"The only thing a record label is good for up front is being a bank for people who might not have the money to start," Pernice affirms. "It's like venture capital. Luckily, we didn't need that."

■ Independent Production: Alex Stone

Alex Stone is a classical guitar player. He self-financed and independently released his debut album, *Timeless*.

What made you decide to record an album?

ALEX STONE: Originally, I didn't have the intention of putting together an album, but people kept asking me if I could make a tape for them. At first, I considered recording at home for these people, but there were more and more people who wanted tapes. I didn't want to do something cheap that wouldn't sound great, so I figured I might as well record something really good, and that's how I decided to make a CD.

How did you put together your own record label?

AS: When I put my album together I simply put the words "produced and published by Alexander Stone" on the CD. I just did it like that.

What advantages have you found doing the music by yourself as opposed to going after a record deal?

AS: The control. I do everything my own way. I don't care what people think; I can do it exactly the way I want it to be. It's important to keep that freedom. I've never worked with a label. Also, I decided that it was better to directly go for the finished product rather than just putting together a demo, because it's probably the same amount of work. In one case, you end up with something you can only show, while in the other case, you end up with something you can sell. The finished product will serve the same purpose as a demo, but it doesn't work the other way around. So it's better to just do the real thing. It forces you to be more professional. With a demo, you may not be so serious, but when you do the finished product you know you have to do it right, so it helps.

In what formats did you release your album?

AS: I chose to put it on CD because of the sound quality and because even if you scratch a CD, you can fix it. It's better for people to buy a CD and copy it on tape; then when the tape goes bad they can make another copy that sounds new again. I've had a lot of people asking for tapes, and some of them wouldn't buy the CD because they have nowhere to play it or record it. It might be better to have a short run of tapes, but I didn't feel like spending extra money on that. The CD is pretty standard. Most people have a CD player, and if they don't have one, their friend might have one.

Lots of people have released music independently. It's certainly nothing to be ashamed of; in fact, it's a glorious opportunity. Beck Hansen—a.k.a. Beck—the offbeat punk, hip-hop, hardcore, folky guy from Los Angeles whom everyone loves, released *Mellow Gold* on Bong Load Records, *One Foot in the Grave* on K Records, and *Stereopathetic Soul Manure* on Flipside—all in 1994. He was doing his best not to become a corporate being.

If you're out there doing your own thing and you're good at it, without a doubt, you'll get noticed. Everyone does.

"If you're selling CDs and doing it as an independent band, at some point, they'll take notice of what's going on," confirms Mark Janowski from Sister Hazel. "If you take things into your own hands, you can't go wrong. Even when you get signed, you still have to be majorly involved. Too many people take it for granted that once you get a deal, you don't have to do anything anymore; you let the record company steer you in the right direction. We're very heavily involved in our careers, because that's exactly what it is—our careers."

■ Rob Zombie: A Long and Varied Career

Rob Zombie had a deal with Geffen Records since the early nineties, first with White Zombie, and then as solo artist and president of his own label, Zombie A Go-Go. When Universal bought Geffen, he got swept up in the mix and continues to carry on. He's one of the lucky ones. Here is the musical story behind the platinum mastermind behind *Astrocreep 2000, Super Sexy Swinging Sounds,* and *La Sexercisto: Devil Music Volume One* and solo albums, *Hellbilly Deluxe* and *The Sinister Urge*.

You recently started Zombie A Go-Go Records. Was that just for fun?
ROB ZOMBIE: I got the record label going. The whole point for me with it is just fun; I wanted it to be fun, I wanted to deal with bands that are fun, I wanted to make the whole thing fun, not this high-pressure thing that has to make money. It's packaged and distributed through Geffen Records, but it's not done on a Geffen level, so the money is really low.

There's not a lot of pressure for these bands, because if they were signed to Geffen, they would surely be dropped because they wouldn't be able to sell enough records to maintain what they're doing. But it's a low-pressure kind of fun thing I want to build and give the bands time to develop.

Is being signed to a major label difficult?
RZ: Not for me, but I've had a deal for a while. With new bands, now what

happens is, bands sign to a major, they give them about a month to do something. If they don't explode, they're history; you never hear from them again. You've got to give a band time to do something, to develop into something, which no one does anymore. Everyone's just looking for that hit of the moment; no one's trying to develop a career.

Are you trying to develop a musical genre with your record label Zombie A Go-Go?
RZ: I wanted the label to be specific so that you could be a fan of the label. You wouldn't even have to know what the band was, you could just see that it was on the label and that you would like it.

How would you describe the music you're releasing on this label?
RZ: It's more like lo-fi trashy psychobilly surf rock nonsense. I hate to try and classify it because it sounds cheap in a way. It's a weird thing, you hear it and people go, Oh I know what you mean. It's just weird monster surf rock music; it's not limited to that, but it fits in that vein. We put out a Halloween compilation with seventeen different bands—they range from the Reverend Horton Heat to Rocket from the Crypt, the Bomboras, the Ghastly Ones, to Southern Culture on the Skids—you can see how they can fall under a certain umbrella. They all have their own identity, but they're all different.

What else is on your plate?
RZ: The main thing is the tour for *Hellbilly Deluxe*.

How do you put together a stage show?
RZ: It gets harder every time, because every time you do it, you figure people expect more than last time. So now the goal is to do something that makes kids go, Oh man, that blows the last tour away. It's that treadmill you get yourself on of always having to top the last thing.

You've worked with some interesting people in the course of your career. Who have been some standouts you've worked with, and why?
RZ: Working with Alice Cooper was a big thing. He was my childhood idol, one of the first things I ever heard when I was a kid and really liked. To get to work with him and do a song, that was pretty cool, and kind of weird.

I wrote the song for the *X-Files* album and he came in and sang on it. It was like me telling him what to do to a point, but I didn't really want to because it just seemed weird.

Same thing with Howard Stern—that was strange and pretty funny. I lived in New York, so I've been listening to him. It's always weird to just meet with somebody, because you can always meet people; but to get to work with them and deal with them one on one is really fun.

What did you learn from Howard?

RZ: The Howard thing was weird because he wanted to do a song, and it became more like my thing. It was just fun—it was a funny project. Howard doesn't make records and he doesn't have a band. He wanted to record a song and his big thing was, "I don't know what to do, you have to make me a rock star. It's up to you to do this." It was kind of funny. It worked out really well.

Do you consider yourself to be a star?

RZ: Not really. If someone says "a star," you think, like, Harrison Ford or something.

Are you successful?

RZ: I consider myself to be successful because that's something you can put facts and figures to. He sold this many records, he made this much money, okay, it was successful; it's like mathematics—you can't really argue it. Whether someone is famous—I don't particularly think anyone in this type of business is famous. Famous is like when everybody in the world knows who you are and you couldn't go anywhere without being swamped. Bruce Willis and Demi Moore can't go anywhere without huge crowds of people forming immediately. That's famous, when you walk down the street and you're stopping traffic.

How has your Zombie image affected your career?

RZ: I had a lot of problems with *Hellbilly Deluxe*—stores won't carry it, malls won't hang up the posters or advertising. And it's not even a specific thing. It just comes down to the fact that you're not something that they want to be promoting in the mall because they're afraid it will be offensive. The world is getting more conservative.

Where do you see yourself in ten years?

RZ: Just doing the same stuff, I presume. I don't see myself being a forty-five-year-old rocker, but I think there's a way that you can get old and still do stuff. It looks embarrassing if you're trying to pretend that you're still young. I don't think anything I've ever done is based around being youthful, so it's not like

I'm ever going to lose it. You're the young cute guy in the spandex, and now you're the old, ugly guy in the spandex; I don't see it.

Has your audience aged as you've aged?
RZ: It's a really wide range of people. Definitely some kids are aging, because if somebody says, Oh man, I've been into you guys for a long time, then they're obviously getting old with you. On the last tour, some of the kids were so young. I know those kids are going to buy the new record and they'll discover me and then they'll go buy the old records, which is good. I don't want to feel like I've trapped myself and am not appealing to new people.

Trends come and go. I never get caught up in trends. I just do what I like; maybe sometimes it seems trendy and sometimes it doesn't. People get caught up in trends because they're just lost. They're like, Oh my god, everybody's cutting off their hair, I'd better cut off my hair! Oh, everyone has a goatee, I'd better grow a goatee. They're so lost, and it just looks embarrassing. It's very obvious. There are bands that can't make up their minds; one minute, they're glam boys, the next minute, they think they're fooling the world because they're putting on flannel shirts. It's a joke.

Once a band has a commercial hit, they always seem to have to go in a more bizarre direction.
RZ: A lot of bands become embarrassed by their success and they seem to want to do everything they can to jeopardize it the next time around. That was kind of a leftover thing from grunge. All those bands—Nirvana, Pearl Jam, whoever—seemed incredibly embarrassed by how successful they were and tried to do everything they could to mess it up next time around. It seemed like they'd do everything in their power to not help it.

After Kiss's *Destroyer*, I don't think Gene sat down and said, Okay, how can I screw up my career? It's a weird mentality; I don't understand it. I think they're too busy worrying about what other people think of their success and not just doing their own thing.

What do you think about your success?
RZ: I think it's great. I certainly don't take it for granted. There was a time you could make a couple of bad records and your fans would still be there for you when you made another good record. Now it's more moment to moment. You have your fans, but if you make a bad record, they're all gone. The market is really singles-oriented. You know the song, you don't know the band, and you certainly cannot even name one person in the band.

There are all these bands—I like to pick on Matchbox 20, because they've probably sold 5 million records—I don't think I could recognize one person in the band if I had to. But they create their own destiny; it's like they go out of their way to seem nondescript.

Did anybody try to package you?
RZ: White Zombie had a good history because we'd gone through the indie route for a long time before signing to Geffen. By the time we were there, I don't even remember anyone trying to direct us whatsoever. I think we were right on the tail end of the time period where you could sneak in and have a career. A lot of bands like Pantera and Slayer don't live or die by a hit song. They have their hardcore fans and it's there. If we have a hit record, we sell more records, but I don't think that it will go away tomorrow because we don't have a hit single.

How did you build your base?
RZ: Touring; it's all about touring. You go and you tour and the kids come. Once a kid comes and sees your show, it's like McDonald's—one billion served. Then you have a real, satisfied fan and he feels the connection.

You know how a record is: you listen to it, you get into it, you forget about it, you throw it into a pile, but you always remember stuff you saw. If a kid enjoys the show and he comes back again, then you have a real fan.

CHAPTER SIX

Making a Record

I don't think I've achieved any fame. It's just my life. I'm

still struggling. I mean . . . I'm nobody. I haven't sold many

albums compared to the Alanis Morissettes of the world. So

I don't think anything's really guaranteed. I just feel really

blessed to do what I like every day and not have to waitress

anymore.

—Jewel, singer/songwriter

Usually—unless you have an unlimited budget or no doubts about your creative capabilities—when you go in to make an album, you have songs that are all ready and rehearsed. You know your bridges, know your breaks, have an idea where to add the oboe. You do preproduction before going into the studio. That way you make the most efficient use of the time and money you have to spend making a record.

"How much preproduction do you have to do before you're ready to go into the studio? Everybody's different," notes producer Steve Addabbo, who has discovered and guided the songs of Suzanne Vega and Shawn Colvin. "Certain bands will be really tight; other bands will have the song half-written. A certain amount of preproduction is important to any band. Too much is not a good thing, and none is not a good thing, either.

"There should be some advance planning," Steve continues, "and that can be defined as anything."

■ The ABCs of Preproduction

Each artist has her own preproduction process. With folkie female artists like Suzanne Vega and Shawn Colvin, preproduction can mean sitting with a singer/ songwriter at her house, listening to songs in their bare form and talking about what she hopes to capture in the recording. Van Halen, who have their own studio and no worries about money, use their recording space as a way to get away from everyone else and be alone with their music.

"When we started work on our blues album, we prepared by playing classic blues songs—'I'm Ready,' by Muddy Waters, 'Shame, Shame, Shame,' by Jimmy Reed . . . and other classics by more obscure artists," shares Aerosmith bass player Tom Hamilton. "We thought we would do an album of cover tunes, but as we cranked away on these old blues songs, new riffs kept popping out. So, by the time we went into the studio, we had several original cuts to put on the album, even though we didn't set out to write any new tunes; it just happened."

If you're recording on a set budget, it's most economical if you already have the basic flow of the song and an idea of who's going to do what.

⋰⋰ **COMMIT IT TO MEMORY:** *Even if you're on a tight budget, leave room for inspiration.*

Those with recording experience advise that you should never go into a studio blind. Even if you're using something as simple as a four-track recorder, you should have an idea about how things should sound on tape beforehand.

"Rehearse in a studio that at least has some kind of cheap recording equipment, so you can get a vibe on how it sounds," advises Tom Viscount of Viscount. "Sometimes people record a song at the wrong speed, because they didn't think about it and they didn't pay attention. There are some issues you can't change after you've laid it down, so be ready."

Preproduction costs are something that most bands are happy to absorb these days, because making music is their craft, and preparing an album is just part of the process. It's when you get into the big studios that charge you five and six hundred dollars an hour that recording gets prohibitive, and you have to be organized as to what you're doing.

"In the studio, I kept some of the pieces the same. With other pieces I kept improvising on the same theme," offers classical composer Alexander Stone.

Sure, you're thinking, Oh we're tight, we play this song live all the time. That doesn't necessarily mean that the tune is going to transfer easily to disc. Sometimes when you take it into the studio, the live arrangement doesn't work as well. Prepare beforehand; play it in rehearsal to see if you need to take things apart and put them back together a little more carefully.

Pop records are made up of parts. You can hear this particularly well with solo acts. Suzanne Vega, for example, is very much a solo artist. When she went into the studio early on, it was Suzanne and her guitar, and Steve Addabbo, her producer, adding different tracks around her to augment what she was doing.

"We began with Suzanne playing live. The sound started to form there, and we took that a little further in the studio," recalls Steve. "On the first record, there are only four or five tracks with a real drummer, and the rest of it is Suzanne with things layered in around her."

■ Making Creative Choices

When you went into the studio, you climbed the first rung of production: you recorded your music. Now you can make more choices in the studio when you hear your music over the speakers.

Listening to your music over powerful speakers will make you realize a lot of things. You can say, This stinks, let's go back to the old idea, or, We really need to take this further, or, This other song does seem too long, let's cut this chorus out. Knowing at what point to develop or stop developing an idea is instinct; it's part of being a musician. When is this idea done? When is this part finished? When is this vocal good enough? Answers to those questions are linked with your instinctual reaction to the music. Your ears will tell you, That part is great! or, We need to do it again because that part is just a slight bit out of time. Then you do it again and it doesn't feel as good as the other one. . . . What do you do? Making an album means weighing quality against emotional content against that indefinable something that makes that vocal performance a take or not a take.

■ Producers

It's an accepted fact that a producer will make your music sound cleaner and more unique. That is a spectacular luxury that a band should experience at least once during its recording career. Using a producer is also a financial luxury. If you're going to go with the industry standard and use a producer, you're going to be paying big dollars. Like recording budgets, producer fees can vary wildly. If you're doing it yourself, it will be totally different than if you're doing a major label gig. Generally, a producer is paid a flat fee for producing an album or a song. On a major label project, the typical producer's fee might be anywhere from $30,000 to $75,000 for producing an album, plus points.

Don't get all panicky now. Generally, some or all of the producer's fee is considered an advance against future royalties on the album, meaning that if the album generates $100,000 in royalties for the producer, the $30,000 to $75,000 already paid to the producer is deducted from the $100,000.

Choosing the right producer for your project is a major decision, as they can affect your sound as drastically as band members can. When deciding on a producer, keep in mind that there are several that may be right for your project. Who works for you will be a combination of factors: timing, personality, and money.

Let's say you've got a nice budget—$35,000—to record a quality album. You are able to spend a little bit of money to make things sound right. You're given the option of working with a producer, an engineer, and a mixer. Who do you use for what?

"Artists shouldn't seek out the most famous producer they can think of," notes Frank McDonough, president of Moir/Marie Entertainment, and manager of many producers. "They should try to find a producer whose work they respect, and who has the time and the inclination to work with an unsigned artist. In this way, it's a mutually beneficial relationship."

"You know what was amazing about having a successful record? On your next record you can record with whomever you want," declares Jacoby Shaddix, vocalist for Papa Roach. "On *Lovehatetragedy* we got to work with our first choice, Brendan O'Brien. We had put that out in the cosmos when we were like seventeen years old. Brendan came in and said, 'At most what I want to do with you guys is get the right arrangement of the song, the right tempo, and put it in the right key.' That was something that we had not really thought about before—what's up with the keys of the song. On *Lovehatetragedy*, there were songs where I couldn't hit the melody because it was a little too high. Brendan suggested we take the guitars down a half step and sing it that way. It was a weird way to make it sound better; it was kind of subliminal to your ear because you don't even notice it. Had I tried to sing the higher version live night after night, I'd be straining, and my voice would just be hurting."

Most everybody's music gets shaped and formed by several sets of ears.

Few individuals have the talent to envision and execute a complete album. Making an audio disc is a group process. Take Mariah Carey's hit single "Honey" from the album *Butterfly*. "Honey" pushed the *Butterfly* album to more than 3 million in sales, making Mariah Carey the only female artist to ever have seven consecutive triple-platinum albums. Figure if anyone has a handle on public taste, it's Mariah. She may write the songs, but taking them from thought to reality is a group process. "Honey" was a joint venture between Mariah and her producer (and former member of the disbanded A Tribe Called Quest), Q-Tip. "It was very much a collaborative effort," Mariah confirmed. "It was Q-Tip's idea to use the loop to the completion of the record."

The producer guides the creative direction of a project. Probably the easiest way to understand this abstract concept is by way of an analogy: film directors do the same thing for movies. Ron Howard and the Coen Brothers might take the same script and make radically different movies, because their perspectives are so different. Similarly, the same song in the hands of two different record producers might come out sounding totally different.

"The producer isn't really in charge of that, anyway. We know how we'd like our individual instruments to sound," observes Edward Van Halen. "The producer is basically an outside objective ear who suggests things here and there, arrangement-wise, song-wise, but no one tells Al how to make his drums sound. Making music is an extension of yourself."

George Drakoulias is the staff producer and A&R executive for American Recordings. On Tom Petty's *Wildflowers* album, George is credited as "consultant on anything really important." As an A&R guy and producer, his role in the project was actually very simple. "I'd go down to the studio and just offer my opinion up; it was a pretty casual thing," recalls George. "I'd go down maybe two or three times a week and hang out for a couple of hours and see what they were doing. I can't think of any major production contribution. It became this thing where I would just show up and expound—whether they wanted to hear it or not."

A producer is the one who's making creative decisions about the music along with the artist. He is the one whom you hire to say, No, this guitar part doesn't work, or This drum sound is not right for this song, and, Let's try this instead. The producer is like a film director, telling the musicians what to do.

"You can only produce a band effectively if you've earned the band's trust," notes George Drakoulias, who signed and produced the Black Crowes, the Jayhawks, and the Freewheelers, among others. "You become very friendly with them and you gain their trust. You court the band; you talk to them; you spend a lot of time with them. You discuss records you like, records they like, then you talk about the songs. So by the time you start recording, they trust you; they know where you're at. They know you're not just saying something because you have to be right about everything. Or you're not just saying it to them just to hear yourself speak, or having an opinion just to have an opinion. You're expressing an opinion because that is your opinion."

The details of what a producer does are varied. On any given project, he may perform any or all of the following tasks:

- Act as referee if two members of a band disagree about a song or instrumentation.
- Help choose which songs should be recorded for an album.
- Encourage an artist to rewrite, add parts, or delete parts of a song.
- Suggest different arrangements for a song.
- Control, either directly or by hiring an engineer, the sonics of a record (i.e., digital recording versus analog, Dolby versus non-Dolby, this microphone versus that one, this guitar amp versus that one).
- Create an environment in which the artist will give his or her best performance. This can take a variety of approaches: candles, carpets, etc., or even making an artist angry while recording to capture the spirit of a song.
- Producers are also sometimes held responsible for making sure that the album is completed on time and within the budget. This isn't the producer's primary function, and, frequently, the administrative aspects of making a record are handled by project coordinators, not producers.

Generally, the producer should be someone whose work the artist admires and respects, making the artist more inclined to take the producer's suggestions seriously. If an artist wants to record her songs exactly as they are, with no changes whatsoever, she doesn't need a producer; she needs an engineer.

■ John Keefe — Producer

John Keefe is the founder of First Generation Recording Studios, and he is constantly at work making music for Midwestern artists, such as the Lamont Cranston band and Pat Hayes. A veteran producer, he shares his thoughts on making a record.

Why do you enjoy what you do?
JOHN KEEFE: Allow me to begin by saying I really like recording. It gives me a chance to work with a lot of different musicians and see a lot of different styles that I probably wouldn't see because I'm playing. I like meeting

and interacting with other musicians. I have a lot of fun doing it and it allows me to be very creative. Thank you for a chance to talk about the recording business.

Once you have the recording done, please explain working with the band or producer on the mixing, or what comes next.
JK: Usually the producers or artists and engineer will sit down and talk about how they want the band to sound. Then they'll talk about the performances and how they rate—whether they are good or mediocre. A [working] mix is then set up to hear how the performances sound. At that point a reference disk may be burned so the producer or artists can take it home and evaluate the performance and/or material.

What are the other steps involved?
JK: Overdubs may be called for to fix weak performances or mistakes. Then finding out what the artists' or producers' visions are of how the material should sound and what route we should take to achieve that.

What are the different roles of engineer, producer, etc., in the final product of a live recording?
JK: An engineer handles the technical part of things. A producer will handle more of the creative end of things. For example, an engineer will handle most of the recording, mixing, editing, EQ setup, and FX setups. A producer would handle song arrangements, performance, feedback, but may also handle some EQ mixing, editing, and FX. A producer may or may not be on hand for the live recording. So the lines get blurred a lot. Some engineers are producers as well. I found myself in the role of producer many times when a band is lacking direction. There are also assistant engineers. I use them a lot on live recordings. You need at least two in order to handle the technical aspects of a live situation.

How important is each role of mixer, engineer, producer, etc., in the final product of a live recording?
JK: Mixers and engineers are the same thing. I'd say the most important thing is the engineer and producer work very closely together and as I said before, the lines are often blurred. Case in point: when Pat and I are working on the live Cranston CD, we're continually bouncing ideas off each other to see what works and what doesn't work, and we don't always agree, although with Pat being the producer, he has the final say. That's probably true in most of the

recording situations. It's the combined efforts that count to make a good recording. Everybody has to be a team player.

Are some producers easier to work with than others? Any stories?
JK: Some producers are easier to work with than others. Some are very technical about what they want. Some are less technical and are looking more at the creative side of things. A good story would be when Steve Miller came into the studio for his first Musicland project, which was a large Broadway production. I had just upgraded to Pro Tools and I only had two weeks to learn the technical aspects of it. So I went on vacation and spent two weeks reading the manuals to try to get a handle on the systems' capabilities and how it worked. As well, Steve was under the gun because it was his first project producing for Musicland. It had to be perfect. The pressure was incredible. I being new to the system, and Steve being new to producing, it was like the blind leading the blind. Our senses of humor helped us handle the pressure. It came out very well, although we went way over budget. And we both ended up eating some of the cost.

Once you are done, what happens next in making the CD?
JK: It goes to a replicating plant. The studio master is burned to a glass master and then the CDs are stamped out. Next, a silk screen design is applied to the nonplayable side of the CD. The booklet is printed; the tray cards are printed. They're all assembled and shrink-wrapped.

■ Your Production Budget

Generally, the amount of money available will dictate how long the artist and producer can spend on an album. Traditionally, if you're making a full-length album, it's going to take you anywhere from fifty hours to a thousand hours to record a complete disc. A major label act with a decent budget and all the time needed to devote to recording an album will take from six weeks to two months to record an album. You probably want to think about the timing and budgeting of a producer this way:

- a week of rehearsal
- a week of basic tracks
- three weeks of overdubbing and vocals
- five to ten days to mix (on smaller budgets you try to mix two songs a day; on bigger budgets you take a day per song)

If you don't have a record deal and you're doing an album because of your creative need to do a record, "two months would be pretty much banging it out. That's basically six days a week; it's working pretty hard," notes producer Fletcher Beasley. "Realistically, if you did a lot of preproduction work and you knew exactly what you were doing, then you could go in and do it in a month's time."

You've heard the generalizations, but, as your album is a unique, creative endeavor, you will have specific time and budget considerations. A producer is brilliant at helping you figure this stuff out. If you're working with a producer, you'll meet with him and figure out how much time you'll need for recording each instrument on each song. He's the guy that knows approximately how long it's going to take to track drums, bass, keyboard, guitar, vocal, sitar, tambourine, whatever.

"I did the production myself," offers Alex Stone. "I realized how much work it was, but I learned. If you rely on other people, very often they might not take it as seriously as you would for yourself, so most likely it's not going to come out the way you want it."

■ Engineers and Mixers

An engineer is responsible for getting the music properly recorded on tape. He is responsible for the technical aspects of recording, like mike placement; he is like the cinematographer running the camera. He helps develop the sounds with you—he'll do a drum sound for you—but it is the producer who will say, Yes, I like it, or, No, I don't.

A lot of producers are engineers. Someone who spends time in a recording studio naturally evolves into an engineer over the years just by doing it; you know what you want and you learn how to go for it.

You need both a producer and an engineer unless the producer can act as an engineer. That is a very, very important factor in having a record sound good. Having a producer and an engineer is also good because everyone does things differently, so you'll get yet another perspective on things.

"I used an engineer because I assumed he would know his part better than I would," observes Alex Stone. "He does that every day and I don't, so he might know little tricks or things that I have absolutely no clue about."

A mixer is someone who comes in at the end when the producer and the engineer have recorded all the music they want. Essentially, a mixer is fresh energy; he is another set of ears to listen to everything and put it together slightly differently or bring some new ideas to the sonics of it. After you've been in the studio for 400–500 hours listening to your songs over and over again, you're used to hearing them a certain way. A mixer will come in with new ears, and can take your music to another level. Think of a mixer as a film editor.

If you're recording on a budget, and don't want to hire a mixer, you could purchase equipment that would mix the album for a similar price. That new toy will not only help you on the new album but it will also help you for the next one.

> ☼ **COMMIT IT TO MEMORY:** *In mixing an album there's a lot of grunt work, and maybe it's a good idea if somebody else does it.*

On the other hand, mixing is an art—a very important art. The benefits of a studio-mixed album can be extremely attractive, perhaps more so than buying a new toy.

Getting forty-eight tracks down to two for a stereo recording is quite a process. Getting the separation and making it sound clean is truly an art form. In the end, all you really want to do is get it to sound like a song, but you've got all these different ingredients that go into it. Some mixes can take two or three days of hard work. That's the luxury of having a mixer come in: he is someone who is sympathetic to what you're doing. Just when you're about to burn out, he gives some gas to that last stage of mixing where everything is on tape and you've got to mix this mélange of tracks down to a two-track tape that's going to be the record. Indeed, this is quite an involved process.

■ Takes

"When we went into the studio, we kept playing the song over and over again," offers Tom Viscount, describing Viscount's recording process. "We all play together live, but we only record the drums. That way the mixer can put in the right dynamics. We take it only one track at a time, but we do it several times and have the whole band playing each song."

You're going to have to record some music so it can be mixed down to exactly what you want, so be prepared to do several takes on each song you record.

"On most of my pieces, I had to do roughly three to four takes until I had one take that was good," shares Alex Stone. "I got it right on the first shot on only one song—that was rare."

Go with your instincts; you know when it sounds the way you want it to sound. You know when you play well, and you know when you screw up.

"I wanted each piece to be recorded in one shot," says Alex. "Sometimes I kept going because I didn't want to stop, but I knew when the take was missed."

■ The Drum Sound

"Drum sounds are like the foundation of your building," notes Steve Addabbo. "It's the superstructure. You're building your rhythm around it. If the drum sounds are badly recorded—there's not a lot of impact to them— you're building on marshmallows and you're not going to have a real strong track."

Everything gets laid on top of the drum sound, so make sure it's done right. Because of the way a drum sound reverberates around the room, each room has its own drum sound to it. Things like size and soundproofing (or lack thereof) matter a lot. You may want to do the drums in a bigger studio to get a bigger sound. A smaller room will give you a more raw feel.

The drums are the backbone of your record; everything else balances on top of the drum sound. The skins set the acoustic balance of the record. The kick drum (the bottom end) and the cymbals (the top end) frame the whole record. A badly recorded drum sound makes it sound weaker, which is why producers and remixers end up replacing drum sounds with their own samples. The drum sound needs to be able to cut through a track. As the mixes get denser, drum sounds need to cut through a little more for the rhythm to come through.

In the old days, when mono and stereo were the way of the recording studio, the vocals were very much the focus of the record, and the drums played along. You had more tracks, three mikes in a studio, and four channels to record music. You'd say, We're ready, let's go, and you'd be done by the end of the day because there was nothing else you could do. Is the song working out? Is the singer any good? Great, can he sing the song?

It's not that simple anymore. As multitrack recording became standard, more attention had to be paid to the drums. Instead of recording the drums with one mike, you had the ability to record them with ten microphones. Magically, you had more control over the tom-tom and the kick drum. When heavy metal ruled in the eighties, the drums ruled. You could find twenty-four-tracks of a recording devoted to just drum sounds. Now it's back in focus.

The role the drums play on a record depends upon the producer. Some are dependent on the drummers doing their job, but there are so many weak drummers out there that others rely on samples, and deal with the drums when they get to the mix. If the band's drummer doesn't work, the producer will throw his sample in instead. That way, you get these very nice, very predictable drum sounds where the snare drum never changes sound, which is definitely not the way it sounds in the real world.

You want drummer consistency, but part of the emotional impact of a drum part is that it does change and that it does go with the song. There's no one way to do it; there's no right way to do it. There are different ways to get the right sound from the drums. Some producers have incredible luck with drum loops, others rely totally on the drummer, and a third breed likes to use the real thing with electronic elements interspersed. Why not? Why limit yourself?

The recording studio is a total fabrication; it's like a movie set. To have someone looking normal on film—say, sitting at a table—takes a crew a half a day to set up. The recording studio is similar to a movie studio in that respect. When you finally get to the point where, Gee, this sounds like a song, you've done an incredible amount of technical work to make it come out of the speaker that way.

Once you get into the studio, it's a totally false situation: there's a tape recorder running and there's a microphone. It's not a live performance. All that stuff goes out the window. All bets are off, so whatever works for you is fine. That is why it takes so much longer now to make a record.

■ Click Tracks

A click track is basically a metronome, which is what you use to keep time. Thus a click track helps you keep the tempo of your music consistent. It is both a great thing and an evil thing. It's great because it gives you the ability to go between different instruments and tracks and still be very sure that your time is right. It's not so great if it makes your performance rigid.

To make a click track, you lay down the tempo of your song on tape. Voilà, you have a basic track that will keep the rhythms steady. It's always a nice thing to have. That way, when you go in later to do an overdub, you don't find one measure where the drummer fell asleep, so it's all out of whack and you can't put anything on top of it without the whole track sounding like it's grinding to a halt.

Certain bands don't need a click track, others do, and some bands can't play to it—these tend to be bands that are new to the studio.

If you're young and up-and-coming and used to playing live, a studio click track may make you give a stiff performance because you're worried about keeping time and aren't focusing on the song.

There are instances where a click track doesn't work and you've got to throw it out. That's just fine. Listen to some of the Beatles' records. Ringo was never a perfect drummer; his time's all over the place. Moving time around is part of an emotional performance, so it's not set in stone that everything should be done to a click track. You have to pick your spots.

■ SMPTE

Ask a dozen people about SMPTE, and though nobody seems to know what it stands for, everybody knows what it's good for. SMPTE code was developed by the film industry to have a specific digital code on tape that was an absolute. Using an SMPTE reader, one could always find a specific spot on tape, enabling one to get the dialog in sync with the talking image on the film. It's far more accurate than the tape counter on a tape machine.

SMPTE keeps time off the click track. It provides a clock source in the studio; it counts the seconds to a song and what's going on at each second. That way, if you do want to add anything, you can digitally dial in the number and make the addition. If you have any problems, and you have the tape tripped with SMPTE, you can correct them by synching up sequencers to it.

"SMPTE, in a recording situation, lets you know where you are on the tape so you can lock things up to it," offers Fletcher Beasley. "It's a timing reference, a clock source."

SMPTE is now used extensively in the studio; the engineer locks the mixing computer to it. If you want to raise the vocal on that one word, it keeps track of that word on an SMPTE number, which is absolute for that song. Every spot has its own number. The SMPTE count equals thirty frames per second, so every one-thirtieth of a second there's a new number you can access. You can synchronize tape machines with that, and have forty-eight tracks synchronized via tape sensors and computers.

■ Capturing a Vocal

One of the trickiest things about making a record is capturing a vocal and knowing when you have it. A big mistake that gets made in the recording process is that people spend a lot of time capturing the big drum sound and the big bass sound, and, all of a sudden, It's time to do your vocals now. The vocalist is expected to immediately sing the vocal performance of a lifetime.

"Our producer, Nick Launay, was actually good about the singing," relates Semisonic's Dan Wilson. "Whenever I would say, 'Come on, let's sing,' he would say, 'Do it.' Generally, he took a let's-get-it-done-as-efficiently-as-possible attitude because we were on a budget and he had to move on to the next project."

A producer should be prepared to do vocals at any time, whenever the vocalist feels like it, not just during the designated vocal week. If you put pressure on the vocalist by giving him specific time slots, nine times out of ten, the artist will get sick that week. Recording the vocals should be the least intimidating process of the whole record, but it is seldom that way.

"It's probably the most intimidating part of the whole record when an artist has to do their vocal performance," confirms Steve Addabbo. "I probably spend most of my life dealing with this part. Sometimes you can get a vocal when you're not even thinking you've got it. I've gotten some of my best vocals when I let the artist think I'm testing the levels. 'Just sing it one time through, I've got to set this up . . .' If I don't have that machine on record, I'm an idiot."

When you listen to the radio, what are you really hearing? You're hearing the beat, but you're hearing the vocal, and that's what's selling the song. If the vocal isn't right, it doesn't matter what kind of drum sound you have—the drums are not going to carry the song. The vocals are the core of it.

The producer should be sharing that intimate experience; he should be inside the headphones when the singer is laying down his performance. That way, the producer is sensitive to what the singer is responding to. The headphone mix should be right for the vocalist, or he's not going to sing the right thing. Perhaps the artist can't use headphones properly. Put the speakers on low in the studio so that he doesn't have to wear headphones. Do it any way you have to do it. There's no one right way. Record it in the artist's shower or living room if there's the need.

"I've done plenty of records where the vocal in the living room maybe doesn't sound as good as the one I can do in the studio, but the artist is relaxed, it sounds like he really means it, and I can make it work," offers Steve. "It's not necessarily the sonics of a song. As a producer, you have to learn to make those choices and to give it up when it's more important for the song."

💡 COMMIT IT TO MEMORY: *In the creative process, there's always going to be some special variable you have to deal with.*

■ When Do You Need a Recording Studio?

A universe of fine equipment does not a complete album make. Even with an array of cool gear, you're probably going to need a better console to mix your album. Inevitably, the stuff in your studio is going to have some problem—it hums, it buzzes, it's just not good enough. So to mix the record you either need to buy a new console, which is expensive (anywhere from $2,000 to $8,000 for something you can actually master onto a hard disc), or DAT (digital audio tape). Do you track at home knowing that you don't have good microphones? Do you bypass that problem and go straight into the hard disc system, then go into the studio and mix it? Or, do you prepare all the material, then rent or buy a DA-88 and dump all the tracks into it, and take a couple of days to do that so you can avoid paying studio expenses, because recording can actually cost a little more than the price of two DATs? Or, do you go into the recording studio and take two to five days and mix the album with an engineer?

When you think about the album, you should make these calculations in your head, and by the time you're actually ready to make a record, know which path you're going to take: spending the hard money on a studio and engineer or getting a new toy and doing it at home. Each way has its advantages.

"I wanted to make my CD, *Timeless,* in a studio," declares Alex Stone. "My feeling is that when you make a CD, because the sound is so clean, if you do it at home chances are there's going to be a hiss or some hum—some kind of noise in the background. That won't sound really professional. I hope, at some point, to have my music on the radio, so you have to stick to a certain quality standard. That doesn't mean you can't stick to a home studio, but it has to have the sound quality."

■ Choosing a Studio

Generally speaking, if you're bringing in musicians, you're going to need to go into a studio. This is obviously a big investment, so you have to choose wisely. Bottom end at odd time slots starts at $50–$100 an hour. If you're working with a producer, he'll try to choose a studio that meets several requirements:

- It fits the budget
- It has gear that the producer likes (Neve board, SSL, outboard, mics)
- It has a good vibe for the artist (i.e., pop artists don't like trashy studios, punk bands don't like really pretty studios)
- It is located somewhere near the producer or the artist or in a place both producer and artist would like to work
- If possible, it's somewhere where the producer has worked before
- It's available during the time frame that works for everyone

"We ended up at a place called Criterion Music in Hollywood. It was suggested to us through a friend, who happens to be our engineer," declares Tom Viscount. "You have to listen to what they do in the studio, then it's all negotiable. If you go with MIDI stuff, you can do a CD real cheaply and still have live drums."

To find a good studio, ask around, or look at the credits on an album that has a sound you like. It may take a while to find a record that was done in your hometown; finding a good studio takes research. People choose studios mostly by sound and word of mouth; did your buddies have a good experience recording in that space?

"For a band picking a studio, there's a cost factor, an availability factor and what the studio has done," informs Steve Addabbo. "If you're a rock and roll band, I don't think you want to go into a singles studio to cut because it's just a different vibe there."

The vibe of a studio is undeniably a very important aspect. "It's as important as the equipment," notes Steve. "When people walk into a room, they like to feel that it's a musical environment—that it sounds good in there, that it's set up by people who understand what musicians need, the headphones sound good, things aren't breaking, the equipment works when you need it. There's nothing more frustrating than being in the middle of an idea and having the whole thing go down on you and you lose all the momentum. The maintenance of a studio is a very important factor. The vibe of the place has to work for you."

Check out studios you might be interested in. Go to a lot of different places and see what feels right. You meet the person in charge, check out the space, and listen to what the studio has done. If you really like it and you're wondering about the investment, talk to other people who've worked there and listen to how their stuff sounds, then ask for their feedback on the recording experience.

Inevitably, the cost of the project will depend upon what you want to do. If you own the equipment and were wise about the decisions you made, you could put out an electronic album, like Alexander Stone's *Timeless*, for $2,000.

"I didn't have to pay for a studio because I had friends. I only had to pay for the actual CD that I had printed and the pressing. That came down to $1,700–$1,800—but if I had had to pay for the studio it would have cost twice as much," offers Alex. "I asked everybody I knew if they knew someone with a studio, and I tried to trade work for studio time because I didn't have the money. Eventually, I found some people who needed help with their band, so I helped them and they let me do my recording."

It's a buyer's market. Home studios have opened up a lot of space in recording studios, so most recording studios have become more affordable and willing to work with you. Ironically, most of the bigger studios are going out of business, because nobody wants to spend that kind of money to make a record.

"If you're recording on a budget, book the studio at off hours, when they don't charge as much," suggests Tom Viscount. "Do a lot of preproduction work, so there's not a lot of guesswork when you get into the studio. Make sure the lead singer knows how to sing the song on pitch. And when you're in the studio, people will get really anal about their little part, so you need to have a big picture in mind when you're recording, or suddenly, you'll be doing things over and over again. That's where people spend a lot of money."

You can't have everyone making decisions in the studio. Allow everyone to give input, but only a couple of people should make the decisions. Different band members are good at different things: some are better at the production side, others are better at the finance side. You need to be able to acquiesce to their knowledge and skill. You can't know everything, so you need to have people who are good at different things contributing to the creative process.

"Long before we had our record deal, we recorded our first album in a basement under a liquor store. We did it for 2,600 bucks, then we got a recording deal," recounts Godsmack vocalist Sully Erna. "When it got released by Republic Records, we just remastered it. We didn't remix it; we didn't rerecord it or anything. We remastered, put some new artwork on it, and it was out in the stores six weeks later."

■ Planning the Studio Session

Let's say the composition you're recording involves cello, viola, violin, contrabass, bamboo flute, and two taiko drums. You can't record that piece in your home studio, so you have to figure out which studio you're going to use, who will be your engineer, and where you can properly record taiko drums. Remember: the instruments—as well as the room—have to sound good for a good recording.

The most efficient way to do it is to have all the parts you want done printed out. Then you hire players for three hours—which is the minimum amount of time you can hire a union player—and skew their arrival times at the studio so you can bring all of your musicians in on one day.

■ The Producer and the Studio

Oftentimes, better-known producers come attached to their own studio. Someone like Bob Rock wants to work at Little Mountain Studios in

Vancouver. Other producers absolutely hate the idea of having their own studio; they don't want the responsibility.

For Steve Addabbo, having his own studio has allowed him to work with groups he wouldn't normally be able to work with because they lacked the budget to go to another studio.

"For someone like me, who finds talent and develops it, it's important to be able to run into the studio and see if it works," notes Steve. "We can do a couple of tracks, and if we like each other, we'll do it. If not, we'll go our own way. It's the quickest way of finding out if a musical relationship is going to work. So, for me, having my own studio has been an invaluable tool to keep my career going, because I'm able to go and develop new things without having to go and hire another studio. The overhead takes care of itself with other bookings."

■ The Reverend Horton Heat: Converting the Masses

Jim Heath, Jim Wallace, and Scott Churilla have been recording as the Reverend Horton Heat for more than a decade. They've always been a profit-making entity, with their albums selling in the 300,000-unit range. Frontman and founding member Jim Heath shares the band's tale of success.

Summarize your career to date.
JIM HEATH: It's been a real success, and everything's been a lot of fun. Nothing's really turned out like I thought it would. I figured if I wrote good songs and I played good guitar and the band had a really kick-ass live show, that record companies would be all over us. I figured the cream would rise to the top, but life isn't always fair. It took a long time, we were passed over by every label in the book. But we're pretty happy where we are.

You got picked up by the legendary Sub Pop Records. How did that happen?
JH: They were the smartest guys in America. When we first started touring, we made a conscious decision to play the punk rock and alternative rooms around the country. By the time we got up to Seattle, we were selling as many other tickets as Sub Pop's other bands—Nirvana, Soundgarden—so it was a logical move for Sub Pop because we were selling out the same venues that it was trying to break its bands in. Sub Pop didn't really have another band like us, so it was kind of a cool deal.

What kind of deal did you get?
JH: We got money to do the recordings, a very simple deal.

Did you get tour support?

JH: No, no tour support from Sub Pop. We're fairly low maintenance; we don't need any tour support to play around America any time we want.

You're now signed to Interscope. What's it like going from an independent label to a major label?

JH: Interscope came and said, "We'll start paying for you to have a bus right now if you sign with us," and we said, "Okay." That's not really smart business, I know . . . but sometimes you just act on instinct.

There are more people that work at Interscope, but to me there really doesn't seem to be any difference. Sub Pop could get our videos played on MTV. Interscope doesn't think that we can do that, so we don't make videos for Interscope.

It must be nice to be making money while making music.

JH: We don't make any money because we've got all this crap we've got to schlep around the country. On our more recent tour we had two buses and two semi trucks—boy, we sure look good onstage and that's all that matters.

You've created an interesting marketing niche for yourself: you're the Reverend and it's Martini Time—all that sort of thing. Did you plan out your marketing campaign and position yourself this way, or is this something that happened?

JH: I'm not really in the business of marketing, so I don't really know. I just play guitar and sing in a band. The whole martini thing came about because it was our idea to call an album *It's Martini Time* and set up a whole theme for the whole CD. We had a song called "It's Martini Time," so some developments are an outgrowth of one idea.

There are a lot of marketing gimmicks that the record company comes up with; I'm just like, Oh, y'all want to do that? Fine . . . Y'all want to spend money on that? Great. . . . It's all about image. There are all these rock stars out there, and they all have these stupid bios that are really 100 percent fake. When they make bios on us, they'll say anything. It's not about politics or anything, I'm not really a big role model like Michael Jordan or something. I don't have to worry about all that crap.

You intended to produce Space Heater, *your third Interscope album, by yourself. How did you evolve to this point?*

JH: We negotiated our contract because we didn't really want some heavy-handed producer with us. We wanted to coproduce *Space Heater*; we really didn't want a producer at all. They gave us the freedom to decide what we wanted to do. We made a little less money—quite a bit less money, to tell you the truth, but they said, Okay, we want to hook you up with a really great engineer. I said okay. Then, all of a sudden, the idea of Ed Stasium came up because Ed is a genius engineer and such a nice guy. When he showed up, it was just beautiful. That's why we went in and gave him producing credits. About halfway through the deal, we said, "Ed, you're so good at this, we're just going to say it was produced by Ed Stasium."

What did Ed do for you?
JH: Some of our old producers, if we had a crazy idea, like, Hey let's sync this spring reverb through my amplifier, would go, Well, Jim, wait a minute, do you really want to do that? If it was Al Jourgensen, we'd sit around and spend two days talking about it. If it was Thom Panunzio, later that night it would be figured out. With Ed, if we said, It would be pretty crazy if we tried this, Ed would go, Hold on a second, take a break. We'd come back ten minutes later and he'd be like, "Hey, this sounds great." We were going, Wow! this guy is on. We're pros now; we go into the studio and we want to work quick. We don't want to sit around all day and ask, Should we do this? Should we do that?

That's one of the things that bothers me about recording: when you try to second-guess instead of just being real bold and adventurous and saying, Yes, let's play the guitar through this stupid little box on this song.

Was Space Heater *your best recording experience to date?*
JH: One of the best ones, yes. There weren't a lot of people, just us and Ed there every day; that was it.

How did you choose your studio?
JH: We choose studios based on where it is comfortable for us to record. We usually cut our basic tracks in Dallas, Texas, where we live. That is about the main consideration. Now, for the mixdown, a lot of times we'll experiment and go different places. This particular time we mixed out in California at a studio that has all vintage gear—old Neve consoles. The console was used to record the theme to "007" in the sixties. It was pretty cool. We didn't do any digital effects on the mixing.

Did you use anything digital?
JH: There's a couple little digital toys that we used. One guy at the studio invented this silly little digital recorder that teaches your parrot how to talk.

You say something into it, put it in your parrot's cage, and it goes off every thirty seconds. I figured out that I could say stuff through it or record stuff with it and then put it over the pickup of my guitar or straight up into the microphone; it was cool. We were playing around with it on a song or two.

One thing was interesting about the way this CD was written. Normally I have everything written before the guys in the band get a chance to hear it. Now we have some money, so, over a period of thirty days, we were in two different demo studios. I had this idea that I could write and record a song a day for thirty days in a row, so when we did the demos for this, we were in there writing every day. It gave my guys a chance to have more creative input with the writing. That was a real different thing.

Did you get a song a day done?
JH: Yes, we did a song a day for thirty days. Some of them, of course, were songs that I'd written a long time ago, and some of them I had an idea for maybe a year or two before I figured how to hone it down on that day. It was a cool deal: we had thirty songs, and I think we ended up with seventeen on the *Space Heater* CD. We wanted to get a lot of songs on the CD to try and have the most value possible.

What do you focus on when you're writing a song?
JH: I want to do each song as well as I can do for that particular time. I'm not thinking, well, how will it fit on the record; is this going to be the first cut or the last one? That's not even a consideration.

Are you very satisfied with Space Heater*?*
JH: I know it's a really good album. Six months from now I might listen to it and say, No, this isn't that good, but we're definitely getting better, so our most recent album is our best one.

You've done several television appearances, on The Drew Carey Show *and* Homicide. *How did you get into TV?*
JH: They asked me. I know it helps us; I don't know if it helps out the show. But Drew Carey is a great guy, and it was a good break for our career.

CHAPTER SEVEN

Recording in the Comfort of Your Home

The music industry was changed so dramatically by the advent of low-cost digital recording gear. Now everybody and their brother can pretty much make a record. You just don't need a quarter-million-dollar record deal to make a record anymore. So you see a lot of people making records and doing jingles and movies and stuff in their home."

— Russ Miller, Professional Drummer

What's happening now in the home studio market is something that was not possible fifteen years ago. Thanks to the advent of low-cost digital recording and digital signal processing, a low-budget option exists. The technology and means are now available to anyone with even a modest budget. In fact, there are now inexpensive units that have mixers, hard drive recorders, various digital signal processors, microphone preamps, headphone preamps, and CD-R burners integrated together in one box. All you do is add a microphone and a pair of self-powered speakers, and you have a self-contained recording studio.

For the musician with the objective of recording an album, the home studio is a necessary way to go.

It allows an artist to record multiple tracks directly to CD and send it to record producers, distribute it cheaply on the Web as MP3 files, or sell the CDs directly from their own Web sites. Personal computers can now host different software applications to record, mix, and dictate signal processing functions. Another nice aspect is that new recording technologies will let you record fine quality music in the environment of your choice. Even Aerosmith, a big-budget band who has been using recording studios for the past twenty years, has taken to setting up a home recording studio on the premises of guitarist Joe Perry's home.

"We're always getting offers to do one-offs of songs or remix this tune or rerecord that track. It's a pain having to go find a studio, usually somewhere outside of Boston, and move everything into it," explains Aerosmith bassist Tom Hamilton. "When we did our *Rocks* album, way back when, we did it at our rehearsal hall in Boston. We have great memories from that record—we really had a good time."

After seventeen albums and a number of years of discussion, Aerosmith and their advisors came to the conclusion that they could cost justify the expense of building a studio.

"Not only can we record our albums here, but there are also 100 other things we can be doing in our studio," elaborates Tom. "Everything from our photo shoots to video stuff, to DVD stuff—a million different things."

■ Russ Miller: Succeeding in the New Millennium

Russ Miller is a professional drummer. He has kept a beat on over 200 records, including Nelly Furtado's first two releases, accompanied international stars from Ray Charles to the Bee Gees, and executed drum work for scores of movie scores. He spends 60 percent of his time in Los Angeles, recording around town, or at home.

Why did you set up a studio at your house?
RUSS MILLER: So a lot of composers and producers that I work for will just come to my place to do drums. This is a big change compared to what used to be.

Does this trend from major-money recording to low-cost production generate new opportunities for independent, freelance musicians to work out of their own homes?
RM: Oh, definitely. There aren't as many opportunities to be doing big, major label records and movies. On the other hand there are a lot of movies and

records getting made at budgets that they couldn't get made for before. There's that whole new grassroots level of production that is happening, and somebody's got to play the music. So there is opportunity there.

When you call someone like me to do a session at a studio, you pay my fee, you pay cartage fees, you have to pay for the studio time, and you have to pay for the engineer, and that ends up being a costly thing, to do a record in a big studio. At the house, I just charge my session fee and a small studio fee, so that's an attractive option for producers.

Do you suggest that musicians spend time building some studio and electronics skills, as opposed to spending all their time becoming a master of the instrument?
RM: We don't have the luxury of just playing our instrument like we used to. I do highly recommend being the best player you can, because it's the only insurance of making a living in this business that you have.

If you're a great player and you don't sleep in your closet and hide from the public, you'll end up floating to the top eventually. But I would never recommend to somebody, "Be an acoustic jazz drum set player and you'll do just fine." I know four or five guys on the planet that can do that and they're the biggest names in the business—and they're making a very average living.

I recommend to everybody that you be the best player you can be and be extremely aware of what's going on with electronics, even if it's just minimal—like having a sampler and a drum machine and a trigger module, so at least you can do tracks or MIDI sequences for someone.

Every pro that I know has a studio in their house. Everyone I know in this business is doing some percentage of their work at home. So, I highly recommend getting those skills.

■ Steve Addabbo: The Home Studio

Producer Steve Addabbo runs his own forty-eight-track studio, Shelter Island Sound, in New York City, but supports the home studio.

How effective is a home studio when it comes to recording an album?
STEVE ADDABBO: The equipment has gotten so good and so inexpensive that it's really hard to tell, quality-wise. If someone has taken the care to do a little homework—if they read *Mix* magazine and learn how to mike things— you can't necessarily tell in the end result if the vocals were recorded in someone's living room or in a $200-an-hour studio.

In the old days there really wasn't a good way to record at home. No one had good microphones, no one had good microphone preamplifiers. Now with the ADATs and everything else, you can get some really good quality that competes with a major studio.

ADATs?

SA: ADAT and DA-88s are digital eight-track tape machines. They're very high quality audio machines for a very low price. The type of recording quality you're getting rivals some of the best multitrack machines that cost $50,000 or more. What it's enabling people to do is get really good quality recordings at home without the big hourly cost of a studio. More and more music is being recorded at a better quality, and it's revolutionized the music industry, because these things are so accessible to people on small budgets.

Hiring a studio is costly—even an inexpensive, $500-a-day studio for two weeks will still cost $7,000. For the same money, you can go out and buy two machines and a little mixer and a microphone and you can pretty much do your album at home. What you're not getting is the advantage of a producer or a really good engineer to make your music sound that much better, but a lot of times it doesn't matter. Certainly in the beginning stages when a band is figuring out their music and figuring out what they sound like it's a valuable tool.

What exactly is a DA-88 and what does it do?

SA: ADATs and DA-88s are just two different formats for recording the same thing. It's like Beta and VHS, essentially—video machines in the old days had two different formats. These also use different tape formats. The DA-88, a machine that was made by Tascan, utilizes a smaller 8-mm high-8 tape and is not compatible with the ADAT, which uses a little bigger VHS-style tape. They both basically sound the same. Their quality is very similar. The DA-88 is preferred by the film industry because it locks up easier to the SMPTE time code that the film people lock onto. The ADAT is a little less friendly in that. That's the difference between the two of them.

The DA-88 machine is more expensive than the ADAT, so the ADAT found favor with musicians more, while the DA-88 found favor with the film postproduction studios. That's the main difference.

How does the home studio differ from the professional studio?

SA: The quality of the equipment, the microphone choices, the acoustic environments. With some home recordings, you get background noise like the oil burner going on. In the final mix you might not hear that stuff, but it tends to cloud recordings—they tend not to be as pristine.

Major studios have equipment and acoustics designed to make the music sound better. And that stuff does add up in the end. There's no doubt that a record done in a recording studio will sound better sonically than one done in a living room. Emotionally, the one done in the living room may sound better, so in the end, maybe the one done in the living room will sell. You can't whistle a console or a studio, but you can whistle a song. The song is still what matters the most, and if that is your approach, you can record almost anywhere.

Does today's low-budget recording process involve both the home studio and the recording studio?
SA: A lot of people still will come to a better studio to mix their record because they're in an environment that's acoustically correct, so they can at least evaluate their mixes. You can do quite a bit with a home recording in a studio when it's time to mix. It would be pretty hard to tell which was done where.

How have ADATs and DA-88s affected the recording industry?
SA: They've made an incredible contribution to it. They've given a lot of artists a lot more creative freedom because of the opportunity to work on their music at home and to really learn. It's given me a bit more freedom in that I don't have to sit there for every nook and cranny on the record. With an ADAT, if you want to try something, you can. If you're on a budget, you really don't have the time to sit there and experiment a lot. You take the piece home, play with it, do your homework and bring it back in. ADATs have become very handy tools, and you can't deny that a lot of people have made hit records on them. They're here to stay.

■ Using Synthesizers and Computers

"If you want to write music, it's really great to have a sequencer on a computer and a sampler," offers Fletcher Beasley. "As a starting point, that gets you pretty far; there are a lot of things you can do with that. Get a multitrack recorder if you play an instrument. You can do a lot of preproduction with those few pieces."

In order to figure out what to buy, you've got to think about what you want to do with your home studio. If you want to use your studio as a writing tool to record ideas for acoustic instruments, get yourself a sampler. If you're playing in a band, get a multitrack recorder.

If you're making music by yourself, the experts recommend a multi-timbral synthesizer that has a lot of sounds on it that you would like to use to write music. Add a computer. You can really do it on any computer that's made now, Mac or PC, though professional audio is still a Mac-based world.

"The computer is just another tool in making music," notes jazz musician Oded Noy. "It's a very powerful tool, but one has to have a level of comfort using it for it to be effective. For digital edits and simple postproduction I use the SAWPlus on my NT box."

"For writing music, I use Logic Audio, which is a MIDI sequencer that does digital audio as well, and I also use Pro Tools," offers Fletcher.

A sampler is good for drum loops and creating complex instruments that don't otherwise exist. A sampler can turn digital audio files into MIDI-driven instruments. If you want to get more creative, add this piece of equipment.

■ Costs Involved

Liken the building of a home studio to buying a car—you can spend some money, or you can spend a lot of money. You can probably integrate some of your existing equipment, such as your stereo and home computer, and you can build some other items that will simplify the process.

☀ **FACT**: *A home recording studio can be as simple as a multitrack cassette deck, a microphone, a musical instrument, and a second stereo recorder for mixing recorded tracks.*

Truth be told, if you're looking to create a product for sale, you will want something better than a cassette multitrack recorder and a microphone. As you progress in the recording process you will want to add additional equipment, which can include more recording equipment, computers, synchronization devices, sequencers, mixers, signal processors, and power. You can sweeten up your acoustics, monitor speakers, and beyond.

Think about your space. If you're in a small room, multiple reflections of sound can muddy the audio, resulting in an uneven recorded sound. You'll want to put up carpeting, egg cartons, or some other type of wall and ceiling treatments to help you control the sound bounce. Other considerations include ambient sound traveling into and out of your studio, as well as the electrical system.

"We went in and gutted the basement and built it up from scratch over the course of two summers," elaborates John Keefe of First Generation Recording Studio. "A friend of mine, Greg Johnson, helped me with the wiring and structure. He's a marvelous carpenter, jack-of-all-trades, and musician. Scott Ludden, the Soulmates's sound engineer/studio engineer, did the design and specifications. I started with [four] ADATs and a 16-track analog tape deck, and a Mackie 32-channel mixing console. In 1998, I switched over to hard disk recording for its editing capabilities and upgraded to an automated console. I use Pro Tools, but still have ADATs and bought a 24-track analog tape recorder. As far as what I can do, I can do most anything. With the advent of digital recording, there is not a whole lot I cannot do. For example, I have software that can take vocals or instruments that are out of tune and put them pitch perfect in tune. A recent example: while recording a CD of Broadway tunes, we had a singer who could not hit a very high note. It was, I believe, a high E. So we had her sing a high D and then we pitch-shifted it to a high E. Listening to it, you would swear she sang that high E. I can take material and speed up or slow down that material with no pitch change. These are just a couple things, but there are many, many more. The computer is a very powerful recording tool. It's amazing."

■ Home Studio Recording FAQ

John J. Volanski, author of *Sound Recording Advice* offers this FAQ regarding home recording studios:

How can I make use of some of these new formats like MiniDisc and MP3s in my home recording studio?
JOHN J. VOLANSKI: Both MiniDisc and MP3 formats use a digital signal processing technology known as audio compression to reduce the amount of information that is needed to be recorded. The good thing about this is that more audio can be recorded onto any given size of digital media. MiniDisc recorders have processors inside of them that can determine what digital information can be deleted from an audio signal and still have it sound good to the human ear. The MiniDisc processor will throw out about 80 percent of the information in the signal and just record the remaining 20 percent of the signal. An MP3 processor will throw out about 90 percent of the information in the signal and just record 10 percent of the signal (and MP3 usually sounds inferior to the MiniDisc). The problem is that once this audio material is thrown out, it can never be recovered. This is called "lossy compression." For this reason, I recommend that MiniDisc and MP3 not be used for multitrack recording or mastering (the final stereo recording that is used for copies to

be made). However, MiniDisc and MP3 are great formats for trading audio recordings with friends (especially sending MP3 files over the Internet) or for personal/portable stereo formats.

How do I get rid of noise in my recordings, such as hiss and 60Hz buzz? How can I record myself with a microphone without picking up equipment noise?

JJV: Noise is the bane of all studio recording, especially for home studios. Noise can come from many different sources, such as from outside of the home studio, poor power filtering, poor electrical grounding or ground loops, crosstalk from other recorded tracks of audio, equipment fan noise within the home studio, tape hiss, and even electrical self-noise from the random collisions of electrons within the electronics of a piece of equipment.

What is the best software to buy so I can use my computer for audio recording? Should I use my computer as the main recorder in my home studio? Is a Mac better than a PC?

JJV: First of all, let's make sure you have a computer that can support the requirements of audio recording. For a PC, you should have at least a 200MHz, Pentium II class of computer. For a Mac, I would recommend at least a Power Mac 9600/200MHz machine. As you start piling on more and more software that must execute in real time, then even those machines might become sluggish. Obviously, the faster and more powerful the computer to be used for audio recording, the better. Currently, the latest PC or Mac machines available on the market are equally able to execute audio recording software for quality results. You can choose whichever computer type makes you feel most comfortable, either the PC or the Mac. If you already have a computer, then you will need to buy a software package written specifically for that type of computer platform. You will also need to buy some sort of hardware that will allow you to plug musical instruments and microphones into your computer for digital recording.

How can I synchronize analog tape recorders with my computer so that audio recorded on both machines plays back at the same time?

JJV: An analog synchronization time code (an audio signal encoded with unique synchronizing signals) can be recorded onto one track of a multitrack analog recorder. A separate hardware processor (such as the JL Cooper PPS2) can then read this synchronizing time code audio from the multitrack analog recorder and convert it into a different digital synchronizing code (usually MIDI Time Code) that can be read by one or more computers (or other digital recorders) in the home studio. The computer will then automatically play and record in perfect synchronization with the analog tape recorder. This is an advanced technique used by home studio owners who want to synchronize multiple audio recorders that use different formats (such as reel-to-reel, standalone digital recorders and computers).

What's the best way to record my [insert instrument name here]?
JJV: Most every acoustic instrument requires a unique miking approach, and that includes the human voice. To complicate matters, there are many different types of microphones that are specifically made to handle different recording situations. Amplified acoustic or electrical instruments present their own recording challenges, especially if a microphone is not used. This subject is so important to making a quality recording that *Sound Recording Advice* dedicates over twenty-four pages to miking and recording various instruments.

Should I buy used equipment? Where should I buy used equipment?
JJV: Absolutely! You should definitely buy used equipment, as this can give the best price/performance ratio available. Also, look for B stock (scratched, dented, open-boxed, or demo new equipment) from vendors. When new equipment is introduced into the market, many vendors sell the older, obsolete (yet new!) equipment at highly reduced prices. You should take advantage of all these low priced sources.

What microphones should I buy?
JJV: As I mentioned, there are many different types of microphones that are specifically made to handle different recording situations. There are microphones made for studio recording that range from $50 to over $5,000. Your budget will largely dictate which microphones you will buy. Keep in mind that the microphone is one of the most important things you can buy for your home studio. If you are spending $1,000 for your home studio equipment, you should spend at least twenty percent of the budget on one good microphone. The book, *Sound Recording Advice,* details the best ones to buy at various price points. It also gives a recommendation for which mic to buy if you can only afford one low-cost microphone for your home studio.

■ Case Study: Oded Noy's Home Studio

Impassioned musicians always have a collection of instruments strewn around the house to meet their creative needs. Oded happens to be a keyboardist who makes music that can best be described as New Age lite jazz. He had everything he needed to record his most recent album, *Silly Little Rain Dance*, at home, although he had a professional do the mix. Here is a tour of Oded's studio:

- 1963 Hammond B3 organ—the highlight of the tour.
- Wurlitzer electric piano. This has sentimental value: the Wurlitzer marks Oded's return to the piano, after not playing it for a long time. "Certain songs sound really good on a Wurlitzer. It's like playing bells; it's awesome," says Oded.
- The Wave Station, one of the few synthesizers that doesn't sound like anything else.
- The XB-2, a MIDI organ left over from band days.
- 2500XS, a control keyboard and sampler which has 64 megs of memory, a piano card, an external CD-ROM for sampling CDs, and various other extensions.
- Roland VS880 hard disc system with eight tracks of audio and a gigabyte inside.
- Atari with Emagic Notator for MIDI sequencing.
- Alysis D-4 drum machine.
- Custom-made Symentrex.
- Fostex console (that needs to be replaced).
- Task MV888.
- Various effects units and microphones.

■ ADAT-XT Eight-Track Digital Audio Recorder

Music historians will someday look back and mark the release of the ADAT as the dawn of the personal digital recording age. Alesis's groundbreaking ADAT Digital Audio recorder changed the way music is recorded, allowing musicians to create professional-quality albums in home and project studios.

The ADAT-XT keeps the ease of use and great sound that made the ADAT the most popular digital multitrack of our time, and adds new tricks of its own. The audio quality actually improves on the ADAT's high standard, recording eight-tracks of audio with eighteen-bit, 128x oversampling, A/D converters, and twenty-bit 8x oversampling D/As. The ADAT format records on readily available S-VHS videocassettes, and up to sixteen ADAT recorders can be linked together for 128 tracks with no external synchronizer required and without sacrificing a track to timecode.

The ADAT-XT offers an improved transport that operates up to four times faster than the original ADAT, with new Dynamic Braking control for more accurate locates and faster lock times. An onboard digital editor allows you to make flawless copy-paste digital edits between tracks on a single unit, or between multiple machines. The XT features tape offset, track copy, track delay, and ten autolocate buttons for sophisticated flexibility and control over your productions. Both +4 dBu-balanced and 10 dBV-unbalanced connections and the ADAT Optical Digital Interface are provided for flexible hookup in your studio, and a comprehensive vacuum fluorescent display provides all the critical information. A rugged six-pound die-cast aluminum chassis offers strength and stability, with lessening torque stress on the transport mechanism.

With its fast, software-controlled transport, onboard digital editor, ten-point autolocator and 100 percent compatibility with over 70,000 ADATs worldwide, the ADAT-XT builds upon the ADAT format as the world's most popular professional multitrack recorder.

■ DA-88 Digital Multitrack Recorder

You'll find a DA-88 in just about every professional audio and video setup. Its rock-solid performance makes it ideal for work on location, and it uses reliable Hi-8mm compact cassettes. Its user-friendly interface includes a jog/shuttle wheel for easy locating, fast transport (fast-forward or rewind an entire hundred-minute recording in eighty seconds) and autolocate features, plus level meters for each track, rehearsal mode, single-button punch-in, and absolute time display. This unit is expandable up to 128 tracks.

Features include:
- One hour and 48 minutes recording time on a single 120 tape
- Expandable up to 128 tracks/sixteen machines
- User-definable track delay and crossfade
- Shuttle and jog capability
- Auto punch with rehearsal
- SMPTE, MIDI, and Sony 9-pin sync capability
- Options include: RC-808/848 remote controllers, IF-88AE/IF-88SD digital interfaces, MU-Series meter bridge MMC-88 MIDI machine control interface, and SY-88 Sync Card

The DA-88 delivers the best of Tascam's Hi8 digital audio format. This is the standard digital multitrack for postproduction, and winner of the coveted Emmy award for technical excellence. Its modular design allows for easy servicing and performance enhancements with third-party products.

The outstanding benefits of digital multitrack recording have unfortunately been an unattainable dream for many personal and professional studios, due to the high costs. The DA-88 dramatically changes this. As the world's first affordable digital multitrack designed for production, the DA-88 opens up a universe of recording options for professionals and enthusiasts alike who want to experience the promise of what the very best digital recording has to offer. Now, any studio can produce master-quality digital tracks without budget or time constraints. For maximum creative control, the DA-88 also provides precise, seamless punch-in/out capability using advanced digital crossfade technology. Every way you look at it, the DA-88 represents a spectacular breakthrough in affordable digital multitrack technology.

For more information about the ADAT-XT and the DA-88, check out *www.sweetwater.com*.

☀ **SOUND ADVICE**: *Read the owner's manuals for the equipment you have (or intend to buy), because no book on general studio recording is going to cover all the details and operational tricks you will find in the owner's manual.*

■ Samples

If you're doing the home studio thing, another good "instrument" to own is a sampler. At this point in history, a sampler is just another instrument.

"A sampler is a dedicated device used for playing back digital recordings of instrument sounds or other musical samples," notes multitalented composer David Javelosa. "A digital recording can be sampled at a variety of sampling rates and dynamic resolutions, depending on capabilities of the particular machine or the style of the intended use."

There are different types of samples. There are the preprogrammed ones that come along with the machine, and there are samples that you can make yourself. If an engineer or a producer has a drummer in the studio and really loves the drum sound, he'll go and have the drummer hit the drums for a while and keep that and later retrigger that sound for another project. This comes in handy if you're a solo artist who has a bunch of songs, and you want to put an album out. If your rhythms are simple enough, you don't have to hire a band; you can use samples to put a different spin on it, throw in a bit of Bjork, or the Chemical Brothers' vibe.

Sampling has become quite an art form. A lot of sampling that's going on with rap and R&B music actually uses snippets of old records, looping them and making them into new songs. The most famous example of this is MC Hammer's multiplatinum hit, "Can't Touch This," which uses a riff from Rick James' "Superfreak." The riff is all-pervasive in the song. Used this way, samples are like an additional instrument. With this type of sampling, you're using someone else's performance or song, and you've got to pay them royalties. That's where it starts to get a little out of hand, but it's become standard in the R&B and rap world, where they often make up songs with no real instruments at all. It's just samples and scratching and voices—a different approach to record-making.

■ Samples: Rights and Royalties

Version 2.0, the 1998 release by the band Garbage, used a couple of different samples and interpolations from well-known sources. The first single, "Push It," uses the phrase "don't worry baby" in the chorus, a quote from the Beach Boys' 1964 hit of the same name. Avoiding any potential legal hassles, Garbage cleared "Push It" with Brian Wilson, who approved the track personally. As a result, the *Version 2.0* CD booklet includes a formal credit for use of what the music industry calls an "interpolation" of "Don't Worry Baby."

Ironically, another song on *Version 2.0* quotes a well-known rock lyric and goes completely uncredited. The Garbage tune "Special" is a tribute to Chrissie Hynde and the Pretenders. Garbage singer Shirley Manson sings it in Hynde's style, and she repeats the words "talk of the town" at the song's end, a direct reference to the Pretenders tune of the same name. The tribute is intentional, but did the band somehow clear the song without a formal credit?

"Definitely," Garbage drummer Butch Vig told the *Wall of Sound* Webzine. "When the label heard a rough mix of 'Special,' someone threw up a red flag and said, 'You can't do that; that's lifting directly.' But Shirley tracked down Chrissie Hynde and called her up, because we had met her before and we are huge fans. Shirley explained that the song was a little bit of an homage to the Pretenders, and you can hear that somewhat in her singing, but at the end of the song, when she drops those lines in, it's pure Chrissie Hynde. So Shirley asked if she could send her the song. Chrissie said, 'No, you don't even have to do that. I love you guys. You can go ahead and do whatever you want to do.' And the next day, we got a fax that read, 'I, Chrissie Hynde, hereby allow the band Garbage to sample my songs, my voice, and indeed my very ass. Love, Chrissie Hynde.'"

To Vig's mind, this is exactly how sample and interpolation clearances should be handled: "Musicians should be able to call up musicians, and either get their blessings or not, and avoid getting attorneys involved, because then it becomes a huge money and legal issue."

In the early days, many sampled records were released without anyone making an effort to clear the rights. The artists and companies often had an attitude along the lines of, If they catch me, I'll make a deal. When the artist did get caught, the deal that was struck meant some money was exchanged and the rights were bought after the fact. Money was then given to the record company owning the sampled recording, but rights are a multilayered thing; the record company's rights aren't the only rights that need to be satisfied. Indeed, the publisher of the sampled musical composition must also be taken care of.

These days, if Red Herring doesn't get permission to use a sample in their song, and they don't pay royalties to everyone, no doubt some federal court will fine Red Herring. Additionally, if Red Herring's song was distributed internationally, their case will get referred to the U.S. Attorney's Office for criminal prosecution, as intentional copyright infringement is a criminal offense.

Be like Garbage; treat sampling with the utmost care and respect. Any respectable record company won't release a record containing samples without knowing that the samples have been cleared. As you'd expect, clearing samples is like any other legal process—a major pain in the butt. And, the owner can always say no. When you ask permission to use a sample, remember that there's no law that requires people to let you use samples of their music; meaning, if they say no, you've got to pull it off your song.

There's also no accepted agreement for licensing samples; you've got to strike the best deal you can. If you have to pay, go for the flat fee. Lawyer Donald Passman, who wrote the best-selling book *All You Need to Know about the Music Business*, suggests that, if it's not a particularly well-known segment from a well-known song, you attempt to buy all of the rights for a flat fee. He suggests a fee of $1,500 to $5,000 for the record company, and about the same amount for the publisher. If the usage is more significant and the song is quite popular, the cost could go up to $25,000 or more.

A buyout of sampling rights is a best-case scenario. Most publishers will instead ask for a piece of your song. The percentage they're going to get is determined after the publisher listens to the tune and negotiates a deal. If you've lifted an entire melody line, they might insist on 50 percent of the song; if it's a more normal use, the range is 10 to 20 percent. They may also ask for a say in how the song is used.

■ Jim Survis, Joe Perry's Guitar Tech, Talks about Aerosmith's Home Studio

Jim Survis has a dream job. He's Joe Perry's guitar tech and Aerosmith's equipment manager. When Joe Perry was constructing his home studio in 2003, Jim was an integral part of the process.

As a kid, did you want to go on tour with a band?
JIM SURVIS: It's funny. When I was a little kid, my fantasy was to run away with the circus. And that's what I've done. With Aerosmith, I put up the big

top up every night. I travel around with a bunch of other freaks and feel like I've gotten away with not ever having to get a job, although my days are often sixteen hours long.

What can you share about Joe Perry's custom home studio, the Bone Yard?
JS: It's on the premises where Joe lives—it's the lower level of his home. He's got a nice studio with beautiful equipment. His recording console is a Neve— a beautiful vintage console from England that's known for its warm sound. That's the centerpiece of the studio.

Is it an analog studio?
JS: It's both analog and digital. He's got Pro Tools digital, as well as analog. He's got everything he needs. Joe works down there all the time when he's off the road because he's an artist. . . . Like Picasso, he just wakes up and goes down and paints, so to speak.

And what part did the Bone Yard play in the recording of Aerosmith's 2004 blues album?
JS: The Bone Yard was where Aerosmith was warming up and putting ideas down. Jack Douglas produced this record. He's worked with the band many times in the past—even as we speak. It's a great energy around the studio. All the band members seem to really like it. We see everybody in here, playing a lot, just jamming creatively, getting loose, and enjoying themselves. They've really been stretching, cutting loose on the blues. After all, the blues is what Aerosmith is all about. Sure, they've got a great reputation for the rock and the pop side of things, but that's not the cloth that they're cut from; they grew up playing the blues.

What's it like to see a great idea emerge?
JS: I feel like a midwife at a birth. It's great to see stuff get born. I can recall hearing the first lick of something and then they built a song around it. That's what gets more of the most about this gig—seeing guys that are this good giving birth. It was thin air a minute ago, and suddenly, they have the nucleus of a song. The next thing you know, something is born.

What's the most satisfying aspect of your job?
JS: My job is pretty different from the studio to the road . . . and I like the immediate gratification of the road. The studio requires a lot of patience; it's

focused and low key, while the road is slamming! WHAM! BAM! We've got a show tonight! We load in in the morning, and eighty guys set up a big arena rock show.

On the road, you've got to be ready. The support act is on at 7 P.M.; there's no 'I can't get ready in time'—that's not an option. Then you knock out the stage and it's showtime. The crowd is screaming and the lights go down and the show is on and there's an immediate adrenaline rush and immediate gratification of putting down a good show. And when you're done with it, you know you've worked hard. You're tired, your body's sore, your ears are ringing, and you know you put in an honest day's work.

So, tell us about a day the in the life of Joe Perry's guitar tech during an Aerosmith tour.
JS: Nowadays, Steven doesn't like to sing two nights in a row because he really puts all his cards on the table at each performance. So our schedule is now is day-on, day-off. We play every other night. We have about fourteen trucks full of gear, and ten buses full of crew, so everywhere we go it's quite the circus. Typically, the production starts loading in at about six in the morning. It starts with staging, then lighting, then sound. Around 11 A.M., the stage is set up, the lights are hanging in the air, the sound is going up, and we start to unload the amplifiers and instruments and all of what we call our "back line equipment." We're usually ready and completely finished with sound check at 5 P.M.

I get there around 9 A.M. I go in early, and the rest of my guys show up between 11 and 12. For me, it's a time when I can FedEx stuff or e-mail somebody, have some breakfast and deal with a few things before my day gets really exciting. My day ends with load-out, so I'm usually done around 1 A.M. and I have the next day off.

Tell us about Joe's road equipment. How many guitars does he travel with, and what are some of his favorite pieces?
JS: We're traveling with around fifty-five guitars. There are a few of the real old vintage pieces that have a real long history for Joe. Those are some of the favorite children, so to speak. He has a 1960 Gibson Les Paul that he's extremely attached to. He's got a nice 1960 Gibson ES 335. But everything is important—we have Flying Vs and Stratocasters and special custom built stuff—like the Billie Guitar.

The Billie Guitar has Joe's wife's picture on it. The custom guitar was painted by the drum tech for ZZ Top. His name is John Douglas and he's also a commercial artist. He's a great artist and he always paints Frank Beard's drum kit. Every ZZ Top tour, he comes up with a new idea for these crazy drum kits.

One time, ZZ Top was doing the David Letterman show as the musical guest, at the same time Joe was sitting in with the Late Night Band as a special guest. John Douglas was setting up a drum kit that was all supermodels that he had airbrushed. Each drum had its own supermodel's face, all airbrushed and stuff; it was just beautiful.

When Joe decided he wanted to paint a guitar, I suggested he give John Douglas a call. He did the Billie guitar—and it's exactly her; you could be looking at a photograph. He did an incredible job.

What amps and effects does Joe prefer, and how does he like them set up?
JS: We tend to tweak and modify stuff every tour. This tour, our wall of doom consists of Gibson GA-30 combo amps, modified Marshall 200-watt guitar amps, and a lot of Marshall 4X12 speaker cabinets. That's the wall that you see behind Joe when you're looking at the stage from the audience. I won't bore you with all the details of how I route the signals. It's way too technical.

Joe has some effects that we use. I run all the effects for him, except for the wah-wah, and if he's got a whammy pedal, for those you need to have a treadle pedal, so you have to be the artist who's playing the instrument do the inflection. But the sound effects that just come and go for solos and special sounds and stuff, he runs around and plays and I take care of all of that for him.

You have a lot of responsibility—all those ears depending upon you.
JS: It's a handful. He changes guitars every song, so I've usually got the next guitar on my shoulder, and doing the tap dance on his pedal board of effects and . . . it's definitely busy. You can't daydream.

What is the most satisfying aspect of your job?
JS: I like the whole ball of wax. I'm glad that I'm able to make a living at something that I'm passionate about that doesn't feel like work, although my days are often sixteen hours. So by any standards, you're putting in twice the hours of the average person at their regular job. It just feels like what you do, and you're into it and you love to rock and it's great, I'm working with people that I've admired since I was a kid.

CHAPTER EIGHT

Timing Is Everything: Planning the Release Date

If you're concentrating on your art, following your instincts, then you're doing your homework, the rest will come. There's going to be an increasing amount of people around you to help get the word out to other people.

—Chris Douridas, DreamWorks Records

In the beginning of their career in the early eighties, Van Halen used to take a week to record such classic albums as *Van Halen II* and *Fair Warning*. In those days, the average album took two hundred hours to record. All that has changed. On more recent records like *Van Halen III*, it takes the current lineup of Van Halen six months to a year to create an album. They go into 5150, Edward Van Halen's home studio, putter around, make a song, try it again. They deliver the record whenever they wish and it inevitably sells a million copies.

You will have to earn the luxury of delivering product on your own time parameters. If you've got any kind of deal at all going, you will have a deadline for finishing the album. It's all part of the cycle. Your record company may schedule your record for release in late July because in August, the company has four big megastars coming out, and has to focus its energies in that direction.

■ Schedules and Deadlines

Once your album is slotted into the release schedule, the record company machine starts working on your behalf. This is where recording an album becomes a group process. The record company needs an adequate amount of time to promote your record, and you need room to set up a proper tour to support your newly released effort. The proper touring and promotion schedule will take anywhere from three to six months to set up and execute.

In the real world of making a career go, album releases, marketing, touring, and television appearances have to be synchronized. You want to have your record out for a month or two before your tour starts so you will have some radio airplay. Obviously, you'll want to go and gig in the markets where radio airplay is happening—that's called building momentum.

"When an album comes out, a band and its record company will set up a schedule of when they're going to radio and what kind of markets they want to be pushing," confirms Virgin Records' Laura Cohen. "Then publicity sends out advances to magazines to start getting some press rolling on it. So when it actually comes out on the release date, there's a little bit of a buzz going with it. Especially on new baby bands. With anticipated bands like Culture Club, Janet Jackson, or the Rolling Stones, people come to us, clamoring for information, so those bands kind of work themselves."

If you are not a megastar, you can't afford to put out a record and decide to tour a year later. It all has to be coordinated so that you have the most impact. If you miss your release date, you'll be sitting around for the next eight months, because everything was planned on a specific agenda.

At this moment in history, there are so many records out there, and so many more records being released every week, that a band needs to milk the most attention they can for each release. If you've got some momentum going, make the most of it. That's where working within the time frame comes in. If the label tells Belly Up to deliver the album in March, then Belly Up should indeed do the utmost to deliver the record by March. That way the record company—the label that Belly Up worked and prayed so hard to get signed to—can get the album released by June, and Belly Up can get on all of those high-exposure summer tours. If the band misses the March deadline, the earliest Belly Up's record can be rescheduled for is the fall. But keep in mind that the autumn—the start of the school year—is when all the big stars put out their records. Autumn is a big time because all the platinum sellers want their albums on display for Christmas. If you're a little band, you tend to get swallowed up by the big guys if you release when they do.

A new band has a definite window of opportunity. In order to take advantage of that window, the project must flow together properly and have a cohesive theme to it.

"Time wasn't really an issue, even though I had to give myself a deadline," offers classical musician Alex Stone. "When two years went by, I realized if I wanted the album to happen, I had to put some limits on how long I spent doing each piece. Basically I had to outline every step that's involved."

Set deadlines and stick to them. If your record is supposed to be done in January, you've got to finish it in January.

※ **COMMIT IT TO MEMORY:** *Keep to your deadlines. It's very easy to fiddle with an album forever and run up a million-dollar tab in the process.*

Very few artists are ever completely satisfied with their finished work, so accept that fact and move on. Find balance for the situation.

"Deadlines are very important; follow them," confirms producer Steve Addabbo. "A big band has already made it and has the money in the bank, so they have the luxury of releasing a record whenever they want. For up-and-coming artists who have to get out there and prove themselves, there are definite scheduling things that have to happen. You have to balance it out."

■ Mastering Your CD

As you draw to the end of your recording process, you need to put the songs in the order they're going to appear on your CD. As you finish mixing, the people in the studio will hand you a CD-R—a recordable CD. This is your premaster. What you're expected to do is listen to your album very carefully to see that nothing is wrong. Decide the best order for your tunes, then have the studio burn a master on CD-R. Once you approve it, a master is done. Make sure it's the way you want it, because after you approve it, whatever is wrong on that master is going to be wrong on all the CDs.

"When I listened to the premaster, the one where I was supposed to choose the song sequence, I realized the drums were too low," shares Alex Stone. "I had to go back to another studio where I actually made the recording of the drums. Then I had to go back to another place where I made the recording of the one song that uses the sequencer. I had to reprogram the whole song module because that guy didn't save the setting, because I wasn't supposed to be back there. I didn't really pay attention to the DAT tape, so the volumes weren't right, and I had to record that over again. It was relatively easy, in the sense that it was a machine, so I didn't have to play it again, but getting it done again was an involved process. Once I fixed the drum sound, it had to be reentered into the computer. Fortunately the settings were better, and I got the master.

"Even then, there was a problem. On the second master they burned, at the very end, maybe ten seconds before the end, there was a click—maybe a quarter second of the music was missing. The computer must have skipped or something, so they had to record it again. That's why it's very important to listen very carefully to that master. The third master that they printed was okay, and I approved it."

■ Cover Art

One thing a band seldom takes into consideration is the time and effort it takes to do the cover art for their CD. If you're a bit overwhelmed, start with a friend who's an artist. They may be totally tickled by the concept of getting their name on an album cover, and they may be willing to do it for free. Otherwise, the project is yours to stress over.

"I didn't even think about the cover until it was time to make the cover. I had to take everything one step at a time so I didn't get scattered," remembers Alex Stone. "Once I had the recording done, the next thing was the cover of the booklet. Basically I looked at fifty CDs to see what the standard was, even though I wasn't going to follow the standard. I wanted to do it my own way, but I had to respect a couple of things that mattered, like clarity and simplicity, as well as legal things like the copyright."

Starting your cover art when your album is finished will only delay your project more. Getting a record out and properly supporting your album release is all about timing. Get yourself a calendar and mark your release date. Now go back six months before that date. That is when you should start thinking about the cover art, not when you finish the CD and know the order of the songs and the length of each piece. The track listing should be the last thing that goes into your package, not the first.

"We usually have a lead time of four months for creating the album cover," offers Robert Fisher, an art director at Interscope Records. "You need time to meet with the band, and find out what they want. Then you have to plan photo shoots and organize any special illustrations that might need to be done. This stuff takes planning."

You may think designing a cover is a relatively simple process, but there are a lot of details involved. Have you thought about the inside booklet? The standard format is three panels, six sides—basically a three-page pullout. Do you want the standard foldout, or do you want a booklet with pages that staple? Or do you want a long foldout, or the kind of thing that folds into a little poster? Silly decisions maybe, but they have to be made, nonetheless.

■ Robert Fisher: Creating the Album Package

Robert Fisher was part of the very talented team of art directors at Geffen Records and Geffen DGC, before the label was absorbed into Interscope. His best-known work is the cover of Nirvana's *Nevermind,* but he's also designed memorable album packaging for the likes of Beck and Urge Overkill, as well. He offers his expertise on creating an album cover.

What's the process of making a CD cover? How do you put the package together?
ROBERT FISHER: The band will come in and meet with the creative director and she'll assign one of the art directors here whose style suits the band. We'll have some meetings and talk about ideas that they have. Sometimes the band will have lots of ideas; sometimes they won't have any.

How do you come up with the original concept?
RF: It's different every time I do a cover. I try to spend a healthy amount of time with the band, getting to know them and getting the feel for what they're about. I listen to the music and try to see them live. I just get into what they're about and try to express that somehow.

What happens after you come up with a cover concept?
RF: Once we get a feel for them, we'll start calling in photographers' books— styles that might work well. Then we'll have them come in and look through books and go through photographers until we finally nail one.

What do you mean, whose style suits the band?
RF: A good art director makes the album package suit the band's vibe. If you went and put your personal stamp on everything, it would look the same. It's important to draw from the band to give them their own style. Photographers all have their own little styles and niches.

We'd hook up the photographer with the band, and after that we'd go over if we wanted to do location or get a studio. If we get a studio, we have to consider dressing the studio with props and backdrops and all that kind of stuff. There's also styling and wardrobe. Some bands are fine on their own;

they have great clothes; sometimes they need some assistance, get some cool clothes in. Sometimes we have hair and makeup for people if they need it. Then we pick a date, do the shoot, go through the photos when they come back, pick the ones they like.

Sometimes the band will want to be on the cover; sometimes they won't. Depends on the band. We usually give them the option of being on the cover. The better-looking the band, the better the result you're going to have with that. Still, it's up to them. We can try and push them in a direction if we think it's going to be right for them.

Say we've got the elements we need. What's the process of putting the album together?
RF: You have the band come in and approve photos. There will be some where their eyes are closed and they're making goofy faces, so you don't want to use those. Edit the pictures, letting the band choose the ones where they like the way they look. Then we'll order prints and I'll go and get them scanned in and start work on computer. If they don't have an idea that they're going for, I'll just start comping ideas, and usually I'll turn in from three to ten cover ideas—that's if we're starting from scratch. If we have a goal that we're aiming at, I'll do two or three.

The band will come in and I'll meet with them and go over things and start fine-tuning it. The band is not that involved with most of the inside art, so I'll do that on my own and show it to them. If they like it they'll say, Yeah, run with it! If not I'll tweak it and resubmit it to them.

Does the band have a choice on how elaborate their package is or does the marketing department say, You have this much you can spend on your packaging?
RF: We have set limits. If you have six panels—three on each side—you get four-color on all of them. If you want to go like four or five panels, you would only get four-color on one side and black and white on the other. If you want to keep it all color you do less panels. Some bands will get more to do a booklet that's color all the way through—that would be a big-selling band. Some bands will pay out of their pockets for extra things.

■ Conceiving Your Package

Unless you're a big-name act, you generally don't get to do your own art. The art department will work with you on it, so creating an album cover is a joint effort. If you're a gold or platinum act, then you have a lot of say-so. Even if you're an act the label sought out, it is still going to want to do your album cover for you. It will always retain the last say on what your album is going to look like, because the record company wants to be able to sell it in Wal-Mart.

If you're very finicky and insist on doing your own art, make sure it's in your contract—because there will definitely be something in your agreement about who gets the authority on your packaging and promotion.

The best way to start planning your album cover is to discuss it with the band. When you have an idea that everyone agrees upon, get it down on paper; do a layout of what you really want.

Also keep in mind that you should design your album packages using the resources available to you. Let's say you have access to a graphics program and you have the ability to scan photos. Sit down one day and start messing on the computer. Get all the words you want in. Talk to all your band members and get all their credits. Then start thinking about what the name of the album will be. How can that be visually represented?

To do a proper album cover, you really should know a computer geek, even if it's just the person at Kinko's. Ask this very precious geek any questions you have about compiling art, color, text, and photos into your vision of the album cover. Doing it this way will help the project maintain a handmade feel, and it won't look as cold and computer-generated. Have a paper copy you can work from, unless you're a visionary. Once you're in front of the computer, having this reference really helps you keep your thoughts straight. A little forethought and direction will save you time when you work on the cover, and will keep you from getting confused about the intention of the project.

Believe it or not, working on a computer is easier than doing it by hand. If you're doing it the traditional way, on paper, and you make a mistake, you have to start all over again. On the computer you can just change the settings and add different colors.

☆ **COMMIT IT TO MEMORY:** *It's not that important to have visually stunning album packaging; it's more important that you have something that reflects who you are as a band, and reflects the theme of the album.*

"My album is called *Glass Half Full*. The theme is that no matter how bad things get, I always tend to look at things on the bright side. This is the running theme throughout all the songs and the album packaging," offers Laura Cohen, manager of publicity for Virgin Records. "Album packaging is totally personal. It doesn't make a bit of difference in terms of sales, but it might make a difference when someone's looking at the work you did, at how much effort you put into your album packaging before presenting the project."

■ Size Matters

Before you start to create your album package, find out the proper specs—the dimensions you should be using to create your art for both the cover and marketing and promotional purposes. The size of the CD is not the size you make the album cover art. It must be larger than the specs indicate, because the printer will trim the booklet, and he needs a little bit of room to work with.

"If I'm working on a CD, I usually go for about seven inches square and 300 dpi, which will blow up to twelve inches and still look good," advises Robert Fisher.

If you know that you're going to want to make a poster of the cover down the line, you're probably going to want to make some files bigger. Don't try to work on the computer with files that are poster-sized just for a CD cover, because it will be really slow and cumbersome to work with.

■ Computer Color

If you're working on your cover art, you're probably using a program like Adobe Photoshop. As you putter around on the program, under the mode heading in Photoshop, you'll find that there are several different types of color—indexed color, lab color, CMYK color, and RGB color. You want CMYK—cyan, magenta, yellow, and black. Those are the four inks they use to print. Working in CMYK will give you the most accurate screen-to-printer color match. If you work in other modes—say RGB (red, green, blue)—the colors that print will not match the colors you so carefully chose as you designed your booklet.

■ The Design Is Done. Now What?

You've done the art on computer, it's the right size, and everything is as it should be. Now how do you get those computer files to become the album art? The file format is very important. If possible, you should give the art to the printer on a Zip disc, or some kind of big disc that can hold all the artwork. Most printers will want files in a tiff format, which will have a suffix of ".tif."

The big label will bring the Zip disc containing the cover art to the graphic arts production department. These people will then send the files out to the separator, who will make four separate pieces of film from your files—one each of cyan, yellow, magenta, and black. These will be layered together to make a composite, which is called a chromalin, which will show you exactly what the cover will look like. It will show you the way everything reads—the type over photos and everything like that. The art department will approve the chromalins, and then it's off to the plant for printing.

If you're an individual or band tight on funds, the thing to do is to take your art to a service bureau who will make your chromalins for you for a nominal charge—usually $150 to $200—depending upon how many pages you have in your album booklet. The best place to find out about service bureaus in your area is from the local Kinko's. If you go straight to a printer, they're going to take your discs, send them off to their buddy at the service bureau, and charge you $500 to $1,000 for the process. That's a big difference in price for the same service. Wouldn't that money be a lot better in your pocket?

■ Printing and Pressing Your Album

Your album cover will be printed in a format called offset litho, on a giant press. What they do is gang a bunch of copies of your CD books together on one three-by-four-foot sheet of paper, run a bunch of those off and then trim them down and fold them.

Generally, the art department of the record label will do a press check. This means they will go to the printing plant (yours will probably be local) and while the album art is on the press and copies are being run off, they will check and make sure that the color is coming out as it's supposed to be. Most printers are really good at that, but once in a while, you have a photograph with some tricky colors in it that you want to make sure you nailed.

Art is done separately; it is printed, dried, cut, stapled, and assembled at its own location, and then it gets shipped to the distribution facility.

If you're looking for good printing deals, NAIL Distribution in Portland, Oregon, has a very reasonable printing and pressing deal. If you give them the chromalins and the master CD, they'll give you a thousand CDs for $1,450. That includes freight to Portland and a four-panel booklet. It's a pretty good deal.

■ UPC Symbols

In order for your item to be easily inventoried and scanned at the checkout register, your CD needs to have a bar code or UPC (Universal Purchase Code) symbol. Getting a UPC symbol is relatively simple. If your album is picked up for distribution, your distributor will assign a symbol and take care of registering it and putting it on the CD. If you don't have distribution, you can buy a UPC symbol from a distributor. NAIL Distribution is very nice and very helpful. In addition to the reasonable print-and-press deal discussed above, the company offers a UPC symbol for $50. Call NAIL at (888) NAIL-INC, or visit *www.naildistribution.com* on the Web.

If you buy the UPC from a distributor, registering it is your responsibility. If you've got lots of things to sell, you can contact the UPC commission, but that's probably not viable, since you have to buy the symbols in bulk.

■ The One Sheet

Along with your CD, you need to have what's called a one sheet—a page with a picture of the album cover on it, a description of the album, and the music. Additionally, there's other vital business information included on the one sheet: your catalog or reference number, the UPC, the price of the record, contact address, and telephone number. A one sheet has all the information a distributor or record store needs to know to order the record, effectively sell it, and pay you for it.

■ Distribution

Once you've got your CD master and your album cover art taken care of, it all goes to the distributor. Every distribution company has their own manufacturing plant where they print the CD, assemble the package in the jewelbox, shrink-wrap the product, and distribute it. The cost is about $1.70 per CD for the first 1,000; then the price drops the more CDs you have pressed.

The major labels all have their own distribution companies and then there are independent distributors for the rest of us. Currently, record distribution is in a very transitional state. Companies are being bought and sold and names are changing.

"The best way to find out who is doing independent distribution is to go to a record store and ask who they buy their records from," informs Kathy Callahan, senior director of western regional sales at BMG Music. "It changes every year as to who's a player and who's not. There's a lot of consolidation on the independent side of music these days."

Getting distribution for a band like Rip Chord is another part of putting the pieces in place. They need a good management company—one with connections. Then Rip Chord needs those other buzz-building elements working for them: a great local base, a good touring reputation, and press. If you've already sold several thousand units out of your trunk, you're a good candidate for independent distribution.

"If you've got those factors working for you, it then becomes a relationship thing," observes Kathy. "You have to find somebody that you like and trust, whether it's a manager or somebody at a record company, that is sending out blind CDs or trying to hook up with somebody who can get you the deal. The toughest thing to do is to find that relationship; who is it going to be that's going to be able to hook you up?"

Alex Stone does not have those contacts in place. Instead, he's trying to do everything for *Timeless* himself, and he's finding it to be a long and tedious process. He has been so overwhelmed by getting his CD out and making a living that he has yet to focus on the distribution and the promotion.

"It's still very blurry for me," he admits. "I'm not sure how it works, the ins and outs. I know I should try for any radio station that's likely to play that kind of music. And, of course, I should have it in any store that's willing to carry the CD, because if they play it on the radio, and nobody can find it in any store, then what good is it really?"

When he finds the time, his intention is to go to all the local music stores, see how they work, who they work with, and try to find the people they work with and find out about distribution. At least he has no debts to pay back on his album.

■ NAIL Distribution: Independent Distributors

NAIL Distribution was founded in 1995 to fill a specific need: to effectively place Northwest independent music in Northwest stores. Their initial family of fifty labels—primarily Northwest artists—has grown to over four hundred labels. NAIL is now proud to offer almost five thousand titles from Northwest/Oregon/Washington artists.

The music they carry is music they like. The staff of NAIL spends many hours trying to get people excited about the music they sell. Alicia Rose is vice president, head buyer, general manager, slave driver, and queen of NAIL Distribution. She is willing to share the secrets on getting distribution.

How does a band find a distributor?
ALICIA ROSE: Most bands are savvy enough to find the CMJ guide or SXSW guide, or they get a list of distributors from a friend who has a label, and they just call up distributors or send distributors packets with a solicitation—a CD and a one sheet. We get them and we look at them. If it looks good, we listen to it; if it doesn't look good, we wait a really long time and listen to it.

How many packages do you get a week?
AR: About fifty.

How do you decide what to distribute?
AR: We're regionally focused. For bands and labels that are regional—in the Northwest—that have an appeal and an audience in this region, we tend to be a little more lenient, especially if it's a band just starting out and they don't

have a label. If a Northwestern regional band is self-releasing, we give them an extra chance to do something because you never know. We take chances all the time on local bands that just want to get their product out there, especially people who play out—but it still has to be quality product.

The artist also has to have some connection with this region and even the rest of the world—something more than just where the band is from. In order for us to distribute an act, they have to have done a good job on their end; they have to go get press; they have to work on radio; they have to work on word of mouth; they have to tour; they have to do everything. All we're here to do is sell records.

Where do you distribute the album?

AR: Nationally and internationally, but NAIL is what you would call a regionally focused national distributor with international exports. Most distributors don't focus on distributing material from a region, but the reason this company has survived is because it is regional.

Do you print and package the CDs as well?

AR: Not for everybody. We do manufacturing, but we're mostly a brokerage service, where Joe Schmidt off the street wants a CD made and we do it. Sometimes we'll do a P&D—pay and distribute—where we pay for records and we distribute them. It gets taken out of the sales. That's pretty standard in the industry; we like those, but they can be complicated. You've really got to find a label that's willing to work with you.

If you're going to distribute a band, what's the general scenario?

AR: If it's someone from the middle of nowhere asking me for distribution, and it's something I'm actually interested in, if it's not a punk or a ska record, I'll probably take fifteen, twenty, maybe thirty maximum. If it's punk or ska, something that really has an audience to it, I'll take anywhere from like eighty to a hundred CDs on our direct-to-retail level.

NAIL functions as a one-stop and a distributor. As a one-stop, I have a whole bunch of labels that are not exclusive that I'm selling to anyone and everyone. We do function as an exclusive distributor for our batch of exclusive and semi-exclusive labels. Our exclusive artists are the ones that have the P&D deal.

If you take thirty CDs, where do they go?

AR: My assistant does a PO, meaning she faxes a purchase order to that label;

they then send us the CDs. Once we get the CDs, we take the one sheet description and put it on our news release fax that goes out every Friday.

What do you charge for your service?

AR: We don't charge for our service; we basically work on a markup of the product. Some distributors do a percentage, and some distributors do markup. Say someone says, I want to sell you my CD for seven dollars. Then the distributor marks up the price of the CD whatever their respective amount is. Some distributors mark up at 16 percent, some distributors are at 30 percent. Then they sell it to the record store for that price to get it to the masses. There is a tremendous amount of satisfaction to be had in taking a release that is drenched in the musicians' and the label's blood, sweat, and tears and adding in our own to make it a success.

■ Home Free

Once you get the distribution deal going, you're set. If your CD is going to a big chain store like Tower or K-Mart, it is sent to the company's regional distribution facility where it is counted, inventoried, and sent off to the appropriate store. The smaller companies get packages drop-shipped to them. It depends upon the number of stores in the chain and the deal that's set up.

Sometimes CDs are sent to a one-stop. The name comes from the term "one-stop shopping"—when you used to be able to buy everything you needed for your record store in one place. A one-stop would sell accessories and whatever you needed to set up shop. These days it's just a place where you can buy every CD available from every different label. The prices are generally a little higher than if you're buying directly from the manufacturer, but it's convenient nonetheless. These days, a one-stop will sell to everybody; they sell to the independent store, to the chain store; they'll sell to whomever has the credit.

■ Roger Stein: Independent Distribution

Roger Stein founded Iguana Records five years ago in New York City. He signs groups in all levels of development. He's partial to bands with finished product that Iguana can put out independently through a distributor that the label uses.

What is your position as an independent label in regard to marketing and distribution?

ROGER STEIN: Our niche, on the first hand, is to develop artists that majors don't see as being able to develop into a successful act.

An independent label is not in a position to compete with Top 40 bands.

Once they're in a trade publication like *Hits* for six weeks, the majors are chasing them. I can't afford to pay $500,000 or more for a project. Once that happens, we're no longer in that mix. We don't have the budget for the marketing and promotion, and don't have the power at Top 40 radio formats.

Where do your strengths lie?
RS: The area an independent label is strong in is on the marketing and promotion side. Obviously, we don't have the funds that a major label has; we don't have a staff of fifteen promotion guys in-house. Instead of competing, we try to do really strong micromarketing; we focus on street and lifestyle promotions.

What kind of bands does Iguana Records sign for distribution?
RS: We just signed a deal with an artist we're working who lives just outside of Boston and sold 15,000 records on his own, and has a little bit of a base to work with. We're distributing him independently because we know that we can tap into what's existing already and have an impact on sales. The style is A3—Adult Album Alternative—modern, adult contemporary top-forty-type of radio-driven band. They're also a good live band.

Who is your distributor?
RS: We have a distribution company called Valley DNA, which is the biggest of the independents that Iguana Records deals with. We'll do some stuff through them, but other things that won't allow us to make an impact with our own distribution, we'll sign with a major.

Where are your strengths in distribution?
RS: We can saturate a market or a region as well as anybody can.

Do you ever hook bands up with major label distribution?
RS: Sometimes we do deals with the majors. Let's say we went out and we saw a real top-forty radio-driven act. There's no way that I can compete in terms of dollars and power to try to really jam something at top-forty radio. But if there was something I thought was a hit, I would do what's called a production deal for the band—meaning I arrange for them to have studio time to record material. Then I try to get the act a deal with a major because I interact with a lot of majors. Therefore, I'm closer to the major labels than any outside musician coming from nowhere might be.

Many of the independent distribution companies have become their own specialized brand of record labels. The person who owns the distribution company has his own retinue of independent labels that do A&R. Essentially, the distributor is signing bands. Wouldn't it be nice if you had somebody on your team who knew this distributor and could get you a deal? Any distributor you're with is basically a good thing. There are very few retailers that are loyal to any one purchasing source.

A distributor will get you a place in the record bin. It takes album sales, money, and/or pull to get your own Rip Chord card in the R section of the CD bin. Another nice record store perk that can be bought is called end capping, which is a way to make your CD stand out from the rest. It's product placement, just like in the grocery store business: they pay for Pepsi to be at eye level and Fritos to have the end of the gondola. End capping is the same thing: the management or record company pays for the space in the end cap, in addition to having your records in the bin. That way people can see them and find them and fall over them. If your record is in an end cap, customers can't walk by without seeing them.

■ SoundScan

SoundScan is what the *Billboard* charts are made of. SoundScan is an information and data sorting service that compiles all of the sales from every store in America. The actual calculation of the sales is done like political exit polls where they take a number of stores in a market and extrapolate from those stores how a record has performed in that market, based on that store's performance and percentage of business in the market.

■ Internet Distribution

In the twenty-first century, the Internet is a new opportunity for CD distribution.

"It appears that it is a huge opportunity," confirms Kathy Callahan. "There's nobody on the Internet that's selling, but it is a tremendous opportunity, and I would think that in a couple years that every distribution company will have a site where they're selling their music and maybe other people's music—similar to the BMG Music Club or the Columbia Record Club."

The music consumer is a very sophisticated person. Oftentimes, consumers go online and do research and then they'll go to a store and buy the record. At the moment, people aren't really buying that much online, but there could be a paradigm shift any second.

The music industry has been delaying this change because it will alter the whole economic structure of the industry, wiping out some record retailers virtually overnight. Remember—record retailers are all set up with their stores, staff, and everything else—they have huge overhead that has to be covered. Business can't change overnight, but the industry, technology-wise, has gotten so sophisticated that it may very well do that. When that happens, the economic impact could be dangerous.

"Retailers are going to have to change, because that day is coming," observes Tony Ferguson, who does A&R over at Interscope Records. "If they don't catch on to the technology and figure out a way of utilizing it for their own good as salesmen, they are going to be out of business. Then all you'll have left is Blockbuster with video and DVD rentals. CDs may very well become a thing of the past, if they're not careful. [We now] have the ability to download music. We're approaching a ramp-up phase—a crossover time period. The technology is practically there. We're getting to the stage now where we don't want to use FedEx or messenger services to listen to mixes. I could be here in my office, and I could have a record being made in Australia downloaded over the phone lines into my computer, and I could hear the finished master. It's going to be a brave new world, that's for sure."

Every genre of music is getting a boost from the Internet, whether it's jazz or New Age. This is happening because rock and roll music appeals to kids, and they love computers, so they find music on the Internet. New Age, classical jazz aficionados are sophisticated and they're early adopters of new technology. While for now the Internet is a good information source, it will soon be a really good revenue source.

■ Steve Summers: Learning the Business

In 1994, 1995, and 1996, Sprung Monkey was voted Band of the Year at the San Diego Music Awards. Cash from club gigs and tape sales financed their first self-released album, *Situation Life*. They made their Surfdog Records debut, *Swirl,* in 1996, and followed it with *Mr. Funny Face* in 1998. That record was picked up by Hollywood Records, and Sprung Monkey became part of the media machine. Vocalist Steve Summers talks about the business of being in Sprung Monkey.

At what point did you become more business-aware?
STEVE SUMMERS: In the first half of 1998, the band's complexion just changed. We did the record, *Mr. Funny Face*, and then Hollywood Records jumped in after the record was done.

When Hollywood Records joined the project, we pretty much instantly felt their impact. Surfdog has always been behind us and done what they could for us, but you can really feel the power of a major industry behind you with Hollywood Records. Like, they have a whole staff of people. I don't know if it was because of their hard work or because our song, "Get 'Em Outta Here," got played on the radio and instantly got a really good response, but things have been going pretty good in the scheme of things.

So the song "Get 'Em Outta Here" is what broke you?
SS: They say the song went to radio at an outstanding rate—station additions picked up every week. The song picked up like sixty stations in three weeks in major markets. Los Angeles jumped in really early and I think that has a big part in why the other stations added—a lot of people look at KROQ's [the Los Angeles modern rock radio station] playlist.

It's weird; you get a song on the radio and everybody thinks you're rich. But we're more broke than ever because we wound up sinking more of our resources into this project to keep it alive and further it. But as much as I might sound like I'm complaining, I'm happier than I've ever been because the band is totally breathing a new life that it never had, and we've been doing this for eight years.

Does success make you feel any different?
SS: I feel a lot more stressed than I ever have. Now I feel like there's something that I really need to look out for. There are a lot of people tugging at us, and we've had to deal with a lot of different things that we thought we'd never run into. We had to figure out: Is this the best option? Is it a lie? Is it true? It gets hard. The hardest thing for me is to split loyalty and friendship and all that kind of stuff that I've grown up believing in, and try and strip all that away and think about business. I don't like business. Sometimes business is motivated by the wrong things. But right now is the time to take the little thing we have and make it grow into something wonderful. For that you need to have a business behind you, a nice effective, efficient business, and when you're first trying to put all those pieces together, it gets hard.

How did you break? What do you attribute it to?
SS: It's Hollywood Records coming into play. The label had shut down and gotten rid of everybody. And the main guy up there had a good relationship with Surfdog Records and that deal went through. The staff had time to work us because they only had two bands at the time they picked us up—Fastball

and Suicide Machine. Fastball, like us, was just going crazy, and I'm sure we scooted through a lot of doors that they had already opened up.

What's the difference between being on a major label and being on an independent label?
SS: Attention for one; not that they're calling me every day to see how I'm doing, but you can feel things. Like, boom, you go to the store, and there's a display of us. That to me was like groundbreaking, the validity of my band and my career.

There's a vibe you can feel, like people in the radio markets coming up to you and telling you, Congratulations, the band is charting. I know Hollywood's really behind us and working for us.

When you were with Surfdog Records, what did they do for you?
SS: Locally in San Diego, we got a lot of airplay. Because of that it trickled into other markets. We were also fortunate enough to be on the MOM records—*Music for Our Mother Ocean*—which was a joint effort with Surfdog and Interscope. On the first one, they chose our song "Good Times" to be the song that represented the album, so Interscope came down and shot a video for it, and worked us into radio. Interscope put some time into it. That did pretty well in the scheme of things so that put our music into a lot of radio people's ears. With *Mr. Funny Face*, I want to believe that the song "Get 'Em Outta Here" is so instantly catchy that that's why they choose to play it. The record company said it was easy for them to break it because it was a good song. I believe in my heart we did something great with this record.

How does marketing differ from an indie to a major?
SS: All I can judge by is what's happened here locally in San Diego, and the first time I opened the magazine here, I saw like a full page ad; there was this total blitz on the radio, on three powerhouse stations. For two weeks before the album came out all you heard about was Sprung Monkey on the radio, so I'm sure they bought a lot of ads to do that, which was incredible. Now we have a Web site, and someone handling all our mail, and they're sending merchandising out all over.

Have you ever seen your T-shirts on people?
SS: Yes, at home in San Diego, we've always done pretty well. Luckily what's sustained the band through our highs and our lows is our local fan base. We've stayed pretty strong. Low periods where we weren't making that much

money, we could always play in San Diego and make enough money to sustain ourselves and at least pay the rent on the studio. So we've always done well at home, and we've done well in the East Coast, mostly Florida.

We've toured around a lot, and made a lot of fans and sold a lot of stuff, but we never really followed it up with the steadiness that you're supposed to. You're supposed to show up in their faces every five months if you can, but it's hard when you try to bankroll everything. Now hopefully that's going to be the difference. Having tour support, we can get a hotel every night.

What did it used to be like?
SS: Well, we bought ourselves a little shuttle bus so we would play here and save a bunch of money, and then go out on the road and waste a bunch of money. It's hard to get big guarantees on the road when you're not going to really draw, so there's a lot of sleeping in the bus.

When you were first starting out, if you had known what you know now, would it have affected the way you approached your career?
SS: Maybe I would have been more ready for it, but that would be the only thing because we always wanted to be in this position; it's just that we never imagined what it might feel like being in this position. It's a different feeling. You read about musicians through the press—some of them are really standoffish and their success has made them somewhat bitter. I always thought, Well, what do you have to be tripping on? You guys are on top of the world—smile and enjoy it! But now I really understand, because we're a pea compared to what these bands are, and I already feel a little of that.

CHAPTER NINE

Getting Heard

It's a cheap out to say that getting on the radio is just about

relationships. Getting on the radio is about relationships,

it's about the music, it's about knowing where you are

going to succeed with this record.

—Kathy Callahan, BMG Music

Radio isn't essential to breaking a band, but it sure makes it easier. The great thing about radio is that it is hypothetically an open market, and it should be free. (There is a fair amount of leverage, bribery, and payola that goes on in the radio industry, but we'll leave that for another book.) Today it really is possible for an indie group to compete with the big labels for those precious few slots on radio playlists, provided you've got the right contacts.

"It's a snap," confirms MCA's Abbey Konowitch. "It's been happening where an independent record that comes out—whether it's 'Firestarter' by Prodigy or whether it's 'Loser' by Beck. Today, radio stations are looking for things to separate themselves from their

competition. They are out there looking for hit records. The chances for getting on the radio are as good as ever, probably better than ever."

■ Independent Promoters

If you're with a band in Woburn, Massachusetts, and you're trying to get your
CD to the program director, join the club. There are a thousand guys who
are trying to get that program director their CDs each year. They're probably
going to hire some independent promotion guy to get to one or two program
directors.

If you're looking to hit at radio, an independent promotion guy, an
"indie," is a magnificent luxury. Radio indies have spent a lot of their lives in
the radio business. They have networks of stations that will follow their lead.
Indies spread the word and make life easier.

Record companies give millions of dollars each year to this tiny clique of
independent consultants who pay annual lump sums to key stations, spon-
sor contests with large prizes for programmers, publish trade tip sheets, and
hand out freebies.

These consultants contend they can influence radio airplay, though how
they can do so is unclear, since it is illegal to trade money or gifts for airplay.
While it is not illegal for a station to take money in exchange for playing a
song, it is illegal to accept money for playing a specific song without disclos-
ing the payment to the public.

Indies have so much power that it has become difficult to determine just
who is setting the agenda these days at radio: the program directors or the
advertising sales managers.

Even if you have a great song, and you are destined to hit, your song is
not going to immediately find twenty or forty radio stations on its own without the help of an indie. If your song is great, you'll pick up airplay on a couple
of stations. But word spreads fast. Some record label president, like Jimmy
Iovine, Jay Boberg, Daniel Glass, or Donny Einer is going to hear about it. It
happens all the time—Hootie and the Blowfish, Goldfinger; the list is long.
Record companies have in-house research departments. They call all of the
local retailers in Woburn, Massachusetts, and ask, What's selling? Because
of the rise in independent success stories, the record company infrastructure
is now focused on finding those few records that are selling regionally.

"What I do for Universal is scour local markets at both radio and retail
for research-oriented bands," confirms Marc Nathan, senior director of A&R
for Universal Records. "I'm looking for bands that have pressed up their own
CD, pressed up a cassette, sell their records at shows, sell them on consign-

ment in record stores, put them out through small distribution avenues and that may be looking to graduate to the major leagues. I'm looking for things that are basically—in baseball terms—in the minor league farm system looking to be promoted to the majors."

■ Targeting Radio

"If your song gets on a commercial radio station, you are guaranteed it's going to be spun almost continuously, around the clock," offers Kathy Callahan. "Once a radio station takes on a song, they pound the record. It's worth a lot."

It's very, very difficult to get on commercial radio. When you're looking to break into commercial radio, target those stations within a market that run specialty shows or local music programming. It's a great way to get your first spins, and then you can expand from there.

If you're an independent act looking to get on the radio, do what the promotion people at record companies do; call on radio stations all over the United States at all hours of the day or night. The graveyard shift is a particularly helpful time. In the smaller markets, there are sixteen-, seventeen-, and eighteen-year-old kids that may be the all-night jocks at a local station somewhere in Montana or Mississippi. There's always a way to get in the door; you just have to figure out how.

"I drove the radio stations nuts," declares Carl Bell of the band Fuel. "I was calling them all of the time. It got to the point where I was on a friendship basis with them, and they were playing the hell out of our music. I would call the radio stations every other day; it reached the point where they would fax me playlists before I could even pick up the phone to call them, because they knew I would be telephoning to find out what was going on. I was checking up on them, seeing how things were going, seeing what their response was for the week, seeing how many spins we were getting, stuff like that. Staying on top of them."

Fuel told their fans to call the radio stations and request their songs. You can do that, too. Or, you can bring your record up to the radio station and explain what your fan base is and how you're trying to create some national awareness. That's an easy and inexpensive way for your band to take it to the next level.

Sure, this sounds simple in concept, but it's not going to be easy. Radio stations have x amount of hours in the day and x amount of slots on their playlist, but if it's a special record it's going to break through. It has happened time and time again.

"It would have to be a really special record because there are only so many slots on any given radio station. All the majors and all of the strong indies are competing for those slots, and in any given week, there may only be one or two or three slots available," notes Universal Records' Marc Nathan. "Hundreds of singles are being pitched at the program directors, but there could be a local new music show, or a specialty show, or a radio station could start to get requests for a record that they don't have because there is a local fan base."

There are several different ways to get airplay. It's not going to be easy to compete at the top forty level with the Celine Dions of the world, but, depending on the format, there are ways to get your record on the air.

■ The Way the Labels Get Radio

"We hire indies, just like everybody else does," offers Roger Stein of Iguana Records. "We'll hire a couple of indies in any given format. We'll see where the song is getting reasonable spins, and we'll try to get the band out to support those stations however we can. Then, we focus on those markets and try and do more micromarketing stuff in those areas. That's more lifestyle stuff—going to the coffee shops, restaurants that are applicable, any place that plays music. Maybe we'll go into a record store and meet with the manager. A kid that's into the music will go in there and play him a song. We throw college listening parties, do interviews with college radio stations—all sorts of ground-level grassroots things—put up posters, do displays at retail, do co-op buys in those particular regions. . . ."

At the major labels, it is the radio department's job to get the label's music exposed at radio. It's the radio department's objective to get the radio station to play that label's song, as opposed to someone else's. It's a lot about relationships; it's a lot about the music itself, but primarily it's relationships.

"You have to have a really good radio team on your side, but you've got to have good music as well," confirms Kathy Callahan. "The radio department has to be smart enough to know where to go with the music. They have to ask themselves, What format does it belong in? Which stations are going to adopt this record? What radio stations does this record sound like? If it's something new that doesn't sound like anything, your radio department has to know which stations are going to take a chance and throw this into their mix, which stations are willing to jar the psyche of the people that are listening to the station."

A lot of radio stations program new tunes in a capitalist manner. The theory is: We've got a lot of advertisements from that label; let's play its new record. Most commercial radio stations work that way—one hand washes the other.

"I've known it to happen," observes Chris Douridas, former music director and host of the KCRW radio program, *Morning Becomes Eclectic,* and current A&R contact at DreamWorks Records. "It's unfortunate. The way it's happening now, it's much more difficult to detect than it was in the past, because there are all sorts of ways of hiding the reality."

■ The Inside Scoop

James Schureck is director of new media for Jeff McClusky & Associates, an independent radio promotion company. James describes his company's work as follows: "All the record labels, all the majors and most of the indies come to us whenever they've got a song they're going to put on the radio. They hire this company as added value to their department because we have a relationship with more than 150 commercial radio stations that matter. Basically, we're the biggest in top 40 and alternative in the United States, and if you want to break our record at radio, you have to utilize our services to make sure that the record gets played at the proper amount of stations—you know, that it gets the proper amount of spins and the proper attention it needs."

How come the record companies haven't been able to take this power away from you?
JAMES SCHURECK: There are five major labels and there are a handful of big indies—and all those people call every radio programmer every week. Who is the programmer to believe? They need a non-biased party to say, "Okay, here's the real deal, here's what's really happening." This label guy is telling you that this is the hottest thing—and no, that's not true. He just has to say that because it's his priority for the week. We work for everybody, so we filter out what's not good and what's better. The radio programmers have a lot more to do than just sit there on the phone and talk to record guys all day. They have to deal with their DJs; they have to deal with a lot of internal issues. They have to be on the air themselves. We don't have to do that. All we have to do is worry about what records go on what radio station.

We can spend the time with the record guys and go, "Look, what can we put together? What kind of promotional deal can we put together to make this more attractive to the station?" So we filter out a lot of that. Even though they still talk to the record guys, they don't have to spend as much time because they're like, "Oh, the guy from McClusky office was telling me this, and I trust what he says because he's never steered me wrong, so he gives me a non-biased opinion and takes care of me."

How do you decide what records to work?

JS: Who's paying us, also if it's a good record. You listen to a record and you can tell. Is it going to be a hit? You do a lot of research: there's call-out research, there's focus group research, there's sales in the marketplace according to SoundScan, there are other radio stations. If KROQ in L.A. or the EDGE in Phoenix adds a record, they're usually an indicator station. They seem to come on records early and 70 percent of records they end up playing become hits in the rest of the country.

You learn to recognize if a label is going to put a lot of money behind this. Do they have a focus and a vision to take this six months, or are they going to let it ride for three or four and, if nothing really happens, they're going to dump the whole project and move on to the next record? Or, are they really committed to this record? So being really close to the record guys and letting them feed us their information, they can say what's happening. Or does a band have a really good, aggressive manager who sometimes will go do his own promotions, and he'll do a lot of things that other managers won't do? Does the manager have a track record of successes? You take all that information into consideration. We work every record, but obviously we work some records more than others. That's based upon:

1. Money
2. If we think it's going to be a hit
3. Do we have a history with the person who hired us on that record?
4. Do we have a history with the management?
5. Do we have a history with the artist?

So, there are a lot of considerations. It's very political. We usually don't work records that don't have push behind them.

How much does it cost to break a record to radio, and what kind of packages can I buy?

JS: It depends so much on an artist; it depends so much on a project. It's very expensive to work commercial radio. We're not the only independent, either—there are other independents. The way it works in the United States is that you pay every independent. We're just one of them, and we happen to be the largest. Usually they have to pay a retainer fee. Let's say Aerosmith has a new record coming out. We are paid a retainer fee to market that on radio. When that record is added to one of the labels where we have an exclusive independent deal, then they pay us an additional fee per station that adds the record.

On top of that, sometimes, to add incentive, they'll put together a bonus package—like, if you get fifteen stations to add the record this week, we'll give you a $10,000 bonus on top of everything else we're doing for you.

How do you break a new band?

JS: Let's take when Britney Spears first came out. You have to have a story—this is a seventeen-year-old girl. This is the writing staff behind her. She's on this label. We've tested it here. We went around and we did radio shows for these particular people. Listen to the music—we guarantee it's going to be a hit. These stations have already committed to the record before we've set a target date to add the record to their playlist. So you try and build a story. A lot of it is promotion, and a lot of it is trust. The fact is that, hey, you guys have told me about things before they were big. So, there are certain stations that, if we sort of lead them in the right direction, they know that we try not to lead them wrong, so they'll add records. Once you get enough stations building that story, then the bigger stations say, "Well, enough of the smaller stations have come in. I think I'm going to take a chance with this record and put it on in a few rotations throughout the week and see what kind of calls will come in and responses from my audience. The more response, the more I'll spin it."

How much of breaking a record is talent and how much of breaking a record is marketing?

JS: It goes both ways. A lot of it has to do with marketing. Take Limp Bizkit for instance. A lot of people think they're a terrible band, but a lot of people think they're a great band and are buying the record. When they came out with "Faith," people were like, "That's the worst record I've heard in my entire life." People didn't get that it was a novelty joke; then when they came out with *"Getcha Groove On,"* people were like, "Oh this is better," but then the older demographic, people who don't like that style of music, thought those guys were completely talentless. It's based on the fact that they pulled every string and they had a great manager and the label was totally behind them.

But then you have other artists who never achieve that kind of success, but are great musicians and great talents—obviously, the jazz community. With Ani DiFranco, a lot of people really, really, really love her music, but she's always considered an independent artist. She doesn't play the game. She refuses to do radio shows; she refuses to go on and do commercial interviews. She only does smaller to-the-left radio stations, if any radio at all. She avoids that commercialism, but if she embraced it, she'd lose a lot of her fans. It's all give or take. If you market the hell out of something, like 80 percent of the time it's going to push. Then there's the 20 percent, no matter what you do, no matter how much money you put behind it, no matter how much of a push, you can't sell it to save your life.

■ College Radio

KCRW, the Santa Monica College station serving the Los Angeles area, is a very unique radio station. Its objective is to create radio with a point of view. College radio is a totally different musical arena than commercial radio—one is driven by passion, the other by dollars. Called college radio, National Public Radio (NPR), or community radio, these privately funded stations are not slaves to the advertiser.

"KCRW is so very valuable as a radio station, due to the fact that it's in Los Angeles and has an audience of people who are doers, producers, filmmakers, directors, record companies, publishers, radio people, people in the entertainment industry—people who are able to take an idea and spread it," declares Chris Douridas. "When people ask me how to get their songs on the radio, I always tell them that one of the first things they can do is send their music to KCRW."

Listen to shows on college radio. Those shows that are playing artists that are in a similar world to your own are an appropriate place to start. Try and get the ear of the person programming that show. Start local; if something gets airplay at a local level and starts to make waves, and starts to build a fire, it's easier for someone in other markets to see some smoke.

Contact the local stations; see if they'll interview you. "We interviewed people all the time," reveals Chris. "The fact that a band had a major label was not why we were interviewing them. We were interviewing them because we loved the music. If the music happened to come by way of a major record label, fine. If we got it by way of cassette from a guy who lives crosstown, then that was fine too.

"We'd just call them up and say, Come on in, we want to put you on the radio," explains Chris. "Beck is an example. I got a copy of a twelve-inch vinyl pressing of *Loser* on Bong Load Records. The day I heard it I called the publishing company, asked for an additional recording because all I had was two songs. They sent me over a cassette that afternoon. I listened to the cassette, called back, and said, 'Tell me more about this guy.' So they said, 'Call him.' So I called him. I found out that he had a show a week later, and I asked him if he wanted to be on the radio that morning before his coffeehouse performance at the Troy Café. He agreed, came in that morning, played on the air live, and that night, at the Troy Café, it was a mob scene."

Other unsigned artists Chris helped promote at KCRW were Gillian Welch, Joan Osborne, and the Eels. His work led to a job with the A&R department of DreamWorks Records. Nice job if you can get it.

People get interviewed on the radio all the time and get their songs played, because that's what radio stations are supposed to do. If a radio station is paying attention to the unsolicited music that's coming in, it will very frequently come across something worth investigating, something worth giving airplay to, and something worth sharing.

The only thing that influences a radio programmer or an A&R person to move forward with an artist is the music itself. At KCRW, the radio programmers have a policy against talking to promotion people; they will talk to artists. Nothing a promotion person will tell them is going to make them want to play the record; it doesn't matter who else is playing it, or what kind of reviews it got. What really matters is the record.

If a disc jockey is trying to present a radio program with a point of view, it has to be his own opinion. If the disc jockey starts programming based on other people's opinions, he loses the rudder that steers the sound. College disc jockeys truly enjoy their independence. Help them assert their individuality—get them your record.

■ Satellite Radio

"There are a number of developing technologies that are going to change the competitive landscape for radio," says Chuck Taylor, the radio editor for *Billboard*. "There's satellite radio, where you have a tiny satellite dish in your car, and radio that you subscribe to—100 stations of it coming into your car, your home, your boom box."

Satellite radio offers dozens of channels of different music formats. Satellite radio isn't free. Consumers need special receivers to capture the satellite signal. Then, there's a monthly service fee—generally between $10 and $15.

Satellite radio will bypass the local stations and beam a signal directly from its two satellites to subscribers, similar to the way satellite TV works. Satellite signals for car radios are constantly improving. Now reception is clear of interference and sounds every bit as good as a tape through the deck.

Portable models come complete with presets, allowing you to move from They Might Be Giants to the Giants game with the touch of a button, and—this is where it gets really good—sixty of the stations are commercial-free.

But the best part of this set is that it offers not only coast-to-coast coverage, but also car-to-office mobility.

"Our goal is to do to radio what DBS [Direct Broadcast Satellite] and cable television did to the TV industry: providing lots more choices," says Hugh Panero, president and CEO of XM Satellite Radio.

■ Internet Radio

Radio airwaves can take only a limited number of niche listening tastes, but Internet radio can provide as many channels as there are music genres. Spinner.com, for example, has 128 channels. Listeners can create their own channels and personalize their Internet radio. Imagine Radio and SonicNet— both recently purchased by MTV—have led the way in offering visitors the capability to program their own channels. By pairing sophisticated Internet tracking tools and niche broadcasting, Web sites can deliver precise psychographics to Internet radio advertisers and brand marketers. In turn, they can provide more targeted messages.

Increasingly, listeners of online streaming music are able to buy music when they hear it. Radio listeners, on the other hand, often aren't even told the name of the song on the air, fumble to find a pencil, and in the end can't find the music when they get to the retail store.

"In the future, with digital delivery, you'll be able to buy a song at a time, and those will probably go for 99 cents," said Ken Wirt of Diamond Multimedia. "So music delivered in that way will probably be a five-times-better value."

For musicians, the Web music revolution could be a way to reclaim artistic freedom.

"We have to go through minefields that we have to negotiate just to reach the listener," says Steve Perry of the Cherry Poppin' Daddies. "It's really kind of up to the [gatekeepers] . . . as to whether or not we reach them."

"With MP3, they can just download the music from us . . . there are a lot of positive benefits to it," notes folksinger Dar Williams, who uses the Web to connect with her client base. "What you do is you build yourself as an artist according to what an audience says about you, as opposed to just submitting a demo tape to someplace and letting a record company take it from there."

Limited bandwidth—the number of streams a server can deliver from a Web site broadcast at any given time—is still a problem.

"Fewer than a million people can hear online radio at any given time," estimates Joe Pezzillo, founder of Eclectic Radio's GoGaGa station. "It would max out the Internet if everyone tried to listen to all Internet radio sites at once—Imagine Radio, all the ShoutCast servers, Spinner. Multicasting would be a partial solution, but has been slow to develop by the telephone companies and others in the business of selling bandwidth because it's less profitable for them. If a Web site's content was differentiated from what anyone else offered, a listener-supported membership model might work."

■ Pay-for-Play

In 1998, a new form of radio broadcasting came into practice. It's called "pay-for-play," and although it's controversial, it's still a form of programming—something like music infomercials. At the time of broadcast, the radio station alerts its audience that the song is paid for; it then bills the record company for playing the song. Some radio stations have even begun to charge record companies simply to announce the names of the songs they play.

"Competition has gotten so steep here for broadcasting market share that record companies are starting to pay for play," notes Richard Branson, the founder of Virgin Records. "What's new? It used to be called payola, and if caught, deejays used to get fired. But now the money goes to owners—and it's legitimate."

The record companies are not entirely uncomfortable with this new trend, because they feel it could offer companies more control over what actually gets played on the radio. It could also help them save money by eliminating the middleman from radio promotion. This is a very new area, and its success has yet to be proven, but major players are partaking in the pay-to-play process. House of Blues (HOB) has been broadcasting using alpha software jointly developed with Microsoft. It charged $4.99 per hour for 300-kbps and faster connections, which also received full-screen video.

"This heralds in a breakthrough in our business model," says Chris Stephenson, HOB senior vice president of marketing. "It told us that we can make money out of the concerts in our archives."

■ What to Send to Radio

If you're in a band and you want to send something to radio, all you need to get them is a seven-inch vinyl, twelve-inch vinyl, a tape, a CD, a DAT, a URL to download an MP3 or listen to streaming audio, whatever—a means by which to listen to the music. If you're smart, you'll mark that tape with a band contact name and phone number. That way, if someone wants to benefit your career, they know how to reach you. It's not necessary to have a lyric sheet or a résumé or press clippings or a photograph or any of that, because if the music's not good, nobody cares. And if they like it, all they really want is the bio; there are no pictures on radio.

On the other hand, there are a lot of music industry people who check out the packaging: Oh he's good-looking, I'll listen to this tape. Or Boy, they've got a quote from *Rolling Stone,* they must be worth checking out. Then there are others that are charmed by a hand-scrawled note wrapped around a cheap cassette.

"We made a policy to listen to everything," remembers Chris. "You could take a very expensive package, and more often than not that would be crap, and the very cheap, crude package would turn out to be the gem. You couldn't make that a rule, of course. There were always exceptions."

■ Beyond Radio

"The A&R process is driven by attorneys more than it is by radio," states Bud Scoppa, vice president of A&R for the Sire Records Group. "It's difficult to speculate on what kinds of music radio is going to be favoring from moment to moment. Let's say you decide to sign an act that's a clone of whatever is the big radio hit at the moment—let's say ska. By the time the deal is completed, the album is made, and the first track goes out to radio, it's at least a year later and ska is no longer being played on radio stations. That's an expensive misjudgment."

Radio simply doesn't have the best interests of young artists in mind. Artist development isn't radio's business. It's necessary for labels to figure out ways of exposing their young artists to audiences without having to rely on radio.

"I don't think radio is the whole story, but it certainly is a major tool in marketing music," sums up Chris. "It has always been and probably always will be—whether it's radio as we know it or some variation on that form."

If you want to sell records, people have to know about you. Get the ball rolling. Get your name and your song out there. Getting on the radio will get you heard. If people like it, they'll buy it. The major labels may be able to get you on the radio, but one thing the record company can't control is buying habits. A record could be getting great exposure—getting thirty plays a week on KROQ in Los Angeles and fifty plays on Z100 in New York, and still no one will buy the record. You can get three plays on a radio station and not be able to keep the records in the stores. Some records are hits, and some aren't. Some make the connection, and some don't.

Record companies are reexamining the hundreds of millions of dollars their companies sink annually into radio promotion. In recent years, several firms have experimented with targeting music fans through print and TV advertising, and by creating "lifestyle marketing" street teams to heighten awareness for underground rap and New Age records—which rarely receive radio airplay—to some success.

Record labels still rely heavily on radio airplay to expose consumers to music by new artists and stimulate record sales. The exposure generated by a radio hit can increase album sales dramatically, transforming unknown acts—such as No Doubt and the Spice Girls—into multimillion-selling pop stars.

■ Chris Douridas: From Radio to Records

Chris Douridas comes from a radio background. In 1990, he moved to Los Angeles to become music director and host of *Morning Becomes Eclectic*, a music program mixing all styles of music for a southern California audience and featuring live performances on a regular basis.

The live performances have been compiled on an album series called *Rare on Air* and are distributed around the world on Mammoth Records. That was Chris's introduction to the record industry. In 1995, he became a record industry consultant in A&R at Geffen Records and, in 1997, moved to Dream-Works as an A&R executive.

When you did your radio show, did you choose your playlist?
CHRIS DOURIDAS: I completely chose my own playlist from the very first moment I got into radio in 1981, to the very last moment I was in radio in 1998. I always picked what I played.

How did you choose what to listen to?
CD: I didn't choose what to listen to. I listened to everything that came in. That was always my policy, and at KCRW it's still the policy—to listen to everything that's sent to us, which is a rare service at radio. But that's how we found things. You can't delegate listening; you can't judge a recording by its cover. You can't judge a recording by the genre or style that might be stamped on the cover. In fact, the most invigorating styles of music integrated all sorts of styles of music and became real hybrids. Why do you play what you play? That's a very difficult question. You go with your instincts; you follow your gut. The things that tended to pop out for me were the things that hit me on an emotional level, whether they touched me emotionally or they made me want to press the gas pedal on my car. Things that really, really soared are the things that I played. I tried not to play things I considered to be mediocre—only things that I really, really loved.

Did you play a lot of unsigned bands?

CD: That was part of the thrill for me, coming across an unsigned artist and giving them some exposure. In essence, I was doing A&R for radio.

Have you signed bands you found at radio?

CD: Yes. The Eels were a band whose demo I was playing at KCRW. At my first interview at DreamWorks, I dropped the demo to the heads of the label. They proceeded to sign the Eels a month later. It was their first new artist signing for DreamWorks Records. The Eels sold a couple hundred thousand records here, so they're definitely doing okay. My first full-fledged signing as an A&R executive was Propellerheads. I was aware of their work from following them as a radio programmer. My second signing was a band called Artificial Intelligence, which came out in early 1999. Their demos came my way because of the relationships I forged at radio.

Now that you're A&R, not radio, do you get more, less, or the same amount of tapes that you got at radio?

CD: There's going to be a drop-off because people don't know where to find me. But I still continue to do work at KCRW in a special project for National Public Radio. I'm not worried about that. But, I'm going to continue the aggressive ear-to-the-ground approach here at the record label that I employed at radio to keep up to date as much as possible.

■ **MTV**

Remember the band a-ha? Or the Whitesnake videos with the girl frolicking across the hood of a Jaguar? At one point in time, MTV could totally make a band's career. Not so at this juncture in history. MTV still has the power, but it doesn't play enough videos to have a real impact. When MTV chooses to get behind you, it has the most power of any force in the industry, but the acts it is getting behind these days are few and far between.

"MTV is a good thing to some degree," offers manager David Krebs. "It's a question of whether television is using music for its own interest, or music is using television for its best interest."

These days, television has the upper hand. MTV caters to as varied an audience as possible, and a healthy chunk of airtime is devoted to programs, not videos, and the videos tend to have an urban music slant. MTV received a lot of criticism a decade ago for not catering to the urban audience. Several years ago, the lightbulb went on and MTV programmers realized it was a huge audience they were missing. The pendulum has perhaps swung a little too far in the other direction; now MTV caters to an urban-style music audience. Is the surge in urban music's popularity directly attributed to MTV? Whether it's the cart leading the horse or the horse leading the cart is a very hotly debated question. But that's still the audience MTV is targeting at this point in time.

■ Making a Video

You're probably wondering, with MTV changing its format, is a band still justified in making a video? The answer is yes, but there's no reason to spend $150,000 on one. Make a video for $25,000; this can be a totally worthwhile investment, especially if you can get something played, whether it's on MTV, local channels, or whatever. But discuss it with the rest of your band; you may be much better off putting that kind of funding into tour support.

■ Performance Nights

Radio airplay is one key to getting yourself heard; the other necessity is playing gigs. A group can build up a solid fan base and eventually support themselves, if not break in a big way, by playing live. When you play out live, people discover you. Time and time again, bands get signed by virtue of having some A&R guy see the way the group turns an audience on and then taking it from there.

Even if you don't get paid for the big gigs, you can get a slot at some of the music festivals. It's a great way to get people to notice you because that's where music people gather. A good place to be discovered is probably on a bill with several other similar artists. Record company people who can hear you and sign you will be there.

"Making a record is only part of the process of getting your music out there," notes Frank McDonough, president of Moir/Marie Entertainment, a company that manages producers. "An artist might make an amazing record, but if they never play out, the odds of getting signed are slim."

The key to a career is touring, and the visceral connection is between the act and the audience. That connection is truly made, at least in rock music, between the act and the audience.

Take Pearl Jam as an example. In the mid to late nineties, Pearl Jam's fan base eroded because the fans lost the visceral connection. All their audience had were the records and music; they had no interviews; they had no press; they had no touring; they didn't even get the image of the band off of MTV. Pearl Jam had pulled away; they became reclusive artists, and their fans lost interest. They rekindled the flame with their 1998 release, *Yield*. Pearl

Jam went back to the recipe that worked so well for them on their 1991 debut: they made videos and toured. After years of being self-indulgent and reclusive, frontman Eddie Vedder regained his integrity, and decided he was ready to give something back. After years of excuses, Senate hearings, and procrastination, Pearl Jam rewarded their fans by going on the road, and their fans rewarded Pearl Jam by buying their albums.

If you're not a name artist, touring will build you a fan base, but you won't necessarily support yourself doing it. There are exceptions to this rule, of course, but in general, you have to really have made a name for yourself before you can go out on the road and make money.

"Touring has become very important again," observes Andy Secher, editor of *Hit Parader* magazine. "During the eighties, it was more of a financial vehicle for the major bands than it was a way of breaking anybody. Back in the sixties and seventies, the only way of breaking a rock band was to slog away on the tour trail and, market by market, get on the radio. It's that way again now—you want to get out there, get a song on the radio, and just play and play and play until you start catching on, because you can't count on the national outlets like MTV to break you."

The first couple of years, until you really make a name for yourself, touring is difficult. The best you can hope for is an opening act slot; that's going to get you in front of enough people that you can start to build your own audience. This is a great thing, but you're still probably not going to make any money at it the first time out.

■ Tour Support

If you're in a label situation where you're lucky enough to get some money to promote your album, think long and hard about how that marketing money is going to be put to use. The $100,000 spent on a video may be your entire marketing budget. If MTV doesn't like it, that $100,000 is down the toilet, and maybe your career is, too. Wiser budgeting can put that money to much better use. One hundred thousand dollars could tour an act for two years.

The marketing campaign for the band Korn, on Epic Records, involved an analysis of the best way to present the band within the budget allowed. It was figured out from the get-go that the act was not going to be embraced by radio or MTV because of the dissonant, aggressive quality of the music. The edict was: put them on the road; let the audience feel the power. Epic spent more than $300,000 on tour support for Korn, and they subsequently went gold. It was money well spent. Korn will have a longer career than 90 percent of the groups that get blasted on MTV with their first single. They will be around a lot longer than Superdrag or Third Eye Blind or any of the bands that get pounded out of the box.

"I don't believe in just sending bands around the country, because that's generally a waste of time," admits Iguana Records' Roger Stein. "The tour market has really dried up over the last couple of years. If you stick a band in a van and have them tour around the country to play, you've got to be willing to do that for like five years to have any impact at all.

"We try to be a lot more intelligent about tour support by acknowledging the fact that randomly doing shows is not going to really do a whole lot for a band. What Iguana Records tries to do is use tour support money as a tool for other things. If we're going to go to Orlando to do a show with a band, it's because we have their song on the radio. As opposed to playing a show, we'll try and do a live radio show. Then we can come back and do a regular show a few months later. Instead of randomly touring, we try to keep the presence of that group growing in that particular market. I wouldn't randomly go to Kansas City for a show with a band just because there's a club there that will have us play for $200."

Touring is a way for a band to spread the word. It's also one of the main reasons people get into making music, to be onstage in front of hundreds of screaming fans. Experienced performers want to make their show something special, something fans will remember and talk about. That keeps the interest up for the performers, who may play as many as 250 gigs a year, and keeps it special for the audience.

"We try to make our shows an event," notes Scott Steen, trumpeter for the swing band Royal Crown Revue. "We don't say, Put on your best duds and come out. We just say, Come out, but people get dressed up when they come to our shows. Rock and roll music has always been about an image along with the music. Swing is no different."

There's a certain state of mind that goes with being on the road. It's got to be something you love to do, otherwise doing it day in and day out will get to you after the first few tours. You're living out of a suitcase. You have no friends or family around except for the band. Doing it year in and year out can become very tedious, unless you love the road and want to set the world on fire.

All musicians are different about touring and about how much of their life they want to devote to being on the road. Veteran folk guitarist Leo Kottke is on the road all the time; he drives his car around and performs, and that's basically what he does. Somebody like jazz legend Etta James doesn't do many gigs, but she makes a lot of money for every one that she does. Everyone has a different touring objective.

"What I want out of our tour is that I'd like to feel like every night the music set me on fire," says Blur's guitarist Graham Coxon. "I don't give a hoot about the charts, I don't care about the reviews; I don't care about anything; I'm not here for statistics. I'm not pressured to sell Blur. If we play well each night, I'm happy."

■ Take Advantage of the Road

When you're on tour, take advantage of the road: do radio interviews, make retail appearances. Work it, baby, work it. When you're in a market, be in a market; don't just go and do a gig and say, Thank you very much, and glad to be here. Do advance press before you get there; make sure you're talking to a radio station or a magazine or a newspaper. Go to retail stores. If you have a deal, make sure you're doing something with the distribution company or the label while you're there. Take full advantage of the time on the road, like any business trip. While touring is great and you get to perform and do what you like to do, it's still a business trip.

■ Merchandising

Merchandising is important. However corporate this sounds, it's about product placement and corporate identity. People respond to bands' logos; kids will put stickers on their loose-leaf binders when they go to school. It's a really important part of spreading the word of music.

When you're on the road, sell T-shirts, bandannas, candles, CDs—whatever you can think of. Be clever in your design—logos are an important part of the image you're creating. What is a T-shirt if it's not a statement of who the wearer is? It's not just loyalty to a band, it's a statement more about the wearers themselves. If you put on a Black Sabbath or a Sepultura T-shirt, it's saying, I am dangerous. If you put on an NSync or Backstreet Boys T-shirt, it says I'm friendly.

Merchandising enables artists to make ancillary income. If you don't do it, some bootlegger is going to slap something together with your name on it, sell it, and pocket the cash. You might as well create a quality product.

Merchandising can keep a band alive. In the early eighties there was a band called Styx that was selling out arenas and basically breaking even on concert ticket revenues. Their merchandising, however, was so lucrative that their tours actually made profits.

Merchandising first became highly profitable in the early eighties, when major companies came along and signed huge bands and fortunes were made. Bands were making millions of dollars in advances off of merchandising deals. Today, the average concertgoer spends $5 per head on merchandising, so if a band gets $10 per head in merchandising, it's truly great. The two hottest acts for merchandising in recent memory are those appealing to the yuppie crowd, the Eagles and KISS. KISS was taking in close to $15 per head and the Eagles were doing about $12.

There is an endless array of places to sell merchandise besides on tour. Lots of CDs come with merchandising inserts, and band Web sites have merchandising pages. Ads strategically placed in newspapers and magazines can also move product. Be creative. Today merchandising extends beyond T-shirts; it can be almost anything. Bands license their name for a lot of things—there are KISS cards and KISS action figures. A band can get involved with many things—and make a lot of ancillary income.

■ Getting Paid to Make Music

Do you do your music anticipating you'll get paid at some point, or do you do this as a labor of love? Most musicians expect to get paid for doing it at some point. They love making music and they want to make a living at what they love to do. It's natural.

When you start gigging around, if you're not offered an up-front fee, you will get paid if you bring enough people into the venues. When you tour early on, don't expect it to be about money; expect it to be about exposure.

Classical guitarist Alex Stone has it easy—it's just him and his guitar. He takes his equipment, goes into a public space, and opens his guitar case. Because he plays on the street, he makes money through tips and by selling the CDs for $15. He figures that if he can sell two hundred of them for $15 each, he covers the cost of recording the CD. Even though he's playing on the street, he's getting exposure. This exposure often leads to gigs.

"Usually when I play in public, people come to me and they ask me if I could play at some party or wedding," Alex offers. "Playing outside is actually a good way to get gigs. It helps to have business cards in a place that's easy to reach, because people don't want to interrupt you while you're playing, and they might not have the time to wait, so they can just take a business card and call you. Another thing that should be obvious: my phone number and mailing address are on the CD, so if somebody has the CD and then they want me to play, that's a way they can get to me."

Figure out where to find your audience. Are they the type that will be hanging out at the House of Blues or some dark little club, or will they be at events in wine country and at jazz festivals? Figure out where your audience hangs out, then go to them.

Once again, if you've got something special to offer, people will find out. The cream rises to the top. Concentrate on sharing your music; if you're good, the rest will come, whether you want it to or not. If you're concentrating on your art, then you're doing your homework, following your muse and your instincts. And there'll be more and more people around you to help you get the word out to other people. Greatness will win out. You can't contain a great work. There's evidence of it all through history.

■ Alternative Markets

You need to take an active role in your own project if you don't have a major record deal. Be creative; use your contacts. Tom Viscount got one of Viscount's songs to be the theme song for a national teen model search. He got Viscount's songs played in a Sears department store for five months. They made about $6,000 off of that deal, and were able to pay back some of the money people had lent them to record the album, *My Name Is Nobody.* Another great promotion he came up with for his band's music was through his day gig with the American Red Cross. Tom got the Red Cross to use one of his songs as the theme tune for one of their blood drives.

"I worked out those deals just by knowing people, networking, and finding out there was a need and submitting the music," shares Tom. "Even if you can get one of your songs in a small movie that doesn't pay much, it gives you exposure."

Get your work out there—the rest will come.

■ Soundtracks

There's one newly discovered driving force in sales that everybody is all over: film and television soundtracks.

"Soundtracks provide me with not only a great opportunity to help DreamWorks artists, but other artists from other labels, and unsigned artists. Not only am I addressing the needs of the DreamWorks features and their soundtracks, but I'm also bringing in soundtracks from films from other studios. Say we might sign a soundtrack for a film that Fox is releasing—we can market our artists on it. So it works two ways: you can put Eels on a Dream-Works film soundtrack, or you can put Eels or Propellerheads on a Warner Bros. film. Furthermore, if the soundtrack's not ours, if the film's not ours, we can still try to get our artists on other company's soundtracks. That's all part of what we do, too," says Chris Douridas.

A soundtrack is a great way to test the waters for an artist. Remember Lisa Loeb? She was an unsigned artist who went to school with the actor Ethan Hawke. When he was doing the movie *Reality Bites,* he brought her music in for soundtrack consideration. RCA put out that soundtrack, and they made a big mistake. They did not put in the contract that they had the option of signing her if her track blew up. Her song became the hit off the soundtrack, and RCA, though they sold a lot of soundtracks, lost the future of Lisa Loeb—an artist that they just spent a lot of dollars marketing. Since that lesson was learned by the soundtrack industry, it's hard to get an unsigned artist on a soundtrack without giving the soundtrack company an option. Still, it's one way of testing the potential of an artist without sacrificing a lot of money.

■ Work for Hire

Selling a song for a soundtrack is a totally different animal than being commissioned to write a song. Suppose Fox Television wants to hire you to write the theme song for their *Lost Universe* TV series. Fox Television (the corporation) becomes the owner of the work, and the person hired to write it disappears from the profit scenario. You'll still get credit for writing the song; you just won't see any back-end money. If you don't mind losing out on royalties, there are plenty of different work-for-hire scenarios: TV shows, jingles for radio, television commercials, video games, industrial films . . . the possibilities are limitless. Find a couple of friends who are directors; if they're busy, they need music made.

According to David Javelosa, who earns a formidable living making music for various projects, a musician can find work-for-hire projects by developing specific skill sets:

- By developing a reputation as someone who does something unique or exceptional
- By maintaining a high profile in one's particular area
- By cold-calling contacts—specifically the producers and managers responsible for hiring musicians

You can generate contacts for work-for-hire projects at trade shows, conferences, seminars, and on other jobs. Basically, networking is what it takes. Eventually you'll develop a growing list of regular clients, periodically keeping in contact with them or servicing them to meet their needs.

■ More than You Could Ever Imagine: Metallica

Metallica has been one of the few bands that have impacted popular music as we know it—they can sell out stadiums from Bangor to Bangkok. The thundering crunch of frontman James Hetfield, drummer Lars Ulrich, guitarist Kirk Hammett, and new bassist Robert Trujillo has sold more than 50 million albums worldwide, and has made Metallica a band that will be remembered a century from now. Lars offers some viewpoints on Metallica's illustrious career. . . .

What is the most challenging part of your songwriting?

LARS ULRICH: None of it really. A lot of the things about the flavor and the direction of the song obviously comes from the lyrics, but the direction of the lyrics comes from the music. For us, songwriting is a very step-by-step process. Here are some ideas; here are some riffs; then this turns into a song. When you get some idea of what the song could be about lyrically, the melodies get words attached to them.

Is it difficult to produce the studio sound live?

LU: I don't worry about that; I got over it a long time ago. They're different beasts. In the studio, you make the best record that you can using whatever way gets you off. Whether that's going in and doing a Green Day and recording a hundred songs in five days or being a Def Leppard and going in and recording five songs in a hundred days, that's something you decide yourself. But the live situation and the studio are two different things, no reason to even sit and worry in the studio about how it is going to work live. You make a record, then you go and play the songs the best you can, the way you feel the most comfortable about playing them.

There have been one or two songs that connected for us in the studio that maybe never worked live, for instance "The Unforgiven," and that's fine. I don't think it has to be either/or.

Do you prefer playing live or making records?

LU: It used to be touring, but I'd say while doing the last two records with Bob Rock (*Load* and *Reload*), the recording process has become a lot more interesting, a lot more challenging, and a lot more fun, so I'm starting to enjoy the recording process more. I'm finding that you're a lot more independent in the studio because you're not set to a schedule. When you're on the road, you know exactly where you're going to be on May 13th at 5 P.M. It's kind of confining after a while.

As I get older, I still get off on the playing side of it, but the endless running around—basically, the other twenty-two hours of the day—are less and less effortless. It used to be effortless for me to travel, and it never used to bother me. The last two, three, four years, it's become more of an effort for me to travel. That's probably got something to do with getting older.

Do you travel with a jet instead of a tour bus now?
LU: We are realizing that we want to sink more and more into being comfortable on the road, because that means we can play better, and play longer tours. We're spoiling ourselves more than we were before. The entourage becomes a little bigger, but you get from A to B quicker than you do any other way.

Is the road still fresh and exciting for you?
LU: That might be pushing it. When you go to Chicago and you play Rosemont Horizon for the eleventh time, I wouldn't say it was fresh and exciting. There is always something that you can focus on to inspire you, and always some new face in the crowd and some new place you can channel some energy from—that's the most important thing.

Certainly what makes it as fresh as possible is that we always seem to play different scenarios, different situations. We'll play the sheds, then we'll play indoors, then we'll play some clubs, then we'll play the stadiums.

How do you design your stage?
LU: We think about the types of venues we'll be playing. If we're doing arenas in winter, we'll do something that would have the whole hockey enclosure as a stage, and that's how we came up with the two-stage idea. There's also been the Snakepit stage, and playing in the round, and so on.

Your stages have gotten so large that sometimes when Metallica performs, the band members are miles away.
LU: You deal with it the best way you can. There are certain advantages and certain disadvantages to playing big stages. The disadvantages are very simple; you don't play together that much and when things fuck up, the fact that you're ninety-five feet away from each other doesn't help. But the advantages so override the few disadvantages that it's great. The fact that we can go on the road and keep it exciting for us as long as we do by playing this way is a lot more inspiring. It's different, and the goal is to keep it as different as you can.

Lollapalooza, Monsters of Rock, Guns 'N Roses—you've done a lot of big shows with other bands. Do you like going out en masse?

LU: I like both. Certainly, you can do a lot more when you're on your own, but there's certainly something to be said about playing with other bands. It definitely has a tendency to keep you on your toes. There's a competitive spirit in those types of situations that's very healthy, both for the bands and the people that watch the shows. That's okay. When you've played 212 gigs in North Dakota by yourself, sometimes, inspiration falls. It's great to have other bands out, especially other bands you respect and other bands you musically admire. If you're having a boring day, it's uplifting to go out and catch thirty minutes of someone like Soundgarden before you play.

What do you like most and least about touring?

LU: I like when we alter the set list; that's the most fun about touring. We're choosing eighteen, nineteen songs out of twenty-five, instead of playing the same set list every night. That makes it a little more refreshing. The thing I like least about it is traveling, probably flying.

Does the band still hang out together on the road?

LU: They're a lot more respectful, a lot more tolerant. We hang out less than we used to. Everybody's going more and more in socially different directions, which is fine. I also find that the tolerance level keeps growing. This is probably because we've become comfortable with each other. A few years ago, there used to be this gang mentality, and whenever anybody would stray outside of this gang mentality, everybody else would frown. Now everybody else is just like, Yeah, whatever. Five years ago if we weren't all wearing black pants, we'd get yelled at by the other three guys.

I'm starting to get more of a life of my own, and feeling less and less fearless about things that go on in my life on a daily basis. When you're just out partying all the time, you just don't care about anything. Now I'm married, I'm a father; I feel different about a lot of things than I used to. I don't have the same "live fearlessly" attitude that I once did.

Do you desire to do any music outside of Metallica in the future?

LU: I'm pretty content. I'm really stoked to be going into the studio and making records more often. That's going to keep my creative juices flowing for quite a while. As you know, I've been into movies for many, many years. One day I might penetrate the movie world at some level, somewhere, somehow. I probably won't tell too many people about it; it's not like a big publicity thing or anything like that. One day—it could be a year, could be five years, could be ten years—I'd like to go into a creative field I know nothing about; it's pretty appealing to me.

CHAPTER TEN

Marketing and Promotion

The difficulty is trying to express music in words. It's like

trying to describe a color to somebody.

—Alex Van Halen, Van Halen

One way to get your band noticed is through publicity—you need to get your name out there. The people who get paid exorbitant amounts of money to calculate statistics figure that an average person has to hear and see a band's name eight times before the group's name starts to register. This means you've got your work cut out for you. You've got to create fan awareness, because if no one knows you're out there, there's no way you're going to build a following. If you only had a limited amount of money to spend on promoting your album, how would you allocate those funds? Cheapie ideas: posters work, gig listings help, but those flyers bands put under windshield wipers at concerts get mixed reviews.

☼ **COMMIT IT TO MEMORY:** *An average person has to hear and see a band's name eight times before the group's name starts to register.*

When consumers hear a single on the radio that they like, it registers, but since most of the time the disc jockey doesn't announce that song, they end up wondering, Oh, what's that song, it's something about old photographs. Then, they're reading an article that talks about the hit single "Wrinkled Pictures," and the lightbulb goes on. The consumer thinks, Oh, that band! I'm going to go pick that album up. Publicity strengthens awareness of the band name and what they're all about, and it gives fans an opportunity to get to know them a bit better.

"There's a huge debate over whether or not publicity sells records," offers Laura Cohen, manager of publicity for Virgin Records. "We know on the highest end—when an artist is showcased on *Saturday Night Live* or *The David Letterman Show*—television definitely sells music. With print, there's a big question of whether or not an article in *Rolling Stone* will sell albums. We think it does, but, at the same time, it's more instrumental in building awareness. If you put everything together without publicity, it's a missing link in a chain of events that's supposed to occur to have a successful album. You hear a band on the radio, you see a band on the cover of a magazine, and it compels you to buy it. You might buy it because you saw it on the cover of a magazine, you might buy it solely because you heard it on the radio, but if you put them all together, it helps emphasize that band."

For the record, publicity expenses come out of the record label's budget, and they don't generally deduct from your share of the back end for promotion. Sure, some things will be deducted, but in general not, so don't stress about those media junkets the label sponsors so that key people can get to know you.

■ Getting Your Vision to the Marketplace

"The real hothouse for the record business right now is in the area of marketing," states Bud Scoppa, vice president of A&R for the Sire Records Group. "If you look at some of the most noteworthy success stories of breaking artists over the last few years, you'll see that these breakthroughs are predicated on creative marketing to a significant degree. One example that I think is noteworthy is Atlantic's work in the initial stages of the Jewel project. They had her out doing regional residencies in coffeehouses in various parts of the country over a period of months. They were really patient as a series of scattered small buzzes in various parts of the country eventually coalesced into a snow-ball effect.

"Hit records aren't made in marketing meetings. They're made in the studio. Fiona Apple's debut album was a great album, but Jeff Ayeroff, the co-president of Sony/Workgroup Records, made a great marketing campaign that broke her."

Any artist—Jewel, Alanis Morissette, or Fiona Apple—has to be positioned in the music marketplace so consumers don't confuse one with another. How an artist is positioned is an outgrowth of meeting with the artist, the artist's manager, and everybody in the record company who's going to be involved with selling the album. The people who are the heads of every department who are going to end up handling the product—radio, marketing sales, international, and everybody in the company who is in a decision-making seat—will sit down and hash it out: How should this go? Where should this be? Who is this artist, and who do they appeal to, and what do we need to do to find their customer base?

Once they figure out how to position the artist, the label then analyzes that talent's sales potential. They figure out how much money they can afford to spend getting the word out while still making a profit, and that's how they get the marketing budget. It's all based on sales projections.

■ Case Study: MSO PR

MSO PR were publicists of Alanis Morissette on the *Jagged Little Pill* album. They were there from the beginning, three or four months before the disc came out. Mitch Schneider, media arsonist and president of MSO PR, recalls the campaign for Alanis Morissette's debut:

> There was no campaign for Alanis's new album—it was like a new artist: send the cassettes out, start generating some interest. We bought back some initial interviews, she did them, and then "You Oughta Know" happened on the radio. It was a wildfire that resulted in $15 million in sales and became the biggest-selling debut album in history.
>
> Part of what we did for Alanis was, we didn't ruin it. Her success happened so fast, and she was entirely grateful for it, but at the same time she didn't want the audience to burn out on it.
>
> In this very media-driven age, there are so many outlets around—particularly cable TV. We got calls from shows like *E! Entertainment Television* asking for permission to show Alanis's video on our credit roll. Her managers,

Scott Welch and Bob Cavallo, said, "Hold them off, wait for another single, it's going to be too much exposure." They said no to TV shows like *Entertainment Tonight* and *Access Hollywood*, places where people are going to see Alanis and just feel oversaturated.

What we did for Alanis was create a subtle campaign. There were major outlets that were turned down, magazine offers that other artists would offer body parts to secure.

Alanis is an artist who wants to hold onto her career, and she felt that it was really important to be subtle. In an age where you're hit over the head with everything, she just wants to be discriminating. She really is a very subtle person. I'm very proud that I was able to contribute to a campaign of subtlety.

■ The Label and the Life of an Artist

It's a commonly held belief that record people can make one or two decisions in the career of an artist that can make the difference between them becoming big or becoming a massive superstar. The thing that great decisions can do is accelerate a group. As everybody keeps saying, great artists are always going to break. Bob Dylan, or Bono, or Bruce Springsteen, or Kurt Cobain, or Eddie Vedder, and on and on and on would not have bombed if they were on Meaningful Records. They would happen on any label because they're great artists. All the record company marketing department can do is accelerate that path.

The record company's role with an artist is to bring the artist's vision to the marketplace. Of course, not everybody always agrees on the artist's vision. Artists and record executives argue constantly. The label might think track number three should be the single, but the band thinks track number one says it all.

"We sit down with the artists, find out what really turns them on, how they want to be perceived in the media," observes Mitch Schneider. "It sounds so basic it's ridiculous, but that's really how you do it. You figure out what is true to them and how they perceive themselves. It's very important to just let the artists explain their vision to you. A good publicist will take good notes, because that's really the key element at that particular point."

■ Priority Artists

Record promotion works on a very logical level. Most record labels have two release cycles every month. Each of those release cycles averages three or four releases. If you look at what bands are happening, you'll realize that each record company has artists who are its priority. The entire label works the album "until it's over"—an arbitrary phrase, indeed. They have allocated a healthy amount of time and marketing budget toward this artist. Radio promotion is continuously working singles, like with the 1997 Janet Jackson album, *The Velvet Rope*. A year after the album was released, Virgin Records was working only on the third single—and that was only partway into the game. Because Virgin paid $50 million for Janet Jackson (it was a record-breaking signing, price-wise), they're going to work that record to try and recoup the best that they can. Virgin had decided to work six singles on the album. More than a year into the album, Janet finally started her tour. The life of *The Velvet Rope* album was three years.

Why a label like Atlantic decides to put their marketing muscle behind Tori Amos, as opposed to Jimmy Page and Robert Plant—that's a decision that's reached after hours of debate about priorities, budget, and future drawing potential behind closed conference room doors.

"Not everything can be a priority at a label," observes Tony Ferguson, who does A&R at Interscope Records. "Acts should realize that when they are being courted by a major label, they are always made to feel that they are going to be the priority. But a major label, upon taking delivery of the record that the act has made, may elect not to make it a priority at that time. That's hard for a band to deal with. I think labels try to push too much product at too high a level and flood the market."

Too many acts are being signed for the wrong reasons. With the success of independent labels over the last few years, the majors suddenly think, Well what are they doing that we're not doing? Just imagine if we, as a major label, signed that act; we'd be even more successful. So, there's a big pressure for A&R people to go out there and sign, sign, sign, and sign. It's kind of like that movie *Glengarry Glen Ross*: Sell those cars! Come on, let's go! Make your quota!

So now the label has eight releases this month and they all have to be marketed. If you're not that high on the list, the record label is not going to try that hard. For a smaller band, the label will put out a single or two. If there's absolutely no radio response, they'll work at press for maybe six months. Then there are other records, which are doing no better, that are still being developed by the record company.

"Everybody knows when they have a racehorse," observes Mitch Schneider. "There's a feeling in a company that this is something that's going to be a really proud record. There are some classic albums that don't sell millions of records, but the integrity value is so huge. It's really important for a record company to recognize what is an integrity record. It raises the corporate profile of the label. It also serves as a magnet to attract other artists."

No one officially says that a band's promotion campaign is over. But around the label you just know it's over because everybody's moved on; it's no longer on the agenda at meetings. Do you want to know how long a record label works a band? Until it's not on the agenda.

■ Marketing Case Study: Joey Kramer's Drum Loops and Samples CD

Always up for an interesting side project, Aerosmith drummer Joey Kramer released a drum loops and samples CD in 2002. Geared for musicians and garnering rave reviews, sales did not live up to Joey's expectations.

Tell us a bit about how Joey Kramer's Drum Loops and Samples *came together.*
JOEY KRAMER: It was my thing to give back a little to an industry that I've taken a lot from. At first I didn't really want to get involved with the idea of doing it, because really, why make myself so available? The whole thing about that is that it's the kind of project, it's about putting yourself out there, it's not really about making money because there's not a lot of money in it to begin with. I did it so kids are able to learn from my experience and hopefully use it as a learning tool, use it for records, or use it for whatever they're using it for, and hope that people enjoy it. It's a little mark that I can leave.

I did the CD with Marti Frederiksen, who is the guy who produced the *Just Push Play* album for us. Marti is also a drummer, and we thought it would be a good, fun, and interesting project. We went into the studio with him and spent days laying down tracks. In doing a drum loop and sample CD, the real work is in the editing. When all is said and done, the CD was a fairly simple thing to do, and it was fun. I got to put together all the artwork for the cover; it was a neat little project for me to do on my own, I enjoyed it.

Are you pleased with the response you've gotten with the CD?
JK: I have not been happy with the sales of the *Drum Loops and Samples* CD because the people that were dealing with it kind of dropped the ball on the project after its release.

How critical is marketing and promotion toward the success of a project?
JK: It's extremely critical because if you have a product and nobody knows that you have it, then it's going to lie on the shelves. If no one is aware of it then what can possibly happen with it? The people who released my *Drum Loops and Samples* CD didn't market it properly; they just threw it in the bin

with everything else that they had. They didn't take advantage of the fact that it was mine and they could have made a special thing out of it, and sold a lot more copies of the product. Instead, they just left it lying there. I was on the road and really wasn't focused in that direction to delve into it properly and make it happen myself, so because they didn't live up to their obligations contractually, and now I have reason to leave them.

■ How Marketing and Promotion Helps

Let's isolate a make-believe band, Smarty Boots. Their music is hard rock with a little bit of alternative and electronica thrown in for good measure. The publicist sends out advance cassettes three or four months before the album comes out. They're getting some stories, but the critical intelligentsia, which encompasses *Rolling Stone, Spin, Musician, Time,* and *Newsweek*—the gatekeepers of taste—are not really jumping on the record. They want to wait and see how it does in the marketplace before they put out their opinions on it. The record company may say, Gee, it seems like we don't have a critical winner here.

Still, they want to recoup on their investment, so they may say, Let's up the radio promotion. When you up the radio promotion budget, that means more airplay should result.

When a publicist is able to go back to the media for round two and say, Hi! This is so-and-so following up on that Smarty Boots CD we sent you. It's been a couple of months since we last spoke, and the song 'Boys or Men' is now getting airplay. It's on thirty to fifty radio stations—a combination of rock and alternative around the country—and it's starting to really take.

They'll definitely get some response back from the journalist, who is usually looking for ways to keep a story up to date, which can be difficult when magazines like *Spin* and *Rolling Stone* have a two- to three-month lead time. The response the publicist gets will probably be something like, Well, okay, but are they touring?

The publicist then says to the label, The press is asking about a tour. Then, the marketing department has to consider what encompasses marketing and promotion—is it tour support? And, if so, they'll get the band on the road.

■ Media and the Road

When your band goes on the road, it becomes an opportunity. There's a whole strata of media that becomes available: local newspapers, television, and fanzines. Most of the fanzines won't talk to a band unless they're going to be in that city.

COMMIT IT TO MEMORY: *When doing tour publicity, you need to start promoting your shows at least six weeks in advance.*

To do the publicity job right, a tour publicist should be given tour dates six weeks in advance, before a group gets to a certain city. That gives a publicist ample time to send out the press kit and the CD to local journalists. The local journalist is anyone from the daily newspaper to the weekly newspaper. In some situations, these publications are monthly, so if you have that six-week window before Smarty Boots' appearance, the publicist may be able to grab a couple of monthlies.

Publicity is an ongoing task. After the records are sent out, the publicist reaches out again. In this day and age you just can't send CDs out to everybody on that first mailing. Hopefully the journalist has gotten a CD from a local record company, so you send the mailing out—press kit photos, bio—and you start to hook a journalist. If they say, They sound interesting; I'd like to hear the music, you get them a CD right away. That becomes the second part of the process. Your publicist has to be efficient in his follow-up because these stories have to appear in advance in order for them to be of any benefit to you. This whole part of the campaign is about selling tickets, so people can come and experience your group.

There are some shows that are sellouts, but you still want your publicist to do tour publicity, because you want to get preview boxes in the papers. Everybody loves a winner. It's great to open up a newspaper and see that Smarty Boots is performing this week at Peabody's in Cleveland and the show is sold out.

Then of course you want the reviews to appear. If you are a punk band, you want the punk 'zines to be there to interview the artist, so that these articles appear in the punk 'zine three months later. That way, when the artist is on round two, that important little community has already been exposed to Smarty Boots.

■ Marketing Novelty: Live CDs of the Show You've Just Seen

Since their 2000 tour, Pearl Jam has been offering "official bootleg" albums chronicling their world tour. The mastered double CDs with custom packaging typically ship two to three days after a concert.

"We decided to do it through the fan club, which is the ideal place for this type of CD," notes Pearl Jam guitarist Stone Gossard. "If you see a spectacular show that everyone is talking about—because we record all the shows, anyway—you can get it right from the source."

It was so successful that bands like the Who and Phish quickly followed suit. Then the suits caught on. In 2003, über-promoter Clear Channel Concerts started burning live CDs at select concerts and offering them for sale within minutes of the final encore.

"We're working collaboratively with artists and songwriters to provide the program at selected events," offers Steve Simon, executive vice president of the music division at Clear Channel Entertainment.

"The value in this is a collectible CD with a spot for your ticket stub, that, if you spent $100 for a concert, gives you more than a T-shirt," said Jake Walker, cofounder of Disclive, a company that offers a similar service.

If you're interested in recording a concert on site, John Keefe, producer at First Generation Recording Studio, explains the nuances of onsite recording.

How do you record a song outside of the studio?

JOHN KEEFE: For onsite recording, we usually show up four to five hours before the show. We bring in MDMs, ADATs; we'll find a spot in the location that can be isolated as much as possible from the stage. Then we'll run what's called a "splitter snake." One half of the snake feeds the house system, the other half feeds the microphone preamps, which in turn, feed the tape decks. We may place some studio mics on stage and use some of the house mics to mic vocals, drums, guitars, keyboards, etc., and then place four microphones around the room to pick up the crowd response. Then the tape decks output to a mixing console, which we can monitor the material being recorded directly to tape through studio monitors and headphones.

From there, the material is recorded digitally onto tape and brought back to the studio, and digitally transferred to hard drives. From there, editing takes place. Editing is a process of removing material that you don't want in the recording. In some cases, we may edit whole parts of a song to shorten the length. In other cases, we edit just parts of tracks to remove mic bleed or any background noise when an instrument isn't playing, which makes for a cleaner recording. After that, then we set up EQs and effects, which is reverb, delay, etc., on the particular tracks to enhance their sonic capabilities, although we try and keep the tracks as natural sounding as possible.

Then, mixing takes place. Mixing can be best described as each instrument having its own place in the song. An example is, rhythm parts have their own amplitude or volume, where solos or lead vocals would have a greater amplitude. You could say that mixing is a bit like cooking: each instrument has its own "flavor," and everything is blended to make the mix in the song. Then EQ and effects are added as the spice. After the mixing process is completed, the tracks are then digitally bounced to a two-track stereo mix. At that point, mastering takes over.

Mastering is like applying a final polishing before replication. It's a process of basically matching all the tracks in amplitude or volume, which is called normalizing, any final EQing, stereo imaging which is widening or narrowing the stereo field and then compressing or limiting the mix to achieve total digital zero output. The problem with digital stuff is, unlike tape, if you go over absolute digital zero, you get instant distortion. So, it's important to try and get the hottest mix without going over digital zero. From there, the tracks are trimmed and ending or beginning fades are applied. Then the tracks are assembled and spaced in the order they will be put on the CD. The CD then goes off to a replicating facility.

How does recording live differ from a studio recording?
JK: The greatest challenge is the location you're at. Not all clubs keep their equipment in top working order. The other challenges—even though we show up four to five hours early—there never seems to be enough time. Also, trying to get the musicians to show up early (two to three hours before the gig) to get a proper recording level and to troubleshoot any potential problems (hum or line buzzes, maybe something that doesn't work). Once we're set up, there's not a lot we can do until the musicians show up and we get proper level checks. In studio recording, you have a very controlled environment and know exactly how something is going to sound when it's recorded down there.

■ Marketing Strategies

When planning a marketing and promotion campaign for a band, the record company needs to think about radio promotion, tour support, and videos. Sometimes a record company won't invest in a video until they see if this song is going to be a hit. If they have faith in the project, there may be video promotion dollars involved with that as well. It's a big project. You're talking $500,000 to properly market a band, and that doesn't include advertising. It may sound like a healthy chunk of change, but in all actuality, it isn't.

Let's say you want to have a group go to London for press promotion, a band like the Beastie Boys. Because every member of the band is recognizable, it can't be just a lead singer; it has to be all three members of the band. Putting a band up in London for three to four nights is an expensive proposition. And while the Beasties are there, the record company is inevitably going to throw a party on their behalf. A lot of times artists say that they should be getting more money from record sales, but a complete publicity campaign eats up profits faster than a dog gobbles treats.

The record companies have to make huge investments on these bands, so the numbers get huge. An artist could wind up with a platinum album on the third record and it wouldn't even make back all the marketing dollars the record company spent on the three albums to get to that point. Being a successful major label artist is a tough business, and there are very few race-horse winners.

■ Publicists

The people who are going to work hardest to get the word out about you are the publicists. Publicists are the liaisons between artists and media. Media includes newspaper, magazines, radio, and television shows that specialize in performance or interview-type situations for an artist. The publicist acts as the contact between the artist and those mediums.

"As publicists, what we're really all about is figuring out a way to bring music to the masses," clarifies Mitch Schneider. "The way to do that is through the media, and media would encompass everything from newspapers to magazine to radio syndication to television outlets and the whole Internet world. We reach out to all the press in those areas and hopefully inspire them to create pieces—feature stories or reviews on our artists."

Once your act's musical genre has been established—whether it's hard rock, New Age, punk, ska, surf, mainstream, or whatever—your publicist will contact the appropriate individual outlets. Each genre comes with its own specialists—writers, photographers, stylists, and beyond. Every genre of music has its own world of magazines; the punk world, the heavy metal world, the R&B world; there are hip-hop magazines, and some magazines that want to write about left-of-center soul music. It's the publicist's job to know these people and their audience and get you press.

Publicists are great because they know media outlets. Magazines are the easiest way to get exposure. It's a good thing to be able to target your band to specific publications, but it's also a lot of work. If you do your own publicity, you have to know the circulation of that magazine, and the demographic of the reader. If you want to do a lot of research, you can find those things out.

■ Independent Publicists

The cost of a professional publicity service can vary from several hundred to several thousand dollars a month. Sometimes a publicist is hired by the band or the artist. In other situations, they're hired by the record company, which feels overwhelmed, because they have a lot of projects going, and they want to put more juice into something. Sometimes there'll be a split; the artist may do half and the record company may do half.

"Our rates vary; I never discuss them," confirms Mitch Schneider. "I will go so far as to say that our rates do vary based upon time consumption. Some bands might only want a punk 'zine campaign; they don't want to be pitched to *Letterman* or *Saturday Night Live* or any of that stuff. There are different rates to reflect each band's needs."

If you only had a limited amount of money to spend on promoting your album, publicity may be a better expenditure than advertising. Through publicity, the publicist would be able to bring back future stories and reviews. The combined costs of that should completely outweigh the cost of advertising. If your publicist scores and brings back a two-page feature for the band, you win, because an ad in a magazine could cost many thousands of dollars.

Publicity is the way to go, especially when you keep in mind that there are publications like *Alternative Press* and *Option* magazine, which will write about something based on the quality of it. Those publications won't ask you how much airplay the song is getting; they don't care. Those publications are an easy way to produce reviews and features based upon the group's musical performance.

■ Doing It Yourself

Publicity is all about getting your name out there—it doesn't have to be *Spin*, *Hit Parader*, or *Rolling Stone*. Figure out what kinds of local newspapers and magazines you can get into without worrying so much about who's reading it, because, in reality, any press is good press.

Start with the local free entertainment papers. Publications like *LA Weekly* cover Los Angeles bands, as well as bands coming through town. Another is *The Detroit Free Press*. Even if you're not signed, they'll give feedback on your demo.

It's pretty easy to get press from local free publications that aren't too big; maybe they're the secondary competition in their market. If you choose this route, you'll be fine. Just don't set your sights too high on places like the *Los Angeles Times*. Forget about national magazines unless you're an established artist with a record label.

Start small; get yourself known. Name recognition, like anything else, comes in degrees. The Geraldine Fibbers, in their own circle in Los Angeles, have name recognition. They're going to sell out in Los Angeles. Send them off to Hansonland—Tulsa, Oklahoma—and no one will know who they are. Like anything, it's degrees. Worldwide name recognition is reserved for those who are superstars. The first place to start is name recognition in your own town. Remember: If you're an unsigned band, think local.

■ Before You Call, Have a Clue

The greatest part about any kind of print publicity is that it's free. It's all free; it's just the cost of a phone call and a CD. What you need to do is determine what you want to accomplish with this phone call to this publication. Do you want to get CD reviews, or do you want press people to come and see you live, and review your live show?

Before harrassing any editors, you have to first pinpoint your immediate goal. Then, when you pinpoint your immediate goal, you have to have a clue about the publications that you're calling. Go get it; look at it. Does the *Orange County Weekly* cover live shows? Don't call them if they don't. You need to know these things.

The approach is simple; say you are an independent publicist representing a band. Call up the publication and see if you can get one of the writers on the phone. Send a package, wait a week, then call to follow up. Call again until you get somebody on the phone. They'll admire your tenacity, and, if they like you, they'll find a place for writing about your music.

"You need any kind of exposure you can get," confirms Tom Viscount. "It's all part of the story, it's all part of the hype. The more people that are interested, the more other people get interested, so hype is really the key. Either you do it or someone else does it for you. It's being tenacious. Unless you get lucky, it's the only way to get the project happening."

Most writers are straight; they'll let you know where you stand after they listen to your album. I'm not into this, can't cover it, don't have room. Or, Yeah, I'll see if I can do something.

■ Getting on Web Sites

Perhaps the easiest way for a band to build up some press clippings is to give material to music Webzines. Online publications, such as *www.rocknworld.com, www.antimusic.com, www.MusicRemedy.com, www.loudside.com, http://altmusic .about.com, http://musicmoz.org, www.konzertfotos.org, www.starpulse.com, www .allschools.net, www.nyrock.com,* and *www.clubcd.com,* are looking for content. Got a Canadian angle? It's easy to get on CanEHdian Features–Canada's entertainment source located at *www.canehdian.com.* With a little creativity, you can have articles all over the Net.

■ Television Publicity

If you can get on television, go for it—ignore all demographic information and just do it. If your band can get on *The David Letterman Show*, dive in without thinking twice. Of course someone like Letterman is not going to put you on his show unless you're big already. Be forewarned: It's really hard getting spots on TV without some sort of story behind you. It's almost a cyclical thing; if you haven't been on television, then you have nothing to show people about what you'll be like on television.

Like anything else, you have to start small, with perhaps a local cable access show. Then you move regional, to *Good Morning Texas*–type shows, then onto the *Regis and Kelly* genre of programming, before you get to do the biggest: *Saturday Night Live*, *The Tonight Show*, and heavily watched late-night programming.

■ Start Simple: Local Cable Access Shows

Local cable access shows are the first step in getting on television. Sure, it's on the tiniest, tiniest level, but there are cable access shows in every city that show videos of unsigned bands and showcase bands performing, so there's an opportunity to get some exposure. You have the flexibility to custom-design your own presentation. Whether it be from a local club or in the studio performing a song and then being interviewed, cable access is one way to go.

You can find out about cable access channels by calling up your cable provider, who will have a listing of cable access shows, or you can do your research by just going through the cable channels. There has yet to be a band that's gone large-scale via cable access, because it's very locally oriented; it's done in one city, for that city.

■ Conan O'Brien

If you're starting to break and you want to go to the next level of television, it's generally agreed that the best place to showcase anybody is on *Conan O'Brien*, because of the show's heavy college audience. It's not like going on *The Tonight Show* or *David Letterman;* those shows are in an earlier time slot and are more high-profile.

The Deftones got on *Conan O'Brien*. Before trying to get on the show, they built a strong buzz. They sold more than 300,000 copies of their second album, *Around the Fur*, with no MTV support and no radio support. MSO put together a strong press-driven campaign for them, and they built a strong résumé, which included articles from *Spin, Rolling Stone, Musician*, a Sunday *Los Angeles Times* feature, etc. Then they hit up *Conan O'Brien* and were invited to do the show. If you don't have critical acclaim and you don't have sales, forget it; you're not going on TV.

"We fought for that booking for two years," confesses Mitch Schneider. "They do not ordinarily book really hard bands, but all the elements were there. It was the right song, 'Be Quiet and Drive,' which actually has shades of the Cure thrown into a very hard rock mix. The Deftones also had a good résumé; you could obviously see the group's growing success."

The *Conan O'Brien* experience had immediate results for the Deftones—they sold a couple thousand more copies of *Around the Fur* in the week following that TV booking.

"That makes me proud as a publicist, when we can have a mark on something," concludes Mitch.

■ Major Television Coverage

If you're connected, you can pitch your music to television shows, whether it be *Melrose Place* or *Northern Exposure,* or you can be the band at the bar in *Buffy the Vampire Slayer.* This placement is a gift, so you definitely have to know someone who knows someone, because there's no way getting on a show is a random act of kindness. If you're with a publicist like MSO, they can suggest that this music be included in an upcoming episode.

"For Aerosmith, we actually sent a package to Matt Groening, creator of *The Simpsons,* suggesting that a song on the *Pump* record called 'FINE' would be perfect for *The Simpsons,*" recalls Mitch. "'FINE' stands for "fucked up, insecure, neurotic, and emotional," but those words were actually never used in the song. Matt Groening's casting people wrote back and said, 'We'd like to go you one better, we'd like to animate Aerosmith and put them on the show.' Aerosmith became the second musical artist [after Michael Jackson] to actually appear on *The Simpsons*. That was huge exposure.

"Of all the stuff I've done in publicity, that may have been the one biggest bang I did for a band, and that all came from my package, and my vision. I just felt that Aerosmith was so special that they deserved that. It was just a remarkable feeling when I called them back; it was like, Oh my god, this is like a winning lottery ticket."

■ Building a Résumé

Even if you're not ready for *The Simpsons,* you should still try and get some TV exposure. Getting things on television gives you the opportunity to get a reel. It's like anything else: as a band, you're building a résumé. Every piece of press that's written about you, every television show, no matter how big or how small, every performance you've ever done of any gig, any radio airplay you've ever gotten, adds to the résumé you're building about your band. It's a story that you're building.

"If you're only selling your own project, it doesn't look so good," offers Tom Viscount, of Viscount. "But it's good when you can tell them that a song's in rotation on a radio station in Los Angeles; it's getting reviewed by *New Times* weekly. When I talk to somebody about myself, I tell them about a bunch of these little things that are going on. They see other people are liking it, and they want to see me."

■ Case Study: Laura Cohen's CD Project

Laura Cohen is manager of publicity for Virgin Records. She specializes in multimedia publicity because she wants to know everything about making and marketing your own music. She tells the story in her own words:

It started back in college, when I was in a very conservative college, on the fast track to becoming a lawyer. Then I gave it all up for my music career because of a personal event that changed my perspective on life.

I had a band in college; we used to play around. I had a great professor who knew I was into doing music. For my senior thesis, for a politics, philosophy, and economics degree, this professor allowed me to record a four-song EP in a studio and write about the marketing and the whole strategy of promoting an album.

I went to all these alumni to try and solicit money, then I went to the school and got a grant to record music. I ended up putting out a four-song EP at a professional studio with a band, as well as a four-track recording of me and my guitar partner, to give an idea of the different sound each type of recording offered.

I wrote a hundred-page thesis on the whole process of writing songs, all the way through to selling albums. That propelled me to get into the music industry and steal whatever information I could from my employers to apply to my own personal knowledge and project.

It's taken forever. I did countless demo tapes in home studios until I finally said, I don't want to go that route. I don't want to do a demo to shop around to a record company and then have the record company do an album. The wave of the future is doing it yourself.

I saved about $5,000, and I went into the studio with my guitar partner and a full band—hired session musicians. We recorded twelve songs in the course of a year. Our album is called *Glass Half Full*. After I finished the record, I worked on the CD cover, remixing, remastering, just trying to get a product that I'd be really proud of.

The next project is getting a Web site, so I can sell my music online, then putting together small tours of cities, either in Los Angeles or surrounding areas. Then I'm pushing like everybody else, trying to get radio play, trying to get myself out there.

The wave of the future is doing it yourself; make your own story and then somebody will notice you. You'll be in a lot better position to negotiate. Be Ani DiFranco; she's an exception; she doesn't want to be signed to a record label. Her goal is to continue to be able to do it herself, which is absolutely something that you can do.

■ Free CDs

As an artist, you've got to be prepared to give away a bunch of CDs to the media and to people who can help promote the word about your band. The percentage of CDs that go for promotion depends upon the album. For a small album release or a reissue, publicity will send out as little as two hundred CDs. For a superstar artist, it can be as many as fifteen hundred.

"I always carry one of my CDs with me. That's a rule with me because you never know who you're going to meet," shares Alex Stone about his album, *Timeless*. "Basically, out of all the CDs, a certain amount has to go for promotion. I probably sell more than I give away, and, because of the cost of the CD, it's reasonable."

If it's a big artist who's going to sell a ton of records, publicity, radio, and promotions want to make sure everybody has one because every publication that you send it to is going to write something about it. For the smaller artists, record companies tailor their mailings. They want to make sure CDs get into the hands of the people who want them.

Each record label has several sets of lists. There's a general product mailing list; these are the heavy hitter writers who get everything. If they happen to write about one of the records that's sent to them, it ends up in a really cool place. As well, there are genre-specific lists that supplement the general product lists. If a journalist we know is into alternative music, and the album being promoted falls into that category, the label will send it to the people on that list as well. If it's music for a college audience, and you're going to be sending CDs to college radio, you want to send them to college papers. It's all logical. Get free music to the people who can best promote your cause.

"Going around town with five or six CDs in your briefcase is not a bad thing; it's how people break in this town," offers Kathy Callahan. "There are ways to do it other than going through majors."

■ Defining a Niche Audience

It's a good idea to think about promotion. Ponder the question, what are you into? Go back to the theme of the album; do you appeal to a certain audience? There are alternative ways of packaging and looking at world music. For example, if you're into computers and your music falls into the jungle of electronica or whatever the Web browsers are listening to, position yourself. Think about why this is music for Netscape voyagers, and that whole market. It's your culture; merge your art with it. Life could be far worse than to have Netscape buy a chunk of your tunes and use it as some kind of music for their thing.

You get your music on Netscape or anywhere else because of contacts. Let's say you've got a New Age album, like Oded Noy's *Dance of Love,* and you want your album to be featured in specific lifestyle catalogs: a New Age products catalog, a crystal catalog, and a massage catalog. That responsibility falls on whoever is marketing the album. Getting placement in catalogs, gift shops, and other alternative markets is all about relationships, networking, and connections.

Let's say your band is playing on National Public Radio. You should try to get into the catalog. If you're not on a label with a good marketing department, the responsibility of getting into the catalog falls onto your band. It will also be the band's responsibility to give the name and contact information for the catalog to the distribution company, who will take the responsibility of distributing the record to the NPR catalog.

Alternative marketing is all about relationships. Call up the catalog you want to be in, find out who is in charge of purchasing and talk to them about what you've got going. If your product is going, it will find a variety of unique homes.

You can ask your distributor about it. Some distribution companies will do alternative marketing for specific artists, but generally this is done through connections or the marketing department. Your distributor will just make sure that your CD gets to these alternative markets.

■ Marketing on the Internet

For an unsigned band, the possibilities the World Wide Web offers are totally exciting, because it's not controlled by anybody. The big print mediums like

Rolling Stone and *Spin* are online. They have their sites and they have their editorial slant that will let them write about the bands they want to write about. But for every *Rolling Stone* and *Spin*, there are a hundred other music sites begging for content. There's a need for content on the Web, so using this space to promote your band is a perfect opportunity. You can read all about the advantages the World Wide Web has to offer in the next chapter.

■ Local H: Making a Profit

Update Nirvana: keep the scathing lyrics, presented in a neat package wrapped with fiercely powerful guitars and pounding drums, and you've got Local H, a new twist on an old patented style. Local H is a power duo consisting of singer/guitarist Scott Lucas and drummer Joe Daniels. We caught up with them while they were marketing and promoting *Pack Up the Cats*, their third album. You may remember them from their release, *As Good As Dead*. Local H got a ton of radio airplay with the sardonic rocker "Bound for the Floor," and racked up fans by opening for the likes of Stone Temple Pilots. *As Good As Dead* went gold. Local H worked on *Pack Up the Cats* with the legendary Roy Thomas Baker (Queen, the Cars) to create an album that has a pop-Nirvana feel, with the hope of expanding their fan base.

How does your third album, Pack Up the Cats, *show your evolution?*
SCOTT LUCAS: We look at what we think our shortcomings are and try to correct them. On this record, we wanted to make sure all the songs tied together. We tried to make music we're not going to get bored with over the next year of touring. We wanted the songs on *Pack Up the Cats* to sound like it was fun, even if the songs are about serious subjects.

Would you say the album has a theme?
SL: Our last record, *As Good As Dead*, had a theme, and we just tried to expand on the sensibility of the last record. It was about being stuck in your hometown—the kind of people that surround you and how they feel, things like that. This new record is an extension of that. The idea behind *Pack Up the Cats* is that your hometown may suck, but if you're unhappy, you'll probably be unhappy anywhere. It doesn't really matter if you live in the city or a small town; you might have fundamental problems with yourself that have nothing to do with the people around you, even though you might want to blame them. The album has to do with getting too big for your britches and forgetting that it might not be everybody else's fault.

How do you build your audience?

JOE DANIELS: By playing to two people, playing to five people, playing to ten people, playing to fifteen. It's rough until you get that break—get a good store, get radio play, get something. Basically, you just play, play, play. That's the old story and that's the new story: playing until you get a break. Any band that keeps digging at it—I don't care if it's ten or fifteen years from now—is eventually going to get somewhere.

You went gold on the last album, As Good As Dead. *How do you feel about how your career is progressing?*

SL: It's flowing along pretty well. One thing that we've always worried about is getting swallowed up, making the wrong move and becoming the whole "Here today, gone tomorrow," scenario. We're careful to take things slowly, to make people view us on the merit of our music; our records are good and the live shows are good. It's not just one single that gets played on the radio and the rest of our music is crap.

JD: The single, "Bound for the Floor," did a lot for us. That single totally made us have a career and made us comfortable.

What did having a hit single do for you?

JD: Basically, it made our wallets fat. It's not like we ended up selling millions of records. We went gold, and Local H is just two guys—our expenses are minimal. If you're a six-piece band, it's not really that lucrative. Taxes are high. You've got your manager, you've got your lawyer, your accountant, your booking agent, and, for a six-piece band, it's kind of tight; you'd better sell a lot of records. Local H is just two of us and our manager. It's a little easier.

We keep our expenses under control; we can make a living off of what we do and that makes it a career. We have a loyal fan base—our fans rock. We do well with merchandise, and we get a lot of airplay. We're fine.

When you started making money, how many different income sources did you make money from?

JD: We broke even with the last record. We owe them money for this record, *Pack Up the Cats,* but if we can sell five hundred thousand of this record, we'll break even. We don't see much money from the record company. Record companies are like one big bank: you just get money when you need it, you recoup it when you can. If not, you don't. Royalty checks—I don't know what band sees royalty checks. It just goes in a circle.

We had radio play, so we got ASCAP publishing checks. We had a lot of radio play, so those are nice healthy checks. Radio is a really good thing.

How lucrative has merchandising been for you?
JD: We've been really good with merchandising. We just happened to come up with cool shirts. They sell.

How well do they sell? What's a good merchandising day for Local H?
JD: If we play a venue that holds twelve hundred, and it's sold out, that's going to be a good merchandising day—we're going to sell about five hundred shirts. Not every band does 30–40 percent, but we do well. It just depends on your shirt designs and how cool you are as a band, whether or not they'll wear your label across their chests.

You make money in a myriad of ways.
JD: We got to the point where we don't really need tour support. That comes from having a great manager who can budget things. Our merchandise and what we make from our shows pays for our crew and our tour bus and our hotel.

Scott and I don't make money on the road right now. We're different from a lot of bands; we're not money-hungry; we'd rather pay for the crew than take tour support.

Local H is a tight little business entity.
JD: I was the business head of our band before our manager, Steve Smith, came on. Scott doesn't care.

How important are your feelings about your music, and how important is your fans' reaction to your music?
SL: When you're writing an album, there's no way you can predict what everyone else is going to think about it, so it becomes more about whether or not you like it. Once the record's out, I start wondering what other people think about it. I can't really think about that while we're making the record or writing the songs. If we did worry about that, I think people would resent us for not taking any risks.
JD: We're not about trying to position ourselves. Our music takes a cue from the bands that we like. Take AC/DC—they just get up there and rock, and it's not really about much more than that. They're incredible, and they've become something great from that—not having to get whatever haircut happens

to be popular at the time. If you set yourself up to be timeless, that is a better business decision than a label trying to make a band out to be whatever the flavor of the moment is.

How much say do you choose to have in the development of the record—let's say, the designing of the album cover?

SL: On our first record, I was under the impression, Well, the label has an art department; they'll pick out photographers and record designers. They know more about it than we do. When you do that, it may turn out fine, but I don't think it reflects the band's personality.

When a record company assigns you to a photographer, chances are they're going to be from New York, and more often than not you're going to get New York-looking pictures. They're going to have a certain attitude to them. If you just let other people make those artistic decisions for you, the art director's personal print is going to go on it, not yours. That would be fine if it was the art director's record, but it's not.

We started taking a pretty active part in the process after the first record. Once we saw a couple of things that weren't up to what we would have liked, it was a pretty big motivator in making us wake up and take control of things. The second and third albums as a whole make more of a statement about Local H.

Do you choose your posters?

SL: We try to have our hands in everything, even down to bios. It's better not to let people who don't know you take control of things like that. As far as the posters go, you're the one who's going to have to look at it. If you don't like the way you're being represented, then you should do something about it.

Does the record company let you take as much control as you want to take?

SL: You'd think that. You'd think that if a record company signs you, they're signing you and they want you, they don't want anybody else, but it turns out that that's not the way it is. They want their own version of what happens to be hot. If another label has a big hot band, each label has to get their own version of that band. A lot of bands find themselves being groomed to become someone else.

JD: At the very least, be true to yourself, and that is going to be more satisfying. You're also setting yourself up to sell records for twenty years, not just one or two years. You'll end up selling a lot more records. I never understand why people are so quick to have a band sell so much right away, when they could just slowly build a band and they would end up selling way more over the years.

What do you think of the business side of making music?
SL: It's shortsighted. I would try to change it by putting people who know a little more about music in positions of power. It always irks me to have to talk to somebody who doesn't really know anything about music, and they're in control of your destiny.

Are there people at the labels who are like that, who don't really know?
SL: I think there are. I've seen plenty of friends in other bands . . . if you're not careful, you can totally get crushed. That's the thing I would hate to be more than anything, some bitter old guy who goes, Yeah, yeah, I had a record out once. I got screwed. I don't think there would be anything sadder than that happening.

Where would you like to get to with Local H?
SL: I'd like to sort of keep moving and not wind up like a dead shark. I have no real desire to be huge tomorrow, but as long as we keep moving at a rate where we'll be able to keep making records and keep interesting ourselves, then that's fine.

CHAPTER ELEVEN

Online

In the long run, everything might be streamed on demand, either online or via satellite, but it will take a while to get from here to there. I will need to have the ability to call up any song that I want anywhere, instantaneously—on my bicycle, in my car, in my house—not just sitting in front of my PC, but on my home stereo, in my Walkman while I'm out jogging. Until I have that level of ability, people will want to possess the physical product. There are generational issues here, whereas I like to hold things. My two year old won't have that issue. So I think the world of downloading and possessing will be with us for a while to come.

—Michael Robertson, founder, MP3.com and Lindows.com

The Internet is a powerful new medium that is in its infancy. Look at our experience with our home and office computers over the last few years, the way that we communicate.

"The music business is well situated to realize how much new technology can help it because music has seen that help in the past," declares John Bates, the Technology Evangelist for Skunk Technologies. "What compact discs did for the music industry was to open it up and make it grow. The World Wide Web is doing the same."

Back before the compact disc hit the market in the early eighties, the digital master recording of any album would be converted to a vinyl disc and pressed like any other vinyl record. The record companies weren't that interested in moving into CDs, as they already had vinyl pressing plants and all the machinery necessary to make records. Finally, when the labels realized that music and technology converged, and there was no other way to go, they made the transition from vinyl to CD.

Now, a highly audiovisual domain like the World Wide Web represents new renewal and growth for the music industry. The facts are all there, laid out clearly in numbers and statistics.

Wascally wabbits on the World Wide Web and music fans like to be on the cutting edge. (Or is that the bleeding edge?) Makes sense. Music people are early adapters. There may be as many music sites on the Web as there are in any other category.

"Look at the number of sites clustered around particular topics on the Web; sex is number one, but nobody talks about that. Number two is music. Just in sheer numbers of sites, it makes you realize that music is playing a big part in what's going on on the Internet," confirms John Bates. "Music drives the Internet technology. A lot of people are working on streaming audio, streaming video, to deliver music across the Internet."

"There's this thought process where people think that the Internet has become the most important thing to the music business," observes Liz Heller, senior vice president for new media at Capitol Records. "In actual fact, music is the most important thing on the Internet. The demographics of the Internet users are very close to music demographics, so that's part of the reason why it's received so much focus."

■ The Web's Appeal

"Music is a global product," notes Larry Rosen, chairman and CEO of N2K and Music Boulevard. "There are no language barriers; people all over the world are into music. And the idea of having a network to link these people together is very, very exciting."

Prior to the World Wide Web, music was broadcast via radio stations. You might have had a radio station in France, another in China, another in Japan, and one in every city in the United States, but there was limited opportunity to broadcast music around the world. The Internet is the infrastructure for a truly global village. It's a very exciting point in the evolution of humankind.

"One of the surprising trends accompanying the rise of the supposedly global Internet has been the creation of a format in which regional songs can thrive again," notes Michael Robertson. "Let's say you're in a band and you want to share your powerful demo tape with your small-but-devoted fan base and local promoters. The Net is a cheaper, easier way to distribute your music than pressing your own discs, even if you're using a CD-ROM drive on a PC. Using the Web, with its easy encoding methods, free servers for small players and enormous audience, you can put products in people's hands for a fraction of what it would have cost you before the Net."

■ Marketing and the Web

The Web makes marketing music easy. When you release a record by an artist, the goal is to have that record become available in every territory of the world, and to promote it and market it on a global basis. Prior to the World Wide Web, international promotion and marketing was difficult. People who were giant fans of a particular artist in Poland might not hear that the artist had a new record out until three months after its release. Now, you can put that information up on the Internet and instantaneously fans around the world can get information on a new release.

The Web is one of the most cost-efficient ways of marketing and promotion. You can put something neat up on the Web that has a life of its own for cheap—basically, the sweat off your brow. To put something on the Web, your biggest expense is time. The amount of money you need to produce something compelling on the Internet can be the cost of the hardware and software that you need to create it.

■ Case Study: Creed's Successful Use of the Internet for Promotion

Creed emerged from a good-sized pack of post-grunge contenders to become one of the biggest-selling rock bands in America during the late '90s. As they've progressed into the new millennium, they have used online marketing to reinforce and expand their fan base. Their success story is shared by Steve Lerner, president of their record label, Wind-up.

How did the Internet play a part in their overall success?
STEVE LERNER: It's been a huge part from the beginning. You can look at it from a developing artist's perspective going back to the first record. When we released the album *My Own Prison*, we had radio in maybe 15 percent of the country. The band had never really toured beyond a small radius of Tallahassee. We used the Internet to build a one-on-one relationship with some

of the tastemakers that could be fans of Creed. In essence, we were just reaching out and connecting with the right people. But we did it subtlety—not from a sales perspective, not with a banner across the top of a Web page. We came up with a marketing approach without feeling as if it's a marketing approach. Early on we were very effective in tying the Net to Creed's touring strategies and looking at local markets and looking at what Web communities would be effected by that and how to become part of it and how to reach the right people.

The first part of being successful on the Net is getting someone interested. The next thing is keeping them entertained and continually keeping them entertained. It's creating the Web site, then creating the content and entertainment to keep the fans coming back.

How important is it, do you think, for a band to keep a handle on their Web site?
SL: It's extremely important because, in this day and age, it is the biggest marketing tool you can have for a band.

Why do you say that? Why is that better than MTV or radio?
SL: All bands would love it if MTV just took their video and played it thirty times. But, MTV has a really short playlist. So, from a reality perspective, what's MTV going to do? They're going to show an image of the band tied to one song. The Web has given the capacity to really develop the one-on-one relationship with a fan for a band.

The real trick is to be very effective on the promotional end, but also to maintain a bit of mystique for the band. Web sites and the Internet have changed things dramatically for music. Before, you just couldn't wait to get your hands on the next record from the band you really liked. You'd learn a little bit more and you'd discover a little bit more. Now things have changed where with a couple of points and a couple of clicks, you really know a lot about that band and of what they're doing at that moment. The mystique factor has changed, but how you present things and how you market on the Web has made it uniquely important to distinguish yourself from just effectively approaching a band's fan base, versus selling to a band's fan base.

What are the elements that helped Creed's second album, Human Clay, *debut at the top of the charts?*
SL: It was Internet driven. We created a unique promotion all tied to the Internet. What we wanted to do was create a triangle. And the triangle was between the brick-and-mortar retailer, the Internet retailer, and radio stations

that are looking to develop traffic on their Web sites. When *Human Clay* was released, we knew there would be a lot of traffic in record stores, so we created a promotion with 3,500 record stores, where we custom created signage for each individual retailer. So the month before the release of the Creed record, anyone who would come into the record store knew that the Creed record was going to be coming out on September 28. The signage was all dictated to driving them to the Web site of the retailer—there being something exclusive at the Web site of the retailer.

In other words, if you went to BestBuy.com, you could download "Higher", which was the single, but you could also stream "What If," and the only place that you could stream "What If" was at BestBuy.com. So Best Buy was able to promote it as an exclusive thing for their Web site. At Tower Records, you could go there to download "Higher" but, exclusively, you could stream "Beautiful"—another Creed song from the record. Transworld had "Say I," Warehouse Music had "Inside Us All," Musicland had "Wrong Way," the Independent Retail Coalition had "Wash Away Those Years." So, we were giving them all something exclusive to wrap their hands around and get all the signage in-store. And also what we were doing was helping them, because they wanted to get people to Telerecords.com, they wanted to get people to Bestbuy.com, Transworld.com, and Warehouse.com. And the online retailers wanted something, so we got CDNow involved and we got Amazon involved and we got Rock Universe involved. And from all the Web sites we got front-of-page promotion where they were promoting Creed. So we're just getting a tremendous amount of visibility for the month prior to the release at the brick-and-mortar locations but also their Web sites.

Then tying into radio, we wanted people to go to the radio station's Web sites and to learn about Creed and to check out the new Creed album. We also wanted to give the radio stations an opportunity to really promote and talk about the new record. So we created a promotion; we got about 200 modern rock and rock radio stations to create a contest where they put Creed on their Web sites where you could download "Higher" and whichever radio station got the most amounts of downloads of "Higher," divided by their latest Arbitron rating, which would create an even playing field between the large markets and the small markets, would win a free Creed concert. So the band would come to their town and do a free concert for the station. With the band selling out 10,000-seat venues, that free concert became meaningful. We got more than 200 radio stations promoting the new record, the single, and our Web site where they could go check everything out. We had a station in Oklahoma that took out a big billboard on Interstate 44 that said something like "Creed, Live In Concert—Yes or No. You Decide at Z94.com." The *Human Clay* promotion was about all these radio stations driving traffic to their Web sites.

In connecting the lines in all these triangles, we used the download "Higher" to raise the awareness that there are other Creed songs out there, but you need to go to these other sites. We helped really bring a lot of traffic to the retail sites and the radio sites. It was a win-win situation. We took great online elements and great offline elements and linked them together. What we got was an unprecedented amount of promotion and we got more than a quarter of a million initiated downloads.

How important is radio versus the Internet?
SL: Radio is still very important. I think that the biggest misconception is that it's only Internet. You cannot break a band just from the Internet, but the Internet and radio combined are a powerful combination. I'll give you an example: look at Bush. Bush was coming off of two multiplatinum records— *Sixteen Stone* and *Razorblade Suitcase*. Bush has been number one at modern rock radio. They came out with *The Science of Things* super-duper early. They debuted at 105,000 units. Creed's *Human Clay* debuted at 350,000 units. And yes, we've had a lot of airplay, but how do you keep the fan into the band and into the music? And, how do you keep developing that relationship? And how do you keep it fresh? That's what the Web has done. It's that link to the fan community and it's how you work that link that's so important and I think that has been a pinnacle to Creed's success.

■ Freedom from Monopolies

From a business standpoint, the Web represents:
- Freedom from distribution strangleholds
- Freedom from being dependent on mass media for marketing and promotion
- The ability to communicate directly to your constituency in a two-way fashion

The Internet will not work effectively as the sole promotional formula; it needs to be synergistically incorporated with other promotions. Remember: people need to hear the band's name at least eight times. When marketing a band, stick your URL on your advertising, put it on your bios, and stick it on the album itself. The Net is another part of the advertising process.

What's particularly cool and effective about having the URL on the album is that it's a good way to cultivate repeat buyers. After Billy Bob in Des Moines buys a Smashing Pumpkins record and plays it 900 times in nine months, one day he's going to look at the CD cover and, Wow! There's a URL on there. Holy moly! A whole new world opens up. Billy Bob downloads the page and finds thirty seconds of a new song from the new album, and then it's the try-it-then-buy-it scenario. Suddenly, you've got something that you just don't get from traditional distribution, and that's a repeat buyer. Try-it-then-buy-it is definitely where it's at, repeat buyers are where it's at, and that's part of the model for the online artist.

"If you look at the statistics on people visiting Web sites, the vast majority of people haven't visited more than fifty sites, and they haven't even visited more than ten in depth," exerts John Bates. "What that says is that you're creating loyal followers to a Web site. Those people are getting the editorial slant from that Web site, finding more groups that they like through the Web site, and then they are able to go and follow the band, buy their CDs, find out more about their concerts. A Web site enables a music following to keep up with what's going on with the band. The Web's creating not only a more loyal following, but enabling the following to be more loyal."

■ Marketing on the Web

The obvious, immediate benefit of the Internet is that it's an easy way to develop a better relationship with potential customers. Labels large and small have set up their own domains.

"Instead of putting a couple of chords out there for five thousand people, three of whom might buy our records, we can focus on the three people that might buy a record. We're turning our marketing method into a better service model," offers Marc Geiger, chairman and CEO of ARTISTdirect and the Ultimate Band List.

"If you're a fan of an artist, you generally learn about the new album through traditional mass media channels. You may pick up a *Rolling Stone* magazine and see an ad, or hear a song on the radio. That media input might motivate you to buy the record; it might not. The Internet offers an economical way to increase consumer awareness, and allows those in charge of marketing and promotion to communicate directly to the artist's fan base.

"That personalized market has never taken place inside the music business before," observes Geiger. "It's way too big. The Web now enables us to do this. If I can get the e-mail address of 40 percent of the people who bought the last Black Crowes record, I can have Chris Robinson do a 50K video interview that I can download to everybody, or send them an e-mail that he personally signs. Those fans would be pretty psyched, and I think that will lead to more sales. If we can sell things that way instead of mass marketing, it will yield more profit."

The Web will let a fan win a signed record from the artist, receive a personal e-mail, or download a spoken interview. Suddenly, he's feeling closer to the band, and gets the impression that the musician really cares about him. The result is that the fan is really going to support the musician.

For an unsigned band, the World Wide Web is a godsend. It's not controlled by anybody, therefore, anybody can play. The Web sites, big print mediums, like *Rolling Stone* and *Spin,* maintain the magazines' editorial slant, and they will continue to write about the music they choose. But for every *Rolling Stone* and *Spin,* there are a hundred other music sites begging for content. There's a need for content on the Web; it's a perfect opportunity.

"If I were an unsigned band, I'd just pretend that I was a writer, write a glowing CD review about my band, and pitch it to anybody that would listen to me, or, I'd make my own Web site," suggests Laura Cohen.

Do searches under the search engines. If you are a folk band, go under folk; maybe there's a folk music Web site that has nothing but unsigned folk bands. There are CitySearches and Sidewalks that are area-specific. Find a local slant for your band (touring is obvious). The sites need to know what's going on in the local area; get them on board. Use your imagination, do searches off of words in your song title; there are an endless number of possibilities that you can go to on the Web, because sites are looking for content and there's an unlimited amount. The Internet is a great way to give yourself exposure.

"Our Web site has definitely helped," confirms Sister Hazel's Mark Janowski. "We update it every day because we're trying to create something that makes people want to come back. We picked up a digital camera and are putting up pictures from the road. On our next record, we're going to do an Interactive CD-ROM on a disc that will work in conjunction with our Web page. So instead of putting our merchandising catalog on paper and inside the disc, we'll put it on the disc, and then, if you're online, boom, you can buy it off our Web site."

You can log in on your computer, talk to people about a concert that you're watching on your TV and listening to over your stereo—pretty obvious, but a great way to stimulate the senses, nonetheless. MTV has hooked up with America Online to let people talk about videos on TV over their computers while they watch the video. Suddenly everyone became Beavis and Butthead, able to publicly critique the material that's out there.

The Web augments all the things that people like to do and offers a richer experience.

When Tom Petty sold out twenty nights at the Fillmore in San Francisco in early 1997, he was changing his song list all the time. Each night, Tom's changed set list was posted on the Internet, so, by the next morning, fans were able to log on and see, What did Tom Petty play last night? It created a lot of fan excitement.

The Internet is its own TV network. Each site is its own network. It truly is. Tune into Tom Petty TV, Hole Online, or the Space Space.

■ Another Effective Revenue Stream: The Fan Club Model

Outsourced fan clubs are an effective way for a band on the rise to capitalize on time and revenue streams. An effective fan management system can turn difficult-to-manage cost centers, such as screening, opening, and responding to fan mail, into turnkey profit centers that create valuable direct sales and marketing relationships with an artist's fan base.

Companies like FansRULE have had success using the fan services model for bands like Aerosmith, John Mellencamp, Christina Aguilera, Jewel, and others.

"Our fans are important to us and we like to make sure that they're taken care of; that's one thing that's always held true with Aerosmith and will always be true," notes Aerosmith guitarist Brad Whitford. "Our fan club is a part of what has helped keep Aerosmith strong over the years. We've been good to them and they've been good to us."

Fan club services can include:

- *Online stores:* Combining both traditional direct mail and catalog sales with online stores and e-mail marketing, the fan can become a direct customer of the artist or celebrity.
- *Ticketing:* In addition to newsletters and other club services, ticketing is a core part of the value proposition that creates a long-lasting subscription relationship between fans and artists. Premium seating available prior to general public on-sale dates, that is based on club seniority keeps a fan renewing their membership year after year.
- *Fan-Mail Processing:* Safe-mail handling procedures and advanced database management capabilities are one of the most difficult and time-consuming aspects of fan club operations.
- *Web Presence:* Creating, hosting, and maintaining vibrant and informative online communities and official fan sites is a key. An effective artist Web site, such as Aeroforceone.com, delivers everything from

dedicated chat rooms, message boards, online stores, and Webcasts, to development of an official fan site that enhances an artist's image and commercial success.

- *Marketing and Product Development:* A well-nurtured fan base can foster fans' willingness to play a "viral" role in the growth of the artist's career. From newsletters and e-mail marketing to merchandise development, interactive media, corporate sponsorship, and venue marketing, artists' development helps artists cultivate and capitalize on the direct artist-fan relationship.

- *Call Center and Fulfillment:* Combining online and offline customer relationship management techniques with our own warehousing and pick/pack/ship capabilitie assists artists on the rise, or an established artist moving into a peak period, such as an album release or movie premiere.

■ Building a Web Site

Now that MTV isn't promoting bands the way they once did, the Web has become the hot new promotional outlet. Do yourself a favor; build a Web site. It's a simple, inexpensive way to get yourself out there.

"The Web is about making information available to people if they want it," states Semisonic vocalist Dan Wilson. "Just put stuff out there—as much as you can. Don't put too much emphasis on giving it a personal touch. If you try to get personal and shake everybody's hand, you're going to miss most people. Let them know that you care about the fans and you want to provide information about you and your music."

Since you're selling music, you should have sound bites: live tracks, outtakes, anything special. Take advantage of all the technology that's out there and make it work for you. Buy a manual. That may sound very geeky, but it's an easy and inexpensive way to get your material up on the Web.

You also have to find someone who can host your Web site. Every America Online member gets a Web page, and they actually give you tools to help you build it. IUMA (discussed later) has a package they sell where they'll host your Web site, build it for you, and maintain it for you. So, there are lots of options, and it's not that expensive. Certainly AOL is not that expensive; it's around $20 a month.

■ Getting Traffic to Your Site

There are a couple of ways to get traffic to your site. You could strike up friendships by chatting online. Check out other AOL members who are into music, and maybe you can swap a little banter, a click button from theirs, a click button from yours. There are Web rings of unsigned artist band sites that are all interconnected—they're part of a central Web site and you can go to their individual pages. Net distribution of music by local bands is an outstanding opportunity for local portals, particularly those associated with radio stations. The local portals get free content, promotion, and traffic, while the bands would get free or low-cost distribution. Both sides might attract new audiences that they'd never reach without the other.

Another plain and simple idea: contact everybody you know who has a Web page and just say, Would you mind placing a link? The more content you have up on the Internet and the more Web sites you have talking about your band, the more links you're going to have to your Web site.

Then there's marketing—getting people to your Web site. There are so many unique strategies that can be used—contests and giveaways, polls, and information.

■ Do Something Interesting

Be creative. A great idea is like a great band—people hear about it. Right now the word is getting out about Ben Harper, a racehorse on Virgin Records. Ben Harper is a perfect example of someone who has name recognition but not the superstardom that translates into album sales. There are diehard Ben Harper fans out there because he is so talented.

Ben's talents parlayed the site. He's an amazing Latin and slide guitar player; one of his fortes is really intricate guitar work. His Web site offers lessons on how to play a Ben Harper song. It lays out the music for you.

Be really creative and be really smart about what you use your Web site for. Post your b-sides, promote your concerts, invite fans to your album release party. If you're going to perform in a local club, maybe you can find a way to cybercast, stream, or download parts of the show on your Web site. Make it all make sense, lead up to something, and build up to something; make it interactive and make it worth somebody's while. Build a fan base, a community, a fan club around your band.

"I've always contended that the Internet site is part of what we call the synergistic package," states David Kessel, president of IUMA/Offline Records. "By having a Web site, you have a centralized location to direct a fanbase, to create a fan base, to give information, and to sell product to a fan base. You can put your URL on any sort of promotional materials you send out. I think by having a Web site you eliminate costly mailings of CDs and all of these colored pictures and brochures that you send to people that actually end up in the trash."

Having a Web site will definitely save you money in the long run. Instead of sending out promo kits of your band, you can send a postcard that says: Check us out, we're hip, we're cool, we make great music, here's our Web site and URL. If you like what you see and hear and you want more, give us a call.

☼ **COMMIT IT TO MEMORY:** *Put your URL on flyers when you play clubs, on posters, on matchbooks—on anything that directs people to a centralized location.*

Having a Web site doesn't take the place of having your act together or trying to work the band in any way you can. It's a beautiful opportunity to have as an add-on to direct people to get a sense of who you are and to get a database and fan base.

Keep that Web site updated! The worst thing if you're a fan is if you don't log on for a couple of weeks and you come back and it's exactly the same as it was last time.

■ A New Creative Emphasis

The Internet is as revolutionary as when the telephone and television first came into our society. It will bring about the evolution of a whole new type of musical artist. In today's world, when an artist makes a record, somebody outside makes the art, and somebody outside makes the video, and the three processes are not necessarily connected. In the future, visionaries such as Peter Gabriel, Linkin Park, Nine Inch Nails, and the Residents will be the norm: artists will conceptualize video, art, and music all at one time and in one place.

This concept is slow to catch on because many traditional artists still see themselves solely as musicians. The concept of multimedia music only came about with the MTV generation. The few musicians who are currently thinking multimedia are producing products that are outside of the mainstream. But bands have thrived incorporating all of their talents.

■ Linkin Park: Going Beyond Making Music

Life is a whirlwind for the members of Linkin Park. Their debut album, *Hybrid Theory,* was released in late 2000 and became one of the biggest selling albums of 2001, thus changing the lives of vocalists Chester Bennington and Mike Shinoda, guitarist Brad Delson, drummer Rob Bourdon, bassist Darren Phoenix Farrell, and samplemaster Joseph Hahn. As Brad offers, one of the secrets to their success has been a multimedia approach to music.

How did you start on your career path?

BRAD DELSON: We started doing our music for fun, just as friends in Mike's bedroom. We really didn't even plan on being a band. But eventually, we got a publishing deal and things just started to happen. When we realized this was more than just a hobby, we decided—just like everything else that you really are passionate about—let's do the best job that we can. That doesn't mean we don't make mistakes—we're obviously learning—but let's pay attention to people and read up on stuff and really take an active roll in not just our creative life, but also our business life. When you relinquish too much control to other people, they can really pervert and distort your goals and your artistic vision, so it is important to have your business life in order.

How do you like the multimedia approach to making music?

BD: Mike Shinoda and Joe Hahn met at Art Center in Pasadena, a very prestigious art school, and they're extremely talented. I did art in high school, and Chester Bennington has done painting, so we're very visually oriented guys. Our visual presentation isn't something we think of after the fact. We're conscious from the get-go of what we can do visually to broaden what Linkin Park means to people.

When you create visual elements you want them to stick in people's heads. You want them to work cohesively with your vision musically so that everything is unified and elements aren't fighting each other. We look forward to anything we do visually.

Like your headlining tour?

BD: Our first headlining tour was incredible. It was the first time we were able to put on a Linkin Park show and not just be an opening element in someone else's show. We tried to integrate everything Linkin Park is about into a live setting. We had the soldier as the backdrop, as well as some other visual elements that Mike and Joe created. We took out Taproot and an L.A. rap group called Styles of Beyond.

How do you plan on expanding the Linkin Park vision?

BD: We want the world to know who we are and what we're trying to do creatively and understand our vision. Our first album, *Hybrid Theory*, established a foundation for our blend of different musical elements. And at the same time we do that, we want to have a lot of fun, show a really positive attitude, and have a really close relationship with our core fan base. That's what we focus on at shows: meeting people and talking to people. We're not about being rock stars and being exclusive. We're about sharing with people.

■ Using the Web to Circulate Your Tape

The average artist, particularly one without a record deal, gets frustrated dealing with record industry people, radio people, and booking agents. If you have a tape, where do you send it to get a deal? Does your band send in promotional material to a radio station? Or to a record company? Or to a booking agent? Or do you just stick it up on one of the numerous download sites and see if anybody notices it?

People in the music industry have a right to be arrogant. It's a supply and demand thing. Radio airplay has a bandwidth problem. There isn't enough space for all the artists to get their message across. Traditional record companies don't have enough money to develop all of the artists who want to record albums. Club bookers don't have enough clubs for all artists to play a date. The current channels of promotion and distribution have a definite bandwidth problem.

Guess what? The Internet doesn't have the bandwidth problem. Online, an artist can get his message out to the people.

"The way for a band to use the Internet is to say, Hey, this is what we're working on," offers musician Oded Noy. "We're working on these demos, we're rehearsing for a live show at this location, and this is what we sound like."

When ambient artisans Massive Attack were preparing to release their album, *Mezzanine,* Virgin Records used the Internet as an instant gratification medium. For the three months before the album was released in April 1998, Virgin put bits and pieces of the album up on the Web.

"For Massive Attack fans, little by little, we were rolling out the album in its entirety to be listened to, over the Internet, before radio got it," recounts Laura Cohen. "So it was a way for fans all over the world to hear the new album before they had a chance to buy it."

The concept of people stealing music off the Web is not a particularly popular belief at the moment.

"I don't worry about that because it's reserved for those that are true hackers," declares Laura. "Ninety-five percent of the people who are on the Internet wouldn't know how to do that. Plus, it's crappy. The difference is like AM and FM or eight-track and CD, so I don't worry about all that downloading stuff. It's a lot easier to go and buy a CD and make a thousand tapes from it."

And certainly the radio stations are not going to download it off the

Internet and play it on the air—that would be like broadcasting the message on somebody's answering machine.

■ Virtual Schoolyard

Most people get into music around high school or college age. Schools are the most wired entertainment palaces on the planet. It goes hand in hand: if you go to school, you can get on the Net. It's also the age at which you're really into girls, surfing, beer, pot, and music.

When you're in school, there's a certain word of mouth that takes place among your friends; usually it's because you play the same sport, take the same drugs, lust after the same guys, and like the same bands. Nowadays, especially on the more fringe stuff, there may not be that many people in your school who dig the same music. Let's say there are four people who like the Bomboras in your school. Go online and you'll find a virtual schoolyard where you can hang out with a thousand people who are like-minded. If I'm in the Bomboras and I make a surprise appearance on that site, it's a big deal to those people.

"One of the inherent values of online communication is the ability to facilitate one-to-one, one-to-many, and many-to-many communication," notes Tony Winders, president of InterActive Agency, an online marketing and promotion firm. "This opens up tremendous possibilities for marketers, because information about a product can be easily disseminated to the people who want or need it most."

Marketers have always known that word of mouth is incredibly powerful. There are opinion leaders out there among every group of friends, and if you can get to those opinion leaders and make them realize how cool your site is, word of mouth is going to spread like wildfire. Oh, Chad says this is really cool. Let's check it out. He knows what he's talking about. Word gets out and then people come there. If the site really is good, they'll tell their friends. Word of mouth is one of the most important ways to promote sites on the Internet.

Another extremely effective way of spreading the word is posting to Usenet newsgroups. Search engines like Yahoo! and AltaVista are able to browse Usenet newsgroups for keywords, so they are becoming a very powerful force to get people to come to your site. Off-line events drive people to online sites, too.

There was an insane Rolling Stones promotion tied into the *Bridges to Babylon* tour. You went online to the Rolling Stones Web site, and you got to vote for which song you wanted them to play that night where they were performing. The song that got the most votes got played that night, and then that song was cybercast at the Rolling Stones Web site. Now, that's a great online event, and it makes sense. It's interactive and you get something back from what you give.

"When you talk about a grassroots or organic way to promote a band, we can do that online," notes Capitol's Liz Heller. "It's a great feeling of excitement and enthusiasm."

One of the goals of the music business is to get as many people online as possible. "What you're going to see in the future is what Napster is doing—ninety-nine cents a track," notes composter David Javelosa. "You can download it to your iPod and you're ready to go."

■ IUMA: The Internet Underground Archive

"IUMA is all about empowering the artist," offers site marketing director Todd Williams. IUMA (*www.iuma.com*) is a fine example of the virtual schoolyard. The site is a platform for independent bands and artists to share their music with the world. The five-year-old site sidesteps the traditional channels of distribution and goes directly to the end user.

IUMA has established a formidable online presence; they get close to four hundred thousand hits per day. There's a real community here, both for musicians and music fans.

Anyone coming to the site can tune into IUMA's radio station. They hook you by telling you: Stop listening to the same ten bands over and over on your local bigwig radio station, and tune in to over a thousand indie artists on IUMA. All you need is the Real Audio plug-in, and the tunes will cease to cease!

Getting heard by who-knows-how-many people on Radio IUMA beats playing in your garage for no one. It gives you a charge and creates a buzz. Bands like tabulaRASA and Creed have written testimonial letters about how having an online presence has given them valuable exposure. IUMA band Battershell had the chance to make it onto the Lilith Fair's Emerging Talent stage during the tour's opening in Portland, Oregon, because people who visited the IUMA site had a chance to vote for them.

"IUMA was fairly small when we joined in," shares Oded. "I sent them a picture, a thing that I wanted for a button, all the text, and a DAT [digital audio tape], and they converted all the stuff, did all the layout, and put three of our songs up. We decided we were going to go with their maximum rate with everything, and it was like $125, and we said, Hey, that's worth it."

Today, it costs $240 for one year of service on IUMA. That base price includes:

- One song
- Up to two pages of text
- Two images (Photos or artwork)
- Online merchandising capability
- One page of lyric text (optional)
- One logo (Artist's logo graphic) (optional)

Additional services:
- Statistical Reports: $60 ($45 if reports can be delivered to an e-mail address). Quarterly statistical reports on audience accesses of songs, images, and text. Accesses are categorized by the user's entry point (i.e., universities, commercial businesses, foreign countries, etc.), and are great for establishing demographic information.
- Video Clips: $90 each, digitized and placed into artists' page.
- Additional Songs: $60 each. Songs in addition to the one song in the basic package (each includes one page of optional lyric text).
- Additional Images: $30 each. Images in addition to the two images and optional logo in the basic service package.
- Additional Text: $30 for two pages of text in addition to the two pages included with the base service.

Just call (800) 850-4862, and IUMA will get your own personal band promotion up and running. Plus, they're linked to several independent record labels, including 3 Foot Records, Offline, Alternet Sonic Reality, Boy's Life, Blue Goat, Evolution, and Gypsy Blues.

Though not everyone on IUMA gets signed, you get feedback from all over the world.

"IUMA is the kind of place you get exposure. Even today, I still get responses," confirms Oded. "There was this guy, Massimo, from the Italian radio; he had his own show about American music. He downloaded a song, and he really liked it. We went back and forth like six or seven times. In the end, he asked for a tape, and he put it on the radio a couple times. He wrote back that people liked it. That's a very satisfying experience.

"Then there was this guy from Russia—he was so excited about seeing our band up on the site, and he asked us how we got there, and blah, blah. He downloaded one of our songs. A week later I asked him if he liked it. He said, 'Yeah, but two days later, somebody stole my sound card.' So there goes Russia.

"Every two weeks, I hear from somebody," concludes Oded. "They say things like, I love that song. My twelve-year-old kid downloaded the whole thing in stereo."

■ Online Events

The Internet is a great way to give a band exposure to a music-hungry audience. The World Wide Web decreases the importance of place, and increases the importance of time. A lot of people would rather be at the concert virtually than see the concert later, in a better manner.

"There's something magical about being in a live situation that will never be duplicated—I don't care how advanced the technology gets," notes Michael Dorf, president of the Knitting Factory, a company that specializes in putting concerts on the Net (*www.knittingfactory.com*). "Everyone's time is getting so scarce, how many concerts a week can you go to? Concerts on the Web give you the opportunity to see something, sample it. To ask yourself, does this look like what I'd like to go to when the show comes to town?"

Online interviews, concerts, and simulcasts are an interesting form of promotion that many groups have effectively utilized. It's like giving a music fan backstage passes and a front row seat to their favorite event. It's a first-rate experience, even though cybercasting is still a very young medium.

"The concept of online appearances is still in its infancy," affirms IUMA's Williams.

■ Michael Dorf: Online Performance

The Knitting Factory started in 1987 as a small performance space in New York City. It grew into an independent record label, but their problem was that records didn't get placed in every major record chain. So they started a Web site, *www.knittingfactory.com,* and began promoting their artists through online concerts and appearances.

The Knitting Factory was the first club to successfully webcast on the Internet twenty-four hours a day. Today, they offer live concerts online every night at 9 P.M. Eastern time. Michael Dorf is president and CEO of the Knitting Factory.

You do online broadcasts regularly . . .

MICHAEL DORF: Every night we do Stream Works videocasting of the shows. You go to the Knitting Factory site. Right on the home page we have this blinking live banner, and it just goes Live . . . Live . . . Live . . . Live. You click on Live to go to the Live page, then you need to download Stream Works. We have a link to Stream Works—it's free—so we make it very easy for people. Once you have that free browser on your hard drive, you're then able to click onto our site and watch the show. It's a little two-by-three-inch color square, which broadcasts five frames per second.

How has webcasting improved since you've started doing it, and where do you see it going?

MD: When we first launched our site, they didn't have anything that could do what we wanted to do. Then in early 1995, CU-C-Me came out from University of Illinois and Cornell. That was a very, very primitive video-conferencing software that really didn't work too well. Stream Works really became something about a year ago, so we immediately jumped on that.

There are constraints to the growth of webcasting. The biggest thing holding all of this back is bandwidth. Until people have a megabyte per second of bandwidth—which is either a cable modem or T-1 level of bandwidth—into the home, it's going to remain a slow, incremental growth. There's only so much compression that can be done. There's only so much stuffing a video signal into telephone lines. We're going to need more bandwidth.

Bandwidth hasn't stopped the Knitting Factory from broadcasting. As a producer, I just will use whatever technology is out there. My concern is to be the conduit; my goal is to get music to people. That's all I'm concerned with.

Three years ago, it was CDs; then that's what I used to get our music out to the people. If today it's Stream Works, then that's what I use. If, next week, Apple Computer comes out with something, I'm going to jump on the bandwagon. I'll go with whatever is available to reach as many people as possible.

Enlighten us about the online broadcasting. How many people listen in? What are the benefits?

MD: The Knitting Factory shows are sold out every night online.

What does sold out mean?

MD: Sold out . . . with a T-1 line, you get 1.5 million bits per second that can go through it. If you divide that up by a 28.8 modem or a 14.4 modem, you get different numbers of people that can view. You divide 1.5 million by 28.8 thousand, you're going to get about eighty-five people that can simultaneously watch.

Most nights that's all we've got available, so at eighty-four people, we're sold out. For certain shows, we will propagate our signal. We'll send it to Sony or Warner Bros. if it's one of their shows. They get one signal and they can turn that into eighty-five per T-1 line. And then they'll take another one of those and send that out, so you can keep multiplying that and get really an unlimited number. On big shows, like Yoko Ono, for example—which was one of our biggest—we had about a thousand people watching. At the Knitting Factory, we had three hundred fifty live in the club and a thousand people online.

Right now, we are getting more people watching and coming to our Web site on a daily basis than we are coming into the club in real space.

Online concerts are an effective promotion technique. It's not that you get a lot of people listening in, because you don't. The average online concert gets an audience of under five hundred people worldwide. After all, to listen to an online concert in decent audio, your computer should be equipped with hardcore UNIX boxes, with the right hardware and software to actually be able to do the CU-C-Me combined with the sound files. But the online event will give the band and the site a lot of really good promotion because it is broadcast over the Internet.

"We did a Spearhead concert online. I don't know how many people were there, but I know a lot of people read about it," observes Liz Heller. "It was in the *Los Angeles Times,* it was in *USA Today*, it was in *People* magazine, it was in all these places that would never have mentioned Spearhead. So everybody felt it was a great success as a result. It's all part of the sum of what you do to promote your acts, to break the artists."

■ Online Chats

The effectiveness of online chats is questionable. Sure, online chats are great if you're a superstar—a lot of people who care about you are on the Internet—if they're checking out your Web site, they'll know about it. It's easy to pump. To effectively host a chat, a band has to have that name recognition in order to get people to log on at a certain time at a certain place. Chats with lesser-known artists are like some site's chat rooms—there's nobody around. If ten people have come to chat with an artist, that is no fun at all and it's embarrassing.

Chats can wait. They don't help; they're a dime a dozen on the Internet these days. You're better off just dropping in on your Web site when you feel like it and chatting that way.

If you're going to do a chat, tie it in with some bigger promotion—like a Rolling Stones chat tied in with their world tour—that makes sense. Celebrities go on *David Letterman* when they have something to promote, because they're building awareness of that property.

■ Michael Robertson: The Internet and the Unsigned Artist

One of the best models for unsigned artists was MP3.com. In its heyday, it was the place for new artists to go and post their music and for the world to download their tunes and check out new artists. Having been purchased by CNET.com, there is now a new unsigned artist Internet presence, *www.music. download.com*, which will offer artists free file hosting and a presence on the Web, and gives music fans free access to a universe of downloadable songs. Michael Robertson, founder of MP3.com, shares his views on how the Internet can be used to promote artists.

What was the role of MP3.com?

MICHAEL ROBERTSON: It is giving an opportunity to artists who have historically been locked out of the music system. The music industry revolves around the platinum sellers— acts selling a million CDs or more. That's where the music industry makes their money. For those artists who sell less than 5,000 CDs, they're really not profitable for the music industry.

Artists who have small followings or are just starting out or don't attract a mainstream listening population really don't fit into the system. The Net and MP3 give that population—which is very big—a distribution system. And to get exposure, which is the most important thing for any artist—to get their music heard. If it doesn't get heard, it doesn't matter how good it is, because you're not going to sell anything.

That's what we were doing at MP3.com. We'd post any artist in the world. They could sell CDs through us and there was no start-up fee, no monthly fees, no binding contracts. We were giving distribution to artists that did not participate in today's music industry system.

How do you think the Internet has affected the music industry?

MR: The music industry represents the legacy. The Net has changed some of those things. The Net has the potential to be a positive for a record label. By their numbers, 85 percent of the bands don't break even. The Net can help them make better choices. Instead of 85 percent of the time, maybe the Net can cut record company misses down to 50 percent. That would have an incredible change to the bottom line for record labels. The music industry has so much to win by merging with new scenarios.

How do you see the financial model shaking out for new bands?

MR: It's important with all artists to focus on revenue potential, not just CD sales. Concert tickets and merchandise all matter. Most people use the barometer of looking at the CD sales component. MP3 really changes some economic principles of the process. For example, when two major record labels merged—Universal merged with Polygram—they dropped a bunch of acts. It's thought that 200,000 units was the cutoff. If you sold less than 200,000 CDs, you got dropped. At 200,000 CDs, the reality is that that artist made no money for himself. But you take that same artist and you put him on the Net, and let's say he sold 40,000—a fifth of what he did at traditional retail. Instead of selling CDs at $16.99, which they traditionally cost in the US, you sell them for $10—a significant price decrease—but the artist gets to keep most of that money for himself.

That same artist who made no money for himself selling 200,000 CDs could move to the Net, sell 40,000 CDs at $10 each and gross $400,000 a year selling CDs. One of the real potentials of the Net is that it's so direct. It really changes the underlying economics.

Some of the old models still apply—CD sales, concert tickets, things like that—but artists have the opportunity to enjoy much greater splits of the revenue than they traditionally have ever seen before.

Going forward we're going to see a lot of new business models to music. The traditional business model is the CD selling model. It's a model of scarcity. You don't get any music until you give me $16—that's the model. It's unlike TV, which is the more people that hear this the more money the acts and the TV channel makes. You might see that with music, you might see ads put on songs, you might see product placement within the song—the song that mentions Diet Pepsi or Chevrolet or Kentucky Fried Chicken. Some artists might say that's heresy, but that's probably one of the models that you see going forward.

You will also see subscription models, à la cable and satellite TV. Pay X dollars a month; get any song you want, any time you want, any way that you want. Maybe that will transform the CD collection into the service, where it's not about collecting CDs, it's about subscribing to this service. How many people really record stuff off of cable TV? Not that many. Music might evolve in that similar strategy as well in the long time.

How will radio change to accommodate the technology and the new artists?
MR: You won't see a lot of changes in traditional radio because there is a limitation on airwaves and channels and regulations. There's a limit on the amount of bandwidth. Radio is really forced to appeal to the broadest population. Off-line, I don't think you're going to see a lot of changes to radio. Online, I see a lot of potential to see enormous changes—micro-broadcasting,

stations that focus on very specific styles of music or artists—Grateful Dead Radio. There's enormous potential to online radio and micro-broadcasting, to interactivity and things like that. Some of that is bandwidth limited and some of it is licensing limitations. But I do think that, going forward, you're going to see some interesting stuff in online radio.

How does online distribution empower an artist?

MR: It helps the artist to communicate directly with the fan, or the potential fan. That's the real power. It's the connection that you make. Reach out and know who that person is and tap into that relationship going forward. Create a special Valentine's Day CD and let your friends know that you've got this great CD that you've made and so if you have a boyfriend or girlfriend, husband, wife, whatever, it's a specialty product; it's part of the benefit of having that relationship one on one with the consumer, and that is the biggest benefit that an artist gains from the Net.

CHAPTER TWELVE

The Future
of the Internet

If radio doesn't give the people what they want, the people

will go to other mediums. Already, the Internet is teeming

with live broadcasts. If you thought TV stole your audience,

wait until cyberspace breaks through in everyone's living

rooms.

—Richard Branson, Founder, Virgin Records

The public is learning that buying things online is no different than purchasing them in a store with a credit card. While 1997 saw $8 billion in business, 2002 found 329 million online users engaging in $333 billion worth of business transacted on the Web—1 percent of the global economy.

An estimated 20 percent of U.S. Internet users regularly purchase recorded music on CD. This indicates an immediately reachable market of 10 to 15 million record buyers on the Internet. These are potential customers who are increasingly comfortable with using the Internet for purchases of lifestyle, as well as technological, products. International Internet growth, particularly in highly developed European

countries and Japan, as well as recorded music and Internet buying charac-
teristics, parallel the U.S. experience.

■ Getting Music Online

The music business is changing its view of the Internet. 2004 was the year
digital downloads hit multilevel marketing. Suddenly, some universal brand
names—Apple, Pepsi, Miller Brewing Company, Napster—chose to target the
download audience by offering millions of free downloads via partnerships
with digital music services.

"The opportunity is to take a power in the brands that we have and merge
it with the ability that we have to meet millions of people with a message,"
elaborates Fred Siebert, president of MTV Networks online. "We can take that
opportunity and merge it with the personalization opportunity of the Internet
and take it to a whole new level of interaction with our users. When we all
figure out a way to do that, then the old media and the new media are going
to have an unbelievable future together."

February 2004 saw the launch of Apple Computer's co-campaign with
Pepsi to give away 100 million iTunes.

"If you recall the Alanis Morisette/Tori Amos promotion on MP3.com, that
was a great example of music as a service, not music as a product," notes entertainment industry attorney Ken Hertz. "It was music as a service, whereby
if you went to that site, you got to hear something by each of those artists that
you couldn't hear anywhere else. It was being streamed on demand and it was
a way for them to get a lot of attention to a tour that sold out relatively quickly
in many cities. It was a big boom to them to presell that many tickets. As a result, the artists wanted it to happen—there were a lot of different value ex-
changes that went on for everybody; that's music as a service."

"As time progresses, you're going to see lots of free music given out via
third-party companies," Buymusic.com founder Scott Blum says. "It's not
going to be Apple and iTunes driving the business. It's going to be companies
like Pepsi and other third parties that are promoting digital music on bottle
caps and on labels."

Brand marketers, particularly beverage companies, are looking to establish broad connections between music and their products—a strategy well-
served by digital music giveaways because studies show that music giveaways
can foster customer loyalty, and should motivate consumers to use the re-
lated products.

"Once marketers have established a relationship with a downloader, they
can start working that database of people who downloaded music, perhaps

offering regular e-mails each month with personalized recommendations," offers Michael Robertson, founder of MP3.com. The internet allows for very precise marketing techniques.

Brand marketers have much bigger marketing and promotion budgets than Web-based businesses. Marketing and co-promotion strategies give download strategies access to a consumer reach outside the scope of most digital music companies.

One trend is to employ strategies like *www.virginradio.co.uk* sponsored with music programming reminiscent of early daytime TV programming.

Youth-oriented lifestyle brands like to piggyback on the strong emotional ties that young consumers have with their favorite songs and artists. Beverage companies have been particularly keen on using music to boost consumer affinity with their brands and are forming more formal relationships with music companies to ensure they have access to relevant music. In 2003, Pepsi united with Sony Music Entertainment for cross-marketing strategies. Coca-Cola did the same with the Universal Music Group.

"The business environment lends itself to partnering," says Geoff Cottrill, group director of music for Coca-Cola North America.

It's a beautiful thing for the record companies, as their profits have been sinking continually since digital downloads first became available. In their negotiations with artists, record companies relinquish several important revenue streams (such as merchandising and co-promotion opportunities). They are always in search of promotional platforms for their artists beyond radio and music video networks.

■ Making Money Online

Record companies have had to expand and reinvent their revenue streams by using the Internet as a form of marketing and promotion, assuming, like everyone else involved on the Net, that the profit model is finally falling into place.

It's been evolving for a while: When the Sex Pistols reunited for their world tour, a gig from the Hollywood Palladium was presented live over the Internet through the Rocktropolis site. The Palladium only holds two thousand people, but four thousand simultaneous Internet listeners were able to hear the entire uncensored live concert and view up-to-the-minute live stills and video segments. The concert was also tied into a competition called "Great Insults on the Internet," whereby entrants e-mailed their favorite put-downs and the most cynical were awarded Sex Pistols swag bags.

"It was as effective as it was offensive, which befits a band like the Sex Pistols," notes Ted Mico, Internet consultant and developer for Virgin Records. "You couldn't do a promotion like this with Julio Iglesias, but it works perfectly for this band. The Internet lets you cater to a group's attitude and vision."

The music industry believes that music fans will beg, borrow, and steal to get more information and music from their favorite bands. And there are probably several thousand people who will, but people throughout the world love the Web because it's free—at least, for the moment.

■ A Logical Introduction to Paying for Downloads

Credit card transactions on the Internet are a way of life. It's no different than using your credit card in a restaurant. Seriously now, when a waiter is taking your card, do you know what the waiter does with it when he's not with you? Maybe they've bought the Taj Mahal in addition to ringing up your bill. Your name is on the card, the expiration is on the card, the card number itself—how can that be any safer than buying something on the Web? And you know that when there's a credit card swipe it's the same electronic transmittal.

Late 2003 saw the launch of reasonably realistic, industry-endorsed online music services charging 99 cents per song. This was Apple Computers's attempt to launch an alternative to free song-swapping services.

■ The Future is Now

The future has arrived. You can now download a disc's worth of album-quality sound. Electronic Commercial Music Distribution (ECMD) is how a new generation of people buys music—pay for it, download it, and access it on a whim.

"Technology holds the promise of revolutionizing the distribution of recorded music," notes Edgar Bronfman, Jr., CEO of the Warner Music Group.

In the perfect cyber-universe, there are mechanisms in place to protect a band's copyrights and the whole nine yards. An artist can sell his product over the Internet and still be protected from the pirating of his music. Consumers can pick and choose the individual songs or albums they wish to purchase, and they can put their music wherever they chose.

■ Larry Rosen: Beyond Bandwidth

Larry Rosen is a partner in CDNow, one of the premier online music entertainment companies and a definitive source for music content, community, and commerce.

Is digital downloading really the way of the future?

LARRY ROSEN: You could actually do it today; it's just a question of band-width and line connections. If you had a T-1 line going to your house directly from the source of the master tape, you could do that today. The biggest prob-lem here is the last hundred yards—you need a fiber-optic connection.

How do you see the upcoming Internet technologies affecting the price of CDs?

LR: In the beginning, the pricing is all going to be exactly the same, but profit levels are going to be somewhat different. It's the same dollars; it's just who gets those dollars and how they are shifted around. We now have the ability to say, I want to buy one song from this guy, and one song from that guy, and one song from this other guy.

The current recording industry model is primarily to use radio and pro-motion to work a single song and drive people to buy the CD. Now that we're shifting to a singles model, how things work could change. You could be re-warded for that one song on some kind of a cross-promotional basis.

What is your long-term view of the online music industry?

LR: How much do you believe in the technology? If everybody in your house is going to have access to a computer, then it's a very large marketplace. Look at the statistics over the last five years: the percentages of sales that were made in record stores have been reduced pretty dramatically. Sales at the traditional record stores have dropped, and alternative methods of distributing albums have grown tremendously—that's everything from the Columbia House Record Club to the BMG Record Club to any other kinds of mail-order op-erations, direct mail, and alternative ways to sell product. And in the United States, the average age of record buyers is getting older and older. The record store itself is designed for a very young kind of clientele.

Have you been into a record store lately? They're paying minimum wage to someone who wants to work in a record store. The guy has purple hair and tattoos all over his body. If you're forty years old and you go in there asking to buy a record by Leonard Bernstein, the guy with the purple hair and tattoos doesn't have a clue who you're talking about.

Online record companies offer a much wider selection of titles.

LR: How you judge the value of a record store is how many turnovers you have on a title per square foot of the store. Stores make the decision that they're not going to carry more in-depth catalog and more slow-moving titles. Mall stores in suburban areas only carry the top pop records that kids want to buy at this particular point. This gives a much greater opportunity to the online world, because in a virtual store, we have a hundred and fifty thousand titles—that's more than the Virgin Megastore. An upper demographic buyer is going to have a hard time finding that depth of catalog and that depth of information in a record store. So, not only is the environment not friendly, but the titles aren't even carried there, which is automatically going to shift people in this direction because this is going to fulfill what they're looking for.

What other benefits are there to shopping online?
LR: You can find out more about the music—you can hear it, touch it, and feel it, so to speak. And you don't have to go anyplace to go get it.

■ Virtual Music

Society is changing. Teens and adults are used to having things and holding things. But, seven year olds are already nonlinear. They don't necessarily have the attachment to physical possessions the same way that we do. As purchasing power is part of the sociological experience, the concept of virtual ownership can be taught, just as citizens of the former Soviet Union learned to work only to meet quotas. If someone grows up knowing that the content they desire will always be available, they'll be less inclined to feel like they need to own it. We're coming upon a whole generation of altered thinking, individuals who will be happy enough with virtual ownership, as opposed to actual ownership.

■ Digital Distribution

"At first, people argued all kinds of cons against digital distribution," declares Michael Dorf, president and CEO of the Knitting Factory. "They said you're going to have no artwork to really be able to present a package, but, actually, it's to the contrary. What the Internet gives you is the opportunity to have an almost unlimited amount of music that can be digitally distributed directly to a consumer. You also have the opportunity to link to all kinds of visuals, or all kinds of hypertext links to the artist's life. Whatever artists would like to share, whatever they want to communicate, they can do over the World Wide Web. If they want to share their list of the top hundred musicians of all time, the best concert they ever saw, their favorite color, their favorite foods . . . whatever artists are willing and wanting to share of themselves can now be attached to their presentation. In that sense, the Web is the ultimate way for them to communicate with their fans."

The big question everyone is asking is, What is the consumer willing to pay for this opportunity? Should accessing special information be a paid service like cable television, or something that's advertising-subsidized, like normal network programming?

■ David Bowie Tests the Waters

One musician who has consistently pushed the envelope is David Bowie. Throughout his career (which began when he changed his name from David Robert Jones to David Bowie in 1966), Bowie has been called a musical chameleon, evolving along with musical fashion and trends. He was one of the first artists to put Internet potential to the test. He released the song "Telling Lies" exclusively on the Internet via his Web site at *www.davidbowie.com.*

"My first working encounter with the Internet was at the beginning of the *Outside* tour in Boston," offers Bowie. "It produced a great response, so I am only happy to take the whole thing to another level and actually release a song on the Web."

Could Virgin Records have charged an additional fee for access to this new Bowie song? Most definitely, but they didn't. It was a test. According to Nancy Berry, executive vice president of Virgin Records Worldwide, "Virgin is always looking for exciting and innovative ways of promoting our artists and getting the music to listeners. So, clearly, we're keen to explore the potential of the World Wide Web."

Exclusive material may be one way to generate additional income in the future. Many are thinking that instead of charging money for Web site access, they should offer customers cool items they can't get through retail.

"Now that the ability to download pristine, quality music has become possible, where does retail fit in?" asks Tony Ferguson of Interscope. "You can now plunk down a credit card and download the whole record. If you want to print out the artwork, it is available, and you have your own file of bands."

■ New Opportunities, an Old Philosophy

"Improved delivery systems surely level the playing field. You can get your record out to as many people as a major artist can," observes Bud Scoppa, vice president of A&R for the Sire Records Group. "But, if those people don't know you exist and you don't have the dollars to tell them you exist, then is the playing field really level?"

If you're a young band, you have to develop some kind of visibility for yourself by doing the things that artists have always done—getting the music out there. As we've discussed throughout this book, that means playing live and allowing people to experience your music firsthand. Your Web site is not going to be a particularly viable promotion entity if there isn't the underlying interest in the band to begin with.

Buy your CD or buy your music over the Web—it doesn't make much difference. Fundamentally the basic law of supply and demand has to be satisfied. People need to be interested enough to put their money out for something—music, merchandising, performance, custom appearances—whatever the market will allow.

■ The Web and Radio

"The World Wide Web is definitely influencing radio," declares A&R maestro Chris Douridas. "It's another platform to market music. When a fan is into a band, they can find out more about the band on the Internet, so the word-of-mouth element definitely comes into play on the Internet."

Audio is one of the things the Web does best. Everybody's computer is at least AM radio-quality, and others are near-CD-perfect, depending on your bandwidth. It's a new technology.

"Internet radio gives you hundreds of channels that you can choose from, so if you have specialized interests, Internet radio can cater to those tastes," states Ted Hooban, director of Digital Media for CDnow. "Whatever music genre you choose, you can probably find a channel that would be convenient. It's more like satellite radio than traditional radio."

■ Case Study: Rapstation.com

Chuck D is the founder of the multiplatinum rap band Public Enemy and one of the most colossal figures in the history of hip-hop, not to mention its most respected intellectual. He redefined hip-hop as music with a message, and his strident radicalism has been a boon to the digital music movement. One of his visionary concepts is *www.rapstation.com*.

What makes Rapstation.com unique?
CHUCK D: Rapstation.com provides a service to the genre we call rap music and hip-hop, something I've been involved with for over twenty years. The traditional areas are not going to expose or expound upon 85 percent of the art form. Radio is an area where only 15 percent of it is accepted into the mainstream because record company politics dictate they should put some finance behind it, and everything else goes by the wayside if it doesn't reach those numbers.

Same thing goes with the video play. You turn on the television and you might never see a video by a certain artist, because they just couldn't get up into that realm. The same thing goes down at retail. Other than people going to the traditional areas and waiting to get programmed, they're waiting for something to happen. With Rapstation, they can actually go to a zone and see it at their disposal. That's the beauty of Rapstation—it's the ESPN of rap and hip-hop.

How have you made it the place where people go to check out what's actually happening?

CD: People are going to say, I want to know what's going on in the rap world, just as in television, when people say, "I want to know what's happening in the sports world," and they go to ESPN or Fox Sports. Same thing we want to do as far as developing this supersite into a superstation: whenever you want to figure out what's happening in the world of rap music and hip-hop, you go to Rapstation. For artists and artists-to-be, this is a perfect vehicle to present their material.

Rapstation is a whole world within itself that exposes and expounds upon the art form, and that's very, very important. Just because you can't get your video played or your song heard, does that mean that your art is wack? Not necessarily. So, these rules have to be built.

If you want to see a rap concert, it's not going to float to those traditional areas. For example, there are such things as rock stations; there are not rap stations. There's not a rap station out there. There are R&B–based music stations. Rap music covers a lot of different musical genres, but most of the time you won't hear it. Most rap music doesn't have a home in traditional areas, so the Internet can be the best vehicle ever for the genre, because it is not in addition to, it is the whole format for it.

What are your goals with Rapstation?

CD: Number one: We're looking to do what MP3.com has done with all of music—just to microfocus it as far as new artists putting up their material and being able to be in the exchange program and a lot of things with their artistry and exposing their art. That's the artists' area.

Number two: Service for even the biggest companies out there to the ones that want to jumpstart a service to expose their art to the public across the world.

Number three: To make the hip-hop world truly the hip-hop world and globalize it—to enlighten and educate as well as to entertain people that are into the genre.

Number four: To have discussions and forums about aspects of the art that might be too detailed to elaborate on in traditional areas, like radio. Why have a deep discussion over rap music and hip-hop when you don't have time to play all the records? This format is perfect for that.

We're lining ourselves up with places like the House of Blues. The Web, we can do for rap music what, maybe, Don Kirshner did for rock. Using the Web, we can do for rap music what Dick Clark and *American Bandstand* did for popular music on TV. We can have correspondence with different parts of the country and the world, responding on rap in those particular regions. We can also expound upon different styles of rap in different countries and how it relates to the particular areas so we can do a lot of things that we couldn't do in traditional areas.

Take your local radio station and couple it with your own order and distribution service, and voilá—you're in business.

⚙ COMMIT IT TO MEMORY: *The World Wide Web is not the panacea, and you may not see immediate returns on your Internet investment.*

The Web is all about community and time—you get to go where you want to by using the Internet—but like everything else, you've got to pay for it. It takes time.

■ The Rise of the Middle-Class Musician

Ellis Paul is a New England songwriter. His best-selling CD, *Stories*, is closing in on 30,000 copies after nearly eight years. But that doesn't mean he's a starving artist. In 2002, Paul played 150 shows and released an album, *The Speed of Trees*. He grossed about $300,000, netting roughly a third of that after expenses—a better bottom line than many major label artists. Ellis plays folk music, like his hero, Woody Guthrie. He also represents a new breed—the middle-class musician.

"I'm making more money now than I ever have," he says. "I couldn't be happier."

⚙ KEEP IT IN MIND: *Entertainment industry attorney Ken Hertz offers these compelling words of wisdom: "Artists don't need to make a lot of money if they're selling a lot of tickets or a lot of merchandise or if they're making a lot of money on airplay or through publishing. In fact, artists look at the record deal as the engine that drives to tour bus."*

He's not a starving troubadour playing for coins people throw in his direction, and he's not riding around in limousines. But, he can live a comfortable life by making music. He makes it work by using the Internet: he offers a Web site, a discussion group, and an e-mail list. He issues albums through his record label, Rounder/Philo. He also sells those albums and self-released projects directly from his Web site and at shows, cutting out the middlemen and earning far more money than he does from store sales. It's a business model that not only yields grassroots artists a good living, but allows them the freedom to pursue their own creative vision.

"Songwriters don't have to deal with the star machinery and the crash-and-burn mentality of the majors when they are on smaller labels," he says. "Having a major label working with me now seems crazy. It would mean the sacrifice of art for commerce."

1994 was the first year Ellis Paul played music full time. He made about $17,000. By keeping track of his databases, he's amassed a loyal group of fans, and several channels for selling to them. Touring income is where Ellis makes his money. A trek around Texas might mean he played to 160 people in Houston on a Thursday, to 100 in Austin on a Friday, and to about 100 in Lubbock on a Saturday. After the promoters took their cut, he earned about $3,500 from ticket sales. He also sold about $2,100 worth of CDs, pocketing about $1,120 after paying Rounder its share.

"Using the Net, artists can realize that they have a pocket of support in Austin, Texas," explains Michael Robertson, founder of MP3.com. "The artist can then go a step further and contact those fans who are near Austin and let them know that, 'Hey, I'm coming to town for a concert.' Those sorts of things are so compelling to a fan."

Ellis also sells CDs via his Web site, along with T-shirts, a DVD of a live performance, and a book of his stories, lyrics, and drawings. Both the book and DVD yield higher profit margins than he earns on CDs. Altogether, Web sales netted him $36,000 in 2002.

Sales of his CDs are split about equally between Ellis's direct vending and stores, but he's still paying back his advance from the store-bought copies.

"Before the Net, the music industry didn't know who their customers were," notes Robertson. "With the Net, the possibility is there to know your customer. The doors that open up allow the artist to have an ongoing relationship with the customer. For an artist to be successful, they need to tap into all of the potential revenue streams that they have—not just CD sales, but merchandising, concert sales, promotion, endorsements. All those aspects are important. And by having that kind of relationship with a customer, you can evolve a lucrative relationship over time."

As 2004 opened, Ellis was marketing his second CD, *Side of the Road*. An interesting concept, the music is a series of cover duets with Vance Gilbert of tunes by well-known songwriters such as Lucinda Williams, Neil Young, and others.

"Every year is a step forward," he says. "I'm happy where I'm at. It's a good living."

■ Make It Known on the Web

The Web is this era's new form of promotion. If you look at the traditional ways artists communicated with their fans, they had their LP and they had an album sleeve. There were interviews in other forms of media, like magazines.

"Back in the late seventies, record labels were more or less dependent on print in order to let people learn about their new releases," states Andy Secher, editor of *Hit Parader* magazine. "This was even before MTV came along! That was a revolution unto itself, but video was only the start of the technological revolution."

In the mid-eighties, a few years after videos became a standard form of promotion, the CD came along. You could put more music on the disc; albums generally can't hold more than an hour's worth of music without a loss of fidelity. CDs allow seventy-four minutes of music, but you have less space for art. The World Wide Web has the potential to be the best of all worlds, for all musicians.

"One of the major benefits the Web offers to music is that it's diversifying the audience and diversifying the type of music that's out there," remarks John Bates. "Because of the diversity, people's tastes are enabled in a much more eclectic manner."

Bandwidth, or the ability to use the existing bandwidth, will make a tremendous difference in the way we can view material on the Web.

"It's going to be easier to find ways to compress and get around needing more bandwidth than it is to install new infrastructure," remarks Bates.

As developers conquer the bandwidth challenge, the Web could feasibly evolve into a perfect substitute for radio. (Not that the capitalists in this country would allow it.) You would listen to music on your computer, and, assuming that the Internet would become the ultimate music archives, you would be able to pick the music you wanted to listen to. Of course, your car radio would still feature FM and AM frequencies.

■ David Kessel: Future Trends

David Kessel is the president of IUMA/Offline Records, an independent record label that is coupled with the Web's leading independent music site.

How will the Web be different for signed bands versus unsigned bands?
DAVID KESSEL: One of the things I see is that a signed act, when their contract is up, and after they've made it—maybe their first two albums are delivered—can maintain electronic distribution rights. All they have to do is go into the studio, produce the music themselves, and sell it digitally. They don't need the record company if they have a fan base.

What they might do then is license the tape to the record company for the archaic in-store stagecoach mode of selling, which there will still be. You will still have those tray lots, whether at the car wash, or the market, or the K-Mart, or wherever—maybe a Top-Ten rack or something like that. It gives you leverage to just sell directly to your fan base.

For instance, if U2 has a new album coming out, they can tell their fans to go to *U2.com* and download the new album. If 5 million people come and download the album, then it has just been direct-marketed to the fans.

Record companies have to start negotiating for the electronic royalties or options on electronic royalties even after the contract expires. They will want to have an option on the electronic distribution because they've taken the time to break the band.

And for unsigned bands?
DK: As far as an unsigned band, if there is a demand for their music, they don't have to press up the CD if they don't have the $2,000. It sure saves some money for Top Ramen and spaghetti. Say they've got a song that's starting to click. They might have a hit digital single. The whole neighborhood gets turned onto it, and they tell friends, who tell their friends—it's just some kind of hip song.

Well, all of a sudden, they go to an Atlantic Records or somebody, and they say: We've just sold like seventy-five thousand songs at 99 cents apiece to seventy-five thousand people." That is a database that says these people have an audience. We should invest in them further as far as promoting them, getting them a booking agent.

I think the record company's role is really going to be in aligning with the booking agent and really being a tag team. By the band going out and working, they're going to sell more units. If they're selling more hard units and getting bigger, that's one way to make up some of the royalties. Maybe the record company can also underwrite the tour, for a percentage, and start getting in the tour business as well, because they already are underwriting things.

■ Be a Player

The Internet Underground Music Archive is the first and one of the largest high-fidelity Internet music outlets, setting the standard and creating the future of music distribution right now. As of May 1998, IUMA received in excess of three hundred thousand accesses per day, and offers the works of over nine hundred independent musicians to an estimated 30 million Internet users. This online community includes a global audience of fans, radio station programmers, club promoters, and music industry A&R representatives who have already signed bands from IUMA to major labels.

For a minimal start-up cost, you can be a player in the Web lottery. If you want to turn it into a small business, be the one who owns the Web site; then, you can be charging a band an initial posting fee to come onto the site. You're actually promoting them, and they actually own a piece of cyber-real estate on your site. There can be an up-front fee to take that band on, and you can take a share in each hit or a CD worth of hits. The customer has an opportunity of buying either a single hit or a full CD worth of hits. So you still have an opportunity for both front-end and back-end revenue in that type of scenario.

■ Generate Hits

Getting people to your site on a regular basis is not a random occurrence. Getting them to visit you is the reward of hard work. It is an outgrowth from your ability to get newspaper, radio, and television exposure, and then also to use the more popular news press agencies like PR Newswire, and get into all the various search engines. Newspaper articles and features should mention your Web site, as should anything on the radio and all press releases. Promotion is the way to get more exposure to your Web site; it gets you more attention and more traffic.

Another way to generate traffic to your site is through MetaNames in the design environment. Meta is using keywords and key elements within the infrastructure of your Web site design. Those key words, those Metas, are built into the site so that when people do keyword searches via a search engine, the search engine will find your site. The more effective you are at building these keywords into your site, the more often you're going to come up in a search engine.

The key is to come up in the top ten, which means using keywords and effectively hyperlinking the site so that you are actually drawn to the top of the search and are coming up in the top ten.

How do you achieve this magical feat? It's all part of effective marketing. It's knowing what the market is calling for. It determines how you structure the elements within, so that you have more of an effective opportunity when people go in and use a search engine and enter keywords. It's really your knowledge of what the market uses, what the strategy is overall.

■ WebTV

The arrival of WebTV means that anyone can surf the Net while leisurely reclining in his La-Z-Boy and slugging a beer. The WebTV revolution began quietly in 1996, when WebTV Networks offered the first link in merging your television set with a computer. Paul Allen, the silent cofounder of Microsoft and owner of WebTV, created a little black box that connected you to the Web and to e-mail through your TV set. WebTV, Inc. has since been bought by former partner Bill Gates and Microsoft. With enhanced operating capital and Microsoft's endorsement, WebTV Plus is one step closer to integrating televisions and computers. WebTV Plus is so well designed, its technology has been selected as the foundation of a new generation of cable-TV boxes. Big cable companies will distribute millions of boxes using WebTV Plus in the future.

"No question. The computer and the television are all going to be in one box, for sure," confirms Capitol Records' Liz Heller.

Cable modems for television are now standard fare; we can stream audio and video from the Web onto our TV sets. Then anyone who wants can surf the Net, or have their own TV show, by creating a Web page.

"Before the World Wide Web proliferates, it must become part of our everyday lives, like the telephone, car, or a television," observes Bryan Biniak, director of business development, Harmonix Music Systems. "WebTV appliances help make the Internet more mainstream and affordable for sending and receiving information: data, voice, video, graphics, and audio."

■ Conclusion

There has never been a time in history when it has been easier and more economical to record and distribute your own music. If you have the desire to make an album, put it in process, as there is nothing to hold you back. You never know what you can accomplish until you try.

Index

Books from Allworth Press

Allworth Press is an imprint of Allworth Communications, Inc. Selected titles are listed below.

Creative Careers in Music, Second Edition
by Josquin des Pres and Mark Landsman (paperback, 6 × 9, 240 pages, $19.95)

Career Solutions for Creative People: How to Balance Artistic Goals with Career Security
by Dr. Ronda Ormont (paperback, 6 × 9, 320 pages, $19.95)

Gigging: A Practical Guide for Musicians
by Patricia Shih (paperback, 6 × 9, 256 pages, $19.95)

The Quotable Musician: From Bach to Tupac
by Sheila E. Anderson (hardcover, 7½ × 7½ , 224 pages, $19.95)

The Secrets of Songwriting: Leading Songwriters Reveal How to Find Inspiration and Success
by Susan Tucker (paperback, 6 × 9, 256 pages, $19.95)

The Art of Writing Great Lyrics
by Pamela Phillips Oland (paperback, 6 × 9, 272 pages, $18.95)

How to Pitch and Promote Your Songs, Third Edition
by Fred Koller (paperback, 6 × 9, 208 pages, $19.95)

The Songwriter's and Musician's Guide to Nashville, Third Edition
by Sherry Bond (paperback, 6 × 9, 256 pages, $19.95)

Moving Up in the Music Business
by Jodi Summers (paperback, 6 × 9, 224 pages, $18.95)

Profiting from Your Music and Sound Project Studio
by Jeffrey Fisher (paperback, 6 × 9, 288 pages, $18.95)

Rock Star 101: A Rock Star's Guide to Survival and Success in the Music Business
by Marc Ferrari (paperback, 5½ × 8½ , 176 pages, $14.95)